NOV 14 2011   P9-DMP-619

Designing for the iPad™
Building Applications that Sell

Designing for the iPad™
Building Applications that Sell

Chris Stevens

A John Wiley and Sons, Ltd, Publication

Dedication

To Peter, Rosemary, Dominic, Louise, and MJ

PUBLISHER'S ACKNOWLEDGMENTS

Some of the people who helped bring this book to market include the following:

Editorial and Production
VP Consumer and Technology Publishing Director: Michelle Leete
Associate Director–Book Content Management: Martin Tribe
Associate Publisher: Chris Webb
Publishing Assistant: Ellie Scott
Development Editor: Kezia Endsley
Copy Editor: Kezia Endsley
Technical Editor: Mike Rundle
Editorial Manager: Jodi Jensen
Senior Project Editor: Sara Shlaer
Editorial Assistant: Leslie Saxman

Marketing
Senior Marketing Manager: Louise Breinholt
Marketing Executive: Kate Parrett

Composition Services
Compositor: Erin Zeltner
Proofreaders: Susan Hobbs, Susan Moritz
Indexer: Ty Koontz

About the Author

Chris Stevens is the designer behind *Alice for the iPad*, which hit the number one spot in the iPad App Store and has remained a bestseller ever since. *Alice* is installed on half a million iPads worldwide and counting. Gizmodo called it "The cleverest iPad book yet" and the BBC said it was "A glimpse of the future of digital reading." *Alice for the iPad* was also featured on *The Oprah Winfrey Show* where Oprah told her audience it would "change the way kids learn."

Chris was formerly a technology columnist for *The Daily Telegraph* newspaper and later wrote for *The Times*. He also presented and directed *Space Bubble*, the popular CNET gadget show. Alongside his writing, Chris is an illustrator and scriptwriter. He has worked for Warner Bros, EMAP, and Wired. Chris won a Guardian Media Award for his work as a journalist and famously discovered reflectoporn.

Today Chris runs Atomic Antelope, the publishing house that created *Alice for the iPad*. He spends his time between London, New York, and Tokyo, working directly with authors on new books.

Author's Acknowledgments

Thank you to my wonderful friend Susan Sunde for finding me a place to write from; I admire you more than all the leaves on all the trees. Thank you to Sacha Taylor for providing mosquito repellant. Thank you to Rishi Anand, Andrew Lim, and the brilliant Ella Morton for keeping me afloat with your good advice. Thank you also to Kezia Endsley, Chris Webb, Ellie Scott, Katherine Parrett, and everyone else at Wiley who made this book a pleasure to write. Finally, thank you to Ben Roberts, the programmer behind *Alice*, for his incredible skills in bringing the designs in *Alice* to life.

Contents

Preface

One week I was on my sofa watching *The Oprah Winfrey Show*, the next week I was on *The Oprah Winfrey Show*. That's how suddenly our two-man iPad developer team, Atomic Antelope, struck iPad app gold.

A year ago, if you snuck over the fence, crossed my garden, and peeked in at the window you would see a sorry sight: A lone man, crouched over his computer, deeply engrossed in Photoshop and Xcode. His mind was focused on one solitary aim: To strike it rich with an iPad app.

A month later I was co-author of the top-grossing children's book on the iPad, *Alice for the iPad*. It was named Oprah's favorite iPad book, and hailed by everyone from *The Financial Times* to *Gizmodo* as the poster child of iPad publishing. Our app appeared on television shows from London to Tokyo and stormed into top position in the App Store, in every international market. *Alice for the iPad* delivered the publishing world its messiah and gave the iPad its first killer app, as shown in the image.

Now I'd like to share my knowledge with you.

Who Should Read This Book?

Anyone who wants to know exactly how to take advantage of the iPad's exciting new features and turn their app ideas into a hit. By the time we're done, you'll be ready to take an app from pencil sketch all the way to the top ten in the iPad App Store. I'll let you into professional secrets so you can grab a lead in the app gold rush, selling fantastic, profitable iPad software. You'll learn exactly how to make your app look beautiful, work intuitively, and sell like crazy.

Why should you trust me to explain how to do this? Why not just stick to the sensible-looking iPad programming manual you were browsing through a moment ago? Well, because unlike that programming manual, I've got proof that this method works. Using the techniques in this book, I designed the top-selling children's book on the iPad. *Alice for the iPad* is installed on hundreds of thousands of iPads and made me rich beyond my wildest dreams. But I'm not going to just sit in my Jacuzzi, tossing hundred dollar bills over the balcony. Instead I'm going to put this knowledge to good use. I'm going to tell you all the tricks I used to win the app gold rush and how you can win it too.

This book is focused on practical steps, not vague suggestions. I'm not going to give you confusing rules to follow or pretend that designing successful apps is all about group brainstorming good ideas—in fact, group brainstorming is a terrible way to come up with ideas, but more on that later.

Whether you're managing a team designing iPad apps, a designer looking for tips, or a programmer who wants to understand the design methodology of a successful iPad app, there's essential knowledge for you here. Let this book be your guide through the horror of the app submission process, and learn how the iPad offers a unique window of opportunity to make best-selling applications using techniques that did not exist before the iPad came along.

The Apple App Store is exceptionally competitive and it's very easy to get lost in the swamp. To make sure that you stand out, you will need tried-and-tested methods of coming up with a sellable idea, refining concepts, prototyping designs, finding a programmer and a designer, and organizing a collaborative project. We're going to take a look at the new code frameworks programmers can use to make exceptional apps. You'll also learn about interface design choices and really get to grips with why the iPad is a substantially different beast from a laptop or iPhone. Most importantly, I'm going to equip you with insider advice on how to get an app to the top of the charts and live the ultimate geek dream.

I'll explain why asking yourself "What would be the coolest app I can make for the iPad?" is a bad place to begin designing an app. If you actually want to make money, the right question is "How will I sell this app?".

The Revival of the Hobbyist Programmer

We live in exciting times. The App Store has hugely democratized the process of writing and distributing software. Apple has led a return to the heyday of garage programmers tapping away on their Spectrums and Commodore 64s. Now a small team of just two or three people can make a best-selling title. A few years ago it was almost impossible to make any money as a lone software retailer, but there's a revolution afoot. If you have $99 to join up as a developer, and a Mac, you have passed the only bar to entry. The rest comes down to your imagination and the information in this book. Sure, there's a lot of criticism leveled at Apple's tight control of the App Store, but, on the other hand, they've made a lot of programmers very happy, and very rich.

Unlike those other books on iPad app development, I'm actually going to give you the cold, hard truth about the iPad app industry. It's dirty down here in the trenches of the App Store, and you might not like what you find, but take my hand and let's go.

TIP

This book is just the beginning. The iPad app scene is constantly evolving. Almost every day I find something new and exciting that an indie development studio has created in an effort to win the gold rush. To keep up to date with the latest app action, visit the official blog for this book at www.AppsThatSell.com or follow me on Twitter: @AppsThatSell.

Part I
Understanding the iPad

The iPad marks the dawn of appliance computing. It is the first true mass-market computer—a device anyone can use without needing special skills. It's also a rare beast among computers because it requires almost no technical support. The iPad is also a true *tabula rasa*, literally a "blank slate" that can transform itself from a keyboard into a guitar, or from a calculator into a sheet of drawing paper. The iPad uses few wires and can be held in one hand. People just seem to *get* the iPad. You only have to watch the numerous videos on YouTube of babies using the iPad to realize that the iPad leads a movement. In this part, I show you how the iPad has kick-started a revolution in software design that focuses on the mass-market user, not on the specialist.

A...T HURT, so she jumped u...ed around.

Chapter 1
Embracing a New Paradigm

You'll notice that the majority of users struggle with the traditional desktop metaphor of windows, icons, mouse, and a pointer (WIMP), but hand them an iPad and they're like a fish to water. The iPad is unusually polite when it's asked to do something. Unlike a desktop OS, the device is quick and responsive to gestures, rarely asking the user to wait. Just like a physical book in the real world doesn't pause for a second before reacting to your touch, rarely does the iPad. Like any device, the iPad has its flaws and niggles, but it's quickly nudging the industry towards a new world dominated by touchscreen inter-activity, and away from traditional desktop computing.

What's most interesting is that this movement is more than a simple change in the tech-nology used by the mass market, it's actually a seismic shift. Touchscreen computing is so universally accessible that it actually appears to have silenced the sighing masses cries of, "I don't understand computers." Apple cleverly trained-up millions of people on the iPhone, so that when the iPad launched it was a much more understandable product for the consumer. But the real magic happens when you hand an iPad to someone who has never interacted with a computer before—a young child or an elderly grandmother—they just seem to *get* it. This is the power of touchscreens and good software design.

A Quick History of User Interface (UI) Design

Desktop computers were not designed for touch, and are hangovers from work done by Xerox PARC in the 1970s and later licensed by Apple. For all its visionary skill, Xerox did not anticipate an era of mass-market touchscreens. The ageing WIMP system uses indirect manipulation—an interface in which the mouse is moved, then causing movement in a pointer on the screen. But this age is over. Now, *indirect*-manipulation methods are being quickly replaced by *direct*-manipulation. This new age is rich in interfaces where objects on the screen are touched and moved directly by the human hand. The reign of WIMP is coming to a close.

The desktop computer's WIMP metaphor, as nostalgically shown in the image, does not extend well to a direct-manipulation interface like the iPad's, and in just a few years it will seem as archaic and peculiar to us as the command-line interface.

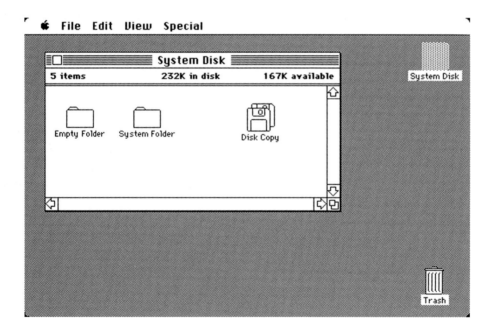

The reason that Microsoft spent more than a decade failing to sell anyone on its vision of tablet computing is that it made the mistake of trying to shoehorn a WIMP system into a touch computer. Microsoft attempted to recycle the UI from its Windows OS, and made the mistake of assuming that the role of the mouse is directly analogous to the human finger. Sadly it is not. It is only recently that the UI designers at Apple developed a practical alternative to a mouse-centric system. In the next few years the industry is set to move beyond the windowed operating system.

However, just because Apple has now figured out a way around the original limitations of touchscreens, there is still plenty of scope to make tragic mistakes when designing iPad apps, especially when adapting desktop software for the new platform.

The iPad blurs the boundary between a user and the computer, marking the transition from a world where we manipulate objects using peripherals, like the mouse and keyboard, to a world where we touch, tilt, and shake our computers. Touchscreen computing is by far the most exciting emerging consumer technology, in fact it will be the fourth largest consumer electronics category by the middle of 2011. The really intriguing thing about it for you, as a developer, is that no one has it all figured out yet. We're only just beginning to explore what the iPad can do.

To give you a sense of the possibilities on offer here, imagine the Apple Macintosh before Photoshop was invented. That's where we are now with software on the iPad. The game is afoot.

Why the iPad Is Not a Big iPhone

If the iPad is just a big iPhone, then a swimming pool is just a big bathtub. The comparison is meaningless in both cases. If there's any sense to be made of this claim, I would argue that you can do a hell of a lot more stuff in a swimming pool than you can in a bathtub, and you do those things very differently. The same is true of the iPad compared to its smaller sibling, the iPhone.

It's an easy mistake to make, and one that trips up many first-time iPad developers, but the iPad is not as closely related to the iPhone as it appears. The ergonomics of the iPad are radically different: The user's finger placement on the iPad is nothing like finger placement on the iPhone. The illusion that you are looking at a scaled-up iPhone is deceptive, and you'll probably end up with an app that will not sell if you simply scale up your iPhone apps to fit the iPad's screen. As an iPad app designer, you will not be able to use the same techniques that you've used for designing iPhone apps.

One of the core principles of design is that form and function are tied; the shape of an object determines how it can be held and used.

Consider how your grip on an object changes as the object grows larger, as illustrated here. Would you grip a tennis ball in the same way that you hold a basketball? What about a ping-pong ball? In the same way, the user's finger-grip and finger-tap patterns on the iPad are different from their finger patterns on the iPhone because the scale of the device has changed. And because the grip pattern has changed, everything has changed.

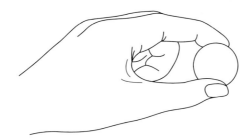

Hand holding ping-pong ball

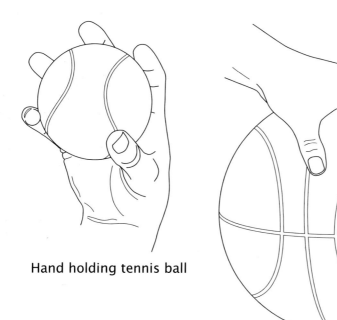

Hand holding tennis ball

Hand holding basketball

This is very important to keep in mind, because the way a user holds the iPad will be your starting point for designing a good user interface in your iPad app. This applies whether you're making a spreadsheet app, a first-person shoot 'em up, or something else entirely.

More Space to Fill

Another interesting difference between the iPad and the iPhone is the size of the screen available for a designer to provide content. This presents an enormous challenge for iPhone interface designers working on iPad apps. The iPad's screen is just nine inches diagonally, and it's tempting to think you can just tweak your iPhone app for the iPad. But, in reality, the iPad will dwarf any iPhone app, making it look ridiculous and impractical to use. It's easy to demonstrate the effect, just download any iPhone app and scale it to fill the iPad's display. Ignore the pixilation, and consider the interface. Is it still an efficient use of the iPad's screen?

Submit It Differently

The iPad differs from the iPhone when you submit your app to Apple, although this is sometimes not obvious until it's too late.

Apple has significantly tightened up the rules on how closely an app has to stick to its interface guidelines for the iPad. On the iPhone, it was often possible to get away with submitting apps to Apple that did not automatically switch screen orientation when the iPhone was rotated. With the iPad, however, Apple's gatekeepers have sharpened their swords and may brutally reject your app if it does not switch orientation when the iPad is turned from landscape to portrait. However, some high-profile apps have crept under the radar, so you never quite know when Apple's reviewers will take objection when you ignore the company's UI guidelines.

As always, Apple's reviewers will make exceptions to the orientation rule, if you can convince them that your app won't work if it switches orientation—some games and Chipmunk Physics-based apps like *Alice for the iPad* being the notable exceptions. However, in the majority of cases, there may be no defense against designing an interface that cannot rotate and Apple may reject your app. You'll read about the issue of rotating interfaces in more detail later in this book.

Pricing Advantages

Finally, for the developer, there is a very exciting difference between the iPhone and the iPad. On the iPad, you can charge more for apps. One study conducted by *Distimo* found that the average iPad app was priced at $4.67, while the average iPhone app cost almost a dollar less at $3.87. But what's more exciting is that, in the pricier categories of the App Store, the iPad market supports even higher app prices. For example, medical apps on the iPad cost an average of $42.11, compared to just $10.74 on the iPhone. Similarly, the average financial application on the iPad costs $18.48, compared to $5.74 on the iPhone. You can begin to see how selling apps for the iPad is a different proposition than the iPhone. Because the software can now do desktop-computing tasks, you can, in some cases, charge desktop-computing prices.

A user's purchases seem more substantial and valuable because the iPad's screen is bigger. The larger screen also opens up the opportunity to develop applications that have a serious business use for which considerable money can be charged. The iPad can transform itself into anything from a portable ECG monitor for a doctor, to a handheld ordering system for a restaurant. Its versatility opens up a whole new world of premium sales to the app developer.

If you want to be involved in designing apps for an interesting and lucrative market, joining some of the most innovative independent developers in the world, you've picked a great platform in the iPad.

Working with a Large Touchscreen

When Steve Jobs called the iPad magical, it wasn't just because he'd eaten too many Twinkies. In a very real sense the iPad is magical, because it is able to assume many forms. I mentioned this idea of a *tabula rasa* or "blank slate" earlier, and herein lies the iPad's magic. When you're using a desktop computer, there's no escaping the fact that you are using a computer—you must interact with it using a mouse and keyboard. No matter what the computer screen shows you—a word processor, or a graphical representation of a Marshall Amp from 1965—you are separated from that graphical representation by your input devices: the mouse and keyboard. But—and here's the magic—when the same representations are shown on the iPad, the iPad seems to *become* those devices. You are allowed to *touch* what you *see*.

Exploring 360 Degrees of Motion

In all the excitement and confusion about the iPad, one of its most interesting features was largely overlooked: the iPad has a portrait mode. Computer monitors across the world are wider than they are tall—a mode known as *landscape*—and in most cases, there's not much the user can do about it. But, like the iPhone before it, the iPad reacts when you rotate it, causing the screen to automatically switch orientation so that everything is the right way up. This means a user can quickly rotate the device to make the best use of the screen for whatever task they're working on.

What sounds like a pretty simple feature is actually a fundamental difference between the iPad and any computing platform you may have designed for in the past. The iPad is now in the curious position of being the world's most popular computer with a portrait mode—this means designers have the option of creating interfaces that occupy more vertical than horizontal space.

The iPad's 360-degree range of rotation also allows graphic elements to react to orientation—changing shape, position, and switching on or off, depending on the way the user holds the device. A good example of this is Apple's *Mail* app, an email manager that displays a different interface depending on which way the iPad is held, shown in the image.

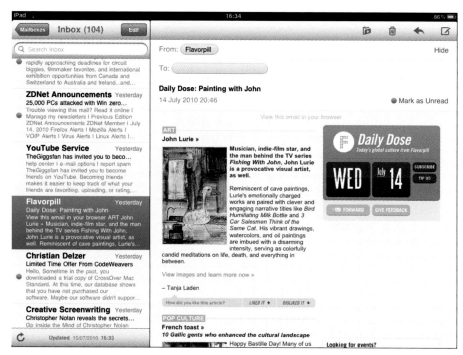

Reproduced with permission of Apple Inc. © 2010 Apple Inc.

In landscape mode, the *Mail* app shows a list of incoming emails in the left pane, and the contents of the currently selected email in the right pane. But if the iPad is rotated 180 degrees, the left pane disappears and the right pane expands to fill the screen. This allows users to get a closer look at the email, causing the iPad to resemble a printed sheet of paper. More importantly, it overcomes a very practical problem: Imagine how the *Mail* app would look in portrait orientation if the left pane did not disappear. The message text would become an extremely thin column, and embedded graphic elements might shift to become illegible.

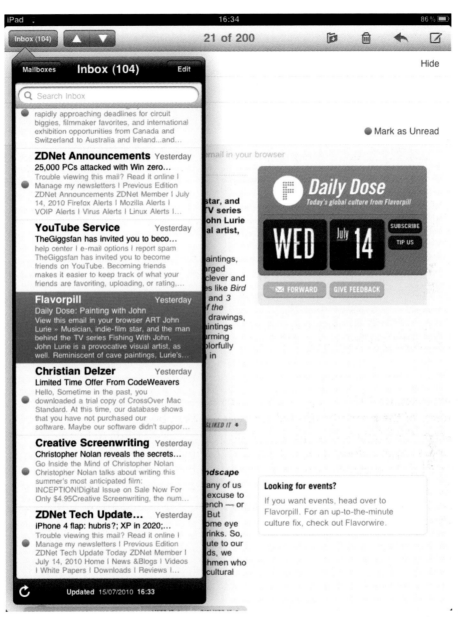

TIP

If you want to make a popular app, it should react to changes in the way the user holds the device. Exactly how the interface changes will depend on what your app does, but if your app doesn't change in any way when the iPad is rotated, you have most likely gone wrong. Stop and reconsider. It's extremely rare for a landscape interface to work equally well in portrait, and this is also true of many interfaces on objects in real life.

Visit www.ngmoco.com
© 2010 Ngmoko Inc.

Currently, iPad game interfaces are less likely to change their appearance when rotated, probably because game designers are traditionally used to coding for very specific, fixed-screen formats. However, many of the best iPad games do re-orientate themselves when rotated. *GodFinger* is one example of an advanced game interface that re-orientates itself as the player rotates the iPad, and is shown in the following images. The game can be played in both portrait and landscape modes and looks very beautiful in both states. The makers of *GodFinger*, Ngmoko, could very easily have insisted on sticking to a single orientation for the game, but one of the reasons their game is very popular is because the designers paid attention to this kind of detail and allowed players a choice. There's also a very cool transition effect that accompanies the shift in appearance.

Other apps, like *Granimator* from ustwo, use very subtle changes when the interface is rotated. *Granimator*'s menu buttons use icons that can be understood in any orientation and it is only when the buttons are tapped that the user discovers that the menus have re-orientated themselves to match the viewer's perspective (see the following images as examples). Of course, the users won't be consciously aware that the menus have changed, but they would certainly notice if this feature was not there—it would be hard, if not impossible, for a users to read the menu text and they would be forced to return the iPad to a landscape orientation. Whether in portrait or landscape mode, the main workspace in Granimator looks the same. However the content of the menus re-orientate themselves to match the current screen orientation.

These are just a few examples of how developers can use the iPad's 360 degrees of rotation, and we'll take a closer look at other ways of using this feature later in this book. Although it is often much harder to design an interface that responds to rotation, it's this kind of attention to detail that makes a killer app.

Visit www.ustwo.co.uk © 2010 ustwo Ltd.

Visit www.ustwo.co.uk © 2010 ustwo Ltd.

Remember: The Human Hand Is Not a Mouse

There are two rules I believe will help you create the best, most imaginative, easy-to-use interfaces on the iPad. I'm going to hammer these into you. Here goes.

Do not do the early layouts of the interface for your iPad app on a desktop computer. Never, ever, ever. Okay?

You can tweak the interface on a desktop computer, you can refine it on a desktop computer, and you can cover it in glossy glass and wood effects in Photoshop on a desktop computer, but absolutely do not layout your early designs on a desktop computer. I'll explain why.

If you jump straight into Photoshop, you will end up designing an interface for use with a computer mouse and not for use with fingers. I almost guarantee it. It'll look great, and the shading will be just right and you'll nudge this pixel into place here, and that one there. Everyone in the board room will applaud you when you present it to your boss or clients, they'll show copies of your designs around the company and you will be loved by the world at large for your marvelous creation.

Except you won't.

What will actually happen then is that the interface will be coded and deployed to your company's iPad and you'll begin testing it. Now everyone will stand around, staring at you confused, wondering why such a fantastic looking design is so terrible to use in reality. Then they'll throw you out onto the street and burn your desk.

TIP

*The problem is that touch interfaces are a whole new beast, and if you're doing your early layout work on a desktop computer, it's almost exactly like being blindfolded. If you want to develop an effective touch-based interface, you'll have to do it using your hands and a real life sketchbook or, alternatively, using your hands and the iPad itself. To design a genuinely brilliant touch-screen interface, you need to be able to touch your work, again and again, until it's right. Then, and **only then,** can you move onto Photoshop to make it look gorgeous. Remember: If you don't touch your designs, your app will suffer for it.*

This brings me to the second rule: *Forget almost everything you know about interface design.*

When approaching iPad interfaces, many designers will suffer from the same problem. Their preconceptions of what interface design is will seep into their work on the iPad. But designing an iPad interface is so unlike designing an interface for a desktop computer that, bizarrely, you are at a huge advantage if you have never designed for a WIMP system.

Of course, interface designers on any platform will have a valuable toolset of ideas and experience, but the biggest risk with the iPad is failing to approach it with fresh eyes. To make an app that sells like mad, forget everything you thought you knew before you picked up an iPad and start again—even if it means getting horribly drunk first.

Adapting iPhone Apps for the iPad

Earlier I discussed why the iPad is not a giant iPhone, and why simply scaling up the interfaces you've used on your iPhone apps will not cut it. So, how should you adapt current iPhone apps for the iPad?

You should list the core functions of your app and start again from scratch.

If you simply make your iPhone app bigger, and move things around a bit, you'll end up in a mess. Controls will be in the wrong place, the app will be inefficient to use, and you'll squander all the advantages of the iPad's larger display. Almost without exception, iPhone apps do not scale well, as shown in the image. This is because the iPad's screen is physically over four times bigger than the iPhone's screen, so the iPhone *Skype* application, for example, scaled up to the size of the iPad's screen, is not an efficient use of available space.

Visit www.skype.com © 2010 Skype Inc.

The most immediate problem you'll face when adapting your iPhone app for the iPad is that you almost have too much screen real estate to fill. Your temptation will be to fill this space with buttons and menus—however, this is also a mistake, because the key to great app design is a balance among features, usability, and good taste.

The Rules of Scalability

Good human-machine interfaces do not often scale with size, they tend to change with size.

Consider some other interfaces as they scale. The physical means, or interface, you use to refuel a lawn-mower is different from the interface you use when refueling a car. Similarly, the interface used to refuel a car differs from the interface you would use to refuel a jet plane. In all these situations the objective is the same, to refuel the vehicle. However, as the vehicle you're dealing with grows bigger, the interface changes, it doesn't simply scale. Try filling up a jet plane using a handheld can if you need any more convincing.

However, because the iPad looks so much like a bigger iPhone, it can be much harder for a first-time designer to recognize the difference between them.

The important point to be clear on is that the iPad is over four times bigger than the iPhone, so the original interface from your iPhone app absolutely needs to change, not just scale.

TIP

Because the importance of the size difference between the iPhone and iPad is lost on most designers, you will stand out from almost every other iPad app designer out there if you recognize this fact.

The best advice I can give you, if you are asked to adapt an iPhone app for the iPad, is to ignore the word "adapt." Approach the project as if you were creating a new piece of software based on the feature objectives of the original iPhone app. Study the original iPhone app in detail, and then forget it. Consciously ignoring the original iPhone app's appearance is the first step towards designing its efficient counterpart on the iPad.

Rethinking Ergonomics

Ergonomics is the scientific study of how the human body fits around its tools and environment. It's the way your hands grip this book, the way your legs fold against the seat you're in, and the way users hold their iPads in their hands.

You might have noticed something unusual about the way Steve Jobs demoed the iPad: He leant back in an armchair, resting the device against his knees, and propped his legs up on a table. Although it looked a bit like Jobs was just relaxing, those quiet actions have now completely changed the ergonomics of home computing. In a few bends of his wizard limbs, Jobs assumed a pose that will dictate many of the design choices you make for your iPad app. We are now dealing with feet-up technology.

Interestingly, the ascent of computer interfaces seems to inversely mimic the ascent of man. While evolution has drawn us ever more upright, computing systems seem to be doing everything in their power to draw us to a state of complete repose. The punchcard and tape-based computers of the 1960 required maintenance and operation from a standing position. Then followed desktop computers, which favored a seated position. Then came laptops, which could be used on a couch, and finally the iPad, which can be used while lying on the floor. However, the iPad is backwards-compatible with all these other postures too, making it an extremely versatile device with few fixed ergonomics.

Exploring Casual Computing

The iPad is an impressive casual computing device. It's much less physically imposing than a laptop or desktop computer, and turns on instantly. However, it's a huge mistake for a designer to assume, because the iPad is at home in a casual setting, that it lacks the sophistication for other uses. While the thin touchscreen display makes it easy to read *Winnie the Pooh* in bed, it also makes it easy to mount the device inside a helicopter, or carry it around the trading floor of a stock market. As with so many aspects of the iPad's design, first impressions are deceptive.

The iPad can be used for computing tasks in situations that computers have not been used in before. This is because iPad software, like all computer software, is designed to fit the situation in which the device running the software will be used. This design process is largely subtle and invisible, and only becomes obvious if you look at very dramatic examples of it in action.

Consider the age when computers were the size of a basement. Back then, you would have been unlikely to design software for a jogger to monitor her running speed through a forest—there would be no way for the computer to monitor the jogger, or for the jogger to see the output. Dragging a five-ton computer around a forest would have been fairly tricky, even for a trained athlete, so no jogging software was produced. Software designers of this era made decisions about what software to build and sell based on ergonomics—where the device running the software could be used and how it could, or couldn't, be held. It's entirely possible that the software designers of the age did not even consider that there might one day be a jogging app, because the ergonomics of computers at that time did not allow it. Today, we take jogging apps for granted on the iPod and iPhone.

Similarly, because we don't expect a professional architect to attempt to design a house on his iPhone—it's just too small a screen for this task—there has been no software built for this purpose. But could such software be a breakthrough product on the iPad?

The point to be made is this: The iPad is ergonomically unique and its size and shape opens up unexplored territory. It is clearly not an iPhone, but neither is it a desktop computer, or a laptop. This means that the environments it can be used in, and the ways in which it is used, should be considered with an extremely open mind. The iPad can find a home in all kinds of weird and wonderful places, from car dashboards to hospital waiting rooms. It is your job as a developer to ignore traditional patterns of computer use and push the iPad into new spaces. Your reward for fresh thinking is the profit you'll make on the iPad App Store. People tend to go crazy with enthusiasm when you show something they have not seen before.

Identifying New Uses

As a powerful, inexpensive touchscreen computer, the iPad can be used to provide a direct-manipulation interface for almost any task you can dream up.

Later in this book, I'll discuss specific uses of the iPad in fields like entertainment, publishing, and music, but first I'd like to give you a broader sense of how to identify new uses for the iPad hardware, and to help you to understand the kind of apps that you could code for these new uses.

There are a few key points to remember about the iPad when you begin to think about how it could be used.

It's Light and Mountable

The iPad can be mounted on objects, or fixed inside objects. For example, with reinforcement, it could be used as the screen and computer controller of an ATM, or it could be used in the back of headrests in passenger planes as an entertainment device. It could be used as a GPS and stereo system in a car, or it could be embedded in a bar to allow drinkers to check sports results. Compare the price of the iPad to the cost of the hardware that could currently do these tasks, and you may find you can easily undercut your competitors in many fields. Think of the iPad as a raw engine that can do many tasks, rather than any specific task.

It's a Touchscreen

Because the iPad is a touchscreen, it can be used in situations where a keyboard would get messy and clogged up—as an ordering system in a restaurant, or as at a check-in point for an airline. Again, the equipment that has traditionally been used for these tasks is expensive, because it is niche and the companies that sell it can charge a fortune. However, the iPad hardware is mass-market and inexpensive, you can use this to your advantage because your iPad-based system can be priced aggressively.

Look around you as you go about your day. Think about the computer systems you use to buy a train ticket, or order food at a restaurant. How expensive is the hardware being used? Could you write an app for the iPad to replace this hardware and capture a new market?

You may find there is resistance to you entering these markets. "The iPad is a toy," you will be told. Ignore these people and follow your vision. The iPad is powerful enough.

Also consider commercial uses of the iPad where there is currently no computer hardware in place. What would it be like if you could tap the ingredients you'd like in your sandwich into mounted iPads while you waited in line for the sandwich to be made?

Could the iPad have uses underwater if it was mounted inside a waterproof case? What could a policeman use the iPad for? What about a carpenter? Ask yourself these kinds of wild questions a lot when you think about app ideas.

It's Low Power

The iPad has very low power requirements. It will run continuously for most of the day on its own charge, or you can plug it into a power supply. The iPad can draw as little as 2.5 watts of power in use, making it perfect for installation in vehicles and other situations where power is limited.

Of course there are also plenty of new uses for the iPad that do not rely on special mounting systems.

So, the iPad is a *tabula rasa*, presents new UI challenges, redefines the ergonomics of computing, and has triggered mass adoption of the touchscreen. Phew. You've definitely picked an interesting time to be developing software. Now that you know the basics, I'm going to tell you exactly how to use the magic of the iPad to turn your app idea into a goldmine.

Chapter 2
Entering the iPad Marketplace

The iPad is already one of the most popular consumer electronics products in history. Apple has been selling a staggering 4 million iPads per quarter. The only other non-phone product that sold in anything like this volume was the DVD player, which shifted a comparatively modest 350,000 units in its first year of release. To put this in perspective, Apple sold over 300,000 iPads on launch day alone, and one million iPads were sold within the following 28 days. The iPad market is enormous and growing. It's the most significant touchscreen computing platform in the world outside of mobile phones. No one knows exactly how big the iPad market will get, but we're told the Oompa-Loompas at Apple's factories are churning out iPads day and night to meet demand. The iPad user base is so big at the moment that a fortune can be made overnight with the right app idea and a clever execution.

As a professional developer, I considered other platforms, like Google's Android, which is being adapted for tablets. But the brutal truth of the matter, at the moment, is that the Android App Store is like the Wild West, and Apple's App Store is more like a polite dinner party where everyone shakes hands and leaves with a nice full feeling in their belly. There may come a point in the future where the Android marketplace becomes a viable and profitable place for developers, but for now the iPad is where the real money is. Analysts predict the iPad will become the fourth-largest consumer electronics category in 2011, making Apple over $9 billion in hardware sales alone—that's not even counting all the money developers will make from apps. If you're still wondering whether you backed the right platform, you can quit worrying. You did.

Making Money

If you want to make money-selling apps independently, the Apple App Store is by far the most financially rewarding option, which is lucky, because as an iPad developer, it's almost the only place you can be. All iPad apps must be sold through the official Apple Store, the only alternative being to buy a special license from Apple to deploy your apps privately to a set number of iPad devices within a single organization.

For most developers, apps will not be sold outside the App Store. But before you throw a fit about Apple's policy here, in their defense I should add that developers for the iPhone and iPad are making a lot more money than developers who are selling apps for "open" alternatives. As much as Apple might annoy us all, it does seem to be getting results. Imagine the enormous cost of building your own payment infrastructure, convincing customers that you are a reliable source, and dealing with sales transactions in hundreds of countries. When you look at it that way, Apple is offering a fairly good exchange for its 30% cut of your app revenue.

There are a few points you should consider when figuring out the size of the market for your app. The first is the current number of iPads sold and the second is the number of those people you think might be interested in buying your app. Broadly, this figure will give you an idea of the market that's relevant to your app. But there is also an entirely different market you can consider: those people you can sell a complete solution to. A complete solution includes iPads as part of the service you provide. For example, if your app is a point-of-sale (POS) app for a shop, or a stock-taking app for a warehouse, you can sell your app as part of a package that includes the iPad hardware. You users wouldn't need to have iPads already, because you can provide iPads to them as part of the cost of the solution you offer. One great example of this kind of app is *Square* by Squareup, a cash-register replacement for restaurants and other businesses, shown in the following image. The Square system was devised by Jack Dorsey, also a co-founder of Twitter. The system uses a small physical credit card reader that's plugged into the audio jack of the iPad, relaying information to the payment software.

Your target market does not necessarily need to own iPads yet. Don't assume that the market for your iPad app is limited to the number of devices currently sold, or to the users who own those devices. You can sell the iPad hardware along with your software as a complete solution.

TIP

Knowing Your Customers

Back in 1979, the brilliant Apple interface designer Jeff Raskin wrote a document describing the way he believed the perfect computer should be built. He called this his *Design Specifications for an Anthropophillic Computer*. In it he laid out his vision of a device that might now sound familiar to you.

Although Raskin's mission statement became the blueprint for the Macintosh, the device he describes sounds a lot more like the iPad. The Macintosh popularized the shift to graphical user interfaces, but it is only the iPad that meets the standards set out in Raskin's plan:

> "This is an outline for a computer designed for the person-in-the-street (or, to abbreviate: the PITS); one that will be truly pleasant to use, that will require the user to do nothing that will threaten his or her perverse delight in being able to say: "I don't know the first thing about computers," and one which will be profitable to sell, service and provide software for… Seeing the guts is taboo. Things in sockets is taboo (unless to make servicing cheaper without imposing too large an initial cost). Billions of keys on the keyboard is taboo. Computerese is taboo. Large manuals, or many of them (large manuals are a sure sign of bad design) is taboo. It is expected that sales of software will be an important part of the profit strategy for the computer."

Raskin made the vital point that computers and computer software should be understood by the person-in-the-street. This person-in-the-street is the average user, and understanding this individual is the key to building great software. This person in the street is exactly who you need to target if you want to build an app that sells like hotcakes.

"Ah," I hear you whimper, "But my app is for a specialist market of experts who get this stuff." Wrong. In almost any discipline you will find that the majority of computer users are confused and bewildered by the devices they use. They may learn how to do specific tasks fairly well, but if anything unexpected happens, they are stuck. I'll let you into one of the biggest secrets of selling successful apps: keep it simple.

TIP

The key paradox of good design, especially good software design, can be summed up in one simple phrase: "Easy is hard." To make software simple, elegant, and practical is very difficult. The majority of programmers and designers churn out monstrosities every day, and very few take the time to make their software elegant. If you want to make a killer iPad app, aim for elegance.

Unless you are writing software for computer scientists, it's very likely that your customer will be the person-in-the-street. It doesn't matter if you're writing software for doctors, fishermen, or stock brokers, the majority of them will get confused by your app unless you focus religiously on their needs.

This does not mean that you should not have respect for your users. You should understand that there is a very good reason why the majority of them have trouble negotiating a computer: It's because the windows, icons, mouse, and pointer (WIMP) system, popularized by MacOS and Microsoft Windows, uses such complex metaphors.

To insiders like you and me, a windowed operating system seems easy to grasp, but as a concept for the person-in-the-street it bears very little relationship to anything else in life outside computers and, as a result, is completely alien to them. As Raskin wrote in his outline, many people take a "perverse delight" in their ignorance; a sort of pride in their inability to understand or engage with computers. And who is to blame for this? Well, us. The designers and programmers.

With the iPad, Apple has reduced the iOS interface to a point of great simplicity, or in many cases removed distracting options from the experience entirely. This will be your approach, too. Sometimes software designed in this way frustrates a small number of technical users, but since the majority of users are not technical, you will make the experience better for the bulk of your customers by making the decision to limit options. This is important to remember when you come to design your app. You may feel the irresistible compulsion to add as many features as possible. Don't do it!

Respecting Your Users

Before Henry Ford invented the motorcar, he didn't go around asking people what he should build, or how he should build it. "If I had asked my customers what they wanted," Ford explained, "they would have said a faster horse."

The same is true for iPad apps. If you ask users what they want, you're very unlikely to get a vision of the future, just a complaint about the present. Most people struggle to imagine a reality that is much different from what's going on around them now. Your customers will be able to tell you if something is wrong (the horse is too slow), but their suggestions on how to fix the problem (a faster horse) are rarely useful. Consider this same effect in the world of software. If you listened to all your users, you'd end up with software that may do more, but just improves the same old ways of doing things, or becomes bloated with niche features.

Software that fulfills hundreds of different user requirements, but does none of them quickly and intuitively, is bad software. Many developers fall into a trap where they feel a kind of desperate need to satisfy each and every whim of their users. To avoid this, trust in your vision and use your skills as a designer to make the experience good for the majority of your users. Observe their difficulties, but understand that the solution to their problems can be found in you, not in the results of a survey. If you really want to make money on the App Store, you'll have to make strong decisions on behalf of your users. Act in their best interests, but don't always listen to them. Respect their wider needs by not doing everything they tell you to do.

Where should you look for answers to how your software can be improved then? Well, observation is one very effective tool, which you'll read about in more detail later. The other is intuition.

Source: Ford Motor Company ©1921

TIP

*Few design classes teach intuition, because it is incredibly hard to formalize the process. The education system likes to teach concepts it can assess empirically, and it would be pretty hard to write an exam on intuition. As a result, there are lots of design "rules" floating about out there, but very few focus on the individual's personal sense of what does and does not work. This innate sense is called **intuition**, and it is one of the most powerful tools you have as a designer or programmer. Albert Einstein came as close to a definition of this tricky creature as I've read when he said, "the intellect has little to do on the road to discovery. There comes a leap in consciousness, call it **intuition** or what you will, the solution comes to you and you don't know how or why."*

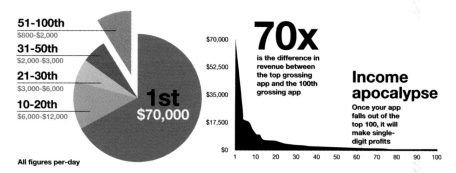

Source: www.appular.com

Your imagination is one of the most essential ingredients in killer iPad software design, so when you are creating an app, try to take a moment now and again to imagine that you are a first-time user of your app, and not the designer of the app. If you knew nothing of how it worked or what you were supposed to do, would it all make sense to you? Really concentrate, and put yourself in the place of this imaginary user; imagine these users sat next to you throughout the design process and make no concessions for faults in the interface. Constantly refine your app with them in mind.

Friends and work peers may be useful guinea pigs for your designs, but try to avoid questioning them. Restrict yourself to observation only. Try to figure out what's going wrong by watching users interact with your prototypes. The solutions to UI problems are more likely to come from watching, not questioning. Often users will be aware that *something* is wrong, but in their effort to articulate what that *something* is they may give you wildly misleading reasons. Trust your own observations.

Focusing on Your Marketing Campaign

Marketing is a dirty word for most programmers. Software designers also tend to deal with the tangible process of creating something, and we see marketing as a fraud, like a deceptive wizard casting a spell over the hapless consumer. When someone says marketing, you probably picture smug men and women in suits running through demographic profiles in a PowerPoint presentation. However, that's not the kind of marketing I'm talking about. I don't want you to create junk and then fool a customer into buying it, but I do want you to be in a position to make money from your app. Understanding marketing, *real* marketing, is the single most important way to make your fortune on the App Store.

Just to be clear on this, by "marketing" I don't mean looking at charts or customer profiles, or modeling long-term trends of late-adopters versus early adopters, or any of that business school nonsense. Instead, I mean telling a compelling story that will provoke an emotional response to your app, and drive a rational decision to purchase it. The narrative of your iPad app must be crystal clear to you, and it must be a story people want to tell each other. Apps sell because people talk about them to each other. If you ignore every other piece of advice in this book, take heed of this chapter. Yes, your app design is important. But, without marketing, nobody will ever see it.

TIP

I give some examples of iPad app marketing techniques in the section entitled "Marketing Your App." You might think the success of your app depends on the code and the graphics, but in fact, it depends on the thing that those two elements produce: A story, or narrative. If there is a good narrative to your app, people will share the story with each other, and the press will cover it. A narrative is not necessarily the story of how you made the app, or necessarily the story in the app. It can also be what the app does and why its uses are interesting. For example, an app that automatically takes photographs at a specified interval is technologically interesting, but the more compelling narrative is that someone attached an iPhone to a weather balloon and shot photographs of space using your app. What your app does is merely words on a page, but how people use it is a compelling human story. Consumers desire products that trigger an emotional response; there is nothing emotionally exciting about a spec sheet. Keep features lists out of your marketing campaign; make it about human stories.

Just in case you're not convinced yet, I'll tell you what will happen if you don't consider the marketing of your app before you start building it.

You will come up with a great idea. Everyone on your team will agree that it is fantastic and cannot fail. You'll explain the idea to friends and family, and they'll stand around and clap enthusiastically, wowed by your remarkable vision. You'll then spend months and months creating this iPad app, convinced that is unlike anything the world has ever seen, beautifully crafted in every way, surely the jewel of the iPad software kingdom. Then, barely alive from all the hard work, you will release your app. It will proudly enter the App Store, instantly fail to make the top ten (because the top ten is already stuffed with top-selling apps), and your app will vanish completely. Forever.

Forever and ever.

Nobody will see it, nobody will buy it, and nobody will care. You just wasted six months. I know because I've been there. The sad reality of the App Store is that you can build some really wonderful iPhone or iPad apps and never sell enough just to cover the food you ate while building them. However, there is one way you can avoid all this heartache and disappointment. You need to consider how you will market your app before you make any attempt to build it. Consider this early iPhone app I worked on, *Bauble*, pictured overleaf. We designed this app from the ground up to focus on a Christmas theme, specifically so that we would be guaranteed press coverage during the slow-news period around December.

To clarify: I don't mean design your app and build it and then start thinking about marketing it. I mean, as I did with *Bauble*, think about the marketing before you even pick up a pencil and start sketching out your first design. Think about the marketing before you open Photoshop, and certainly before you open Xcode. If you're no good at marketing, find a friend who is, or hire someone. You should hire someone who's good at marketing before you think about hiring a second programmer. There is nothing more important.

Consider the first app I designed, *Twitch Origins*. I didn't for a moment think about how the hell our team was going to communicate what it was, so Ben Roberts and I wasted a huge amount of time—months and months of hard graft, for nothing. *Twitch Origins* made a few hundred dollars, and vanished into the wilderness.

But then we got wise.

Our second app, *Bauble,* was designed from the very start to be demonstrable, and instantly desirable, in a 30-second YouTube video. For you, the first question before starting work on any app now is, "Can I sell this in 30 seconds on YouTube?" If there's any doubt at all about it, choose another app idea.

With *Alice for the iPad*, we took this idea even further. Before beginning the project, I had a long think about how what book to adapt and how to sell it. The *Alice in Wonderland* book stood out, not purely because it would make a great app, but most importantly because I knew I could sell the idea in a short viral video. We timed it to launch around the time of the Tim Burton movie remake, and we took a new piece of technology (Chipmunk Physics) and used it in a way nobody had ever seen before. Take a look at how many hits the video showing *Alice for the iPad* got on YouTube. Over 1.4 million people have watched this promo and many of them bought the app as a result. None of these people would have found us in the App Store, it's just too crowded.

TIP

*Remember, the App Store will not sell your app for you. It will stock it and make it available, but the only way people will buy it is if **you** advertise it. Apple won't tell you this, and most app designers don't realize it either, but 90% of app design is about discarding app ideas that will not sell before you waste time on them, and developing the ones that you have a clear marketing plan for.*

Assuming you have no money to advertise, the only real option is to use YouTube as your advertising platform. In which case, pitch your app ideas from this perspective when you're discussing them. Don't pitch the app idea; pitch the video that will sell the app on YouTube. Customers won't buy your app based on the features you've listed on a sheet of paper; they will buy it based on what they see in your 30-second YouTube video. The deeper excellence of your app will keep people coming back, and recommending you to their friends, but without YouTube you will never get your customers through the door. *Remember: Marketing idea first, app later.*

Alice for the iPad

Alice for the iPad is a trademark of Atomic Antelope LTD.

Dreaming Up App Ideas

What is every other app developer out there doing? Maybe you should take a look around the App Store and find out? Although this seems like a good strategy, it's a waste of time and a very easy mistake to make. If you seek inspiration from the App Store you'll likely end up trying to improve on someone else's product, fighting it out for a tiny slice of a crowded marketplace. The App Store is a graveyard for creative thought. Killer apps come from you.

If you really want to shake things up, look for your inspiration anywhere except the App Store. In fact, look for inspiration outside of the media that other developers are likely to be looking at. Most iPad developers watch television, so steer clear of television. Most developers read blogs and design websites, so avoid spending too much time on these. Have a think about fun things to do that most developers are unlikely to be doing. Will many developers be reading 19th century literature? Probably not. Get yourself a bunch of Mary Shelley novels, and a book of paintings by Paul Cézanne. Most developers don't go to pottery classes or browse the botanical illustrations of Ferdinand Bauer. Walk around your town or city, explore junk shops, pick a book at random from the library, sit in a cafe and watch people for half an hour. Listen to their conversations.

No programming manual in the world is likely to give you this advice, and that is one of the big reasons why software design has, until very recently, been dominated by sprawling, badly thought-out ideas. But if you look for inspiration outside the world of computing, and you search for it in mediums that no other developer has considered, you will end up equipped with a weapon that is far more powerful and compelling than any other: *Originality*.

It's only because Steve Jobs took calligraphy classes that the Macintosh computer had proportionally spaced fonts. Think about that for a moment. The whole reason the desktop publishing revolution began is because Steve Jobs took a calligraphy class. Most people would tell you that if you wanted to develop software to replace the printing press you should learn all about printing presses. But the reverse is true. If you really want to create an amazing app that takes a new creative approach, open your senses. Don't explore the world assuming that you should restrict your interests to pursue a specific goal. Wander into different experiences and disciplines because these will guide you to a new, more interesting goal. Great app design comes from exploration.

TIP

The actor and comedy writer John Cleese gave what I find is very good advice for coming up with iPad app ideas. He suggests that you create a "tortoise enclosure" for your creative mind—a safe area where ideas can surface and you don't feel stressed out or put upon by the bustle of the modern world. Cleese views the creative mind as a nervous tortoise that will only sneak out and look around if it feels safe in an enclosure. Cleese creates for himself "boundaries of space, and boundaries of time." The boundaries of space keep interruptions away from him, and this involves finding a quiet place to work. The boundaries of time keep him relaxed and focused. By designating a time and place to work, you create an oasis for the subconscious mind to come up with ideas. Of course, you might find you get your best ideas skydiving. Each to their own.

Getting Press Coverage for Your App

I worked as a journalist in the national newspaper industry for many years, and I noticed something interesting that newspapers and magazines do to organize their features content. Consider this strange occurrence: If you pick up a newspaper on Napoleon's birthday, you're likely to find yourself reading a feature about his great battles. If you pick up a magazine around Christmas, you're likely to find yourself reading about the top ten Christmas presents, or the top ten Christmas iPad apps. This is because the editors of these publications theme articles around calendar events. They write features and news stories pinned on holidays, celebrations, seasons, and the anniversaries of historical events. If you sat in an editorial meeting at *The Times* in London at Christmas time, you would hear discussion after discussion about how to theme the newspaper's content around Christmas.

Remember, the first question you should ask yourself before starting work on any app now is, "Can I sell this in 30 seconds on YouTube?" If there's any doubt at all about it, choose another app idea.

TIP

So, given that these publications are already desperate to fill their pages with stories that relate to these calendar events, what could you do that would make them likely to print news about your app? The answer is this: Build apps themed around these calendar events and launch them to coincide with that event. The advantage of this approach is that newspapers and magazines are already hungry to print stories about these topics, and your press release will perfectly coincide with their editorial theme. This makes it a hundred times more likely that they will write about your app.

Here are a few examples of events you could theme your app around.

Special Holidays

National holidays, especially Christmas, are great calendar dates to theme your app around. Christmas is a particularly slow time for news. Nothing much happens in the late winter months, and so you're likely to get picked up by many news sources if your app is well designed and Christmas-themed. The App Store is flooded with Christmas apps each year, but very few of them are any good. I saw an opportunity here one year, and so we made the app I mentioned earlier, *Bauble.* It used Chipmunk Physics to simulate a Christmas tree decoration. The user could shake his hand from side to side and the bauble would bounce around the screen. The app also let you pick from a selection of decorations, and choose from one of many backgrounds—all picked from public domain art.

The next thing I did was make a video where I embedded the iPhone into the front of a Christmas card, to create *The World's Most Expensive Christmas Card*, which I then filmed myself posting into a mailbox. The result was hundreds of thousands of views on YouTube and a global frenzy to make Christmas cards like the one we'd created. The app sold thousands.

Although it helped that the app was a great design, we didn't even start developing it until we had picked a press-friendly theme—Christmas—and decided on our YouTube marketing campaign—making *The World's Most Expensive Christmas Card*. If you want to sell thousands of copies of your app, these are the kinds of decisions you need to make before you write a single line of code.

New Film Releases

Is there a film adaptation of a book about to be released? You could ride on the back of publicity surrounding that film by making that book into an app. You can either write to the book publisher to secure the rights, or even better, only pick book titles that are in the public domain and can be used for free. Many of the world's most popular stories have fallen out of copyright, as have many gorgeous old illustrations like this Edmund Dulac print for *The Princess and the Pea*. Keep checking the film release schedules on imdb.com—you can see what's coming out months in advance. This is exactly what we did with *Alice for the iPad*. There was a natural resurgence of interest in Alice because of the Tim Burton movie adaptation. It didn't hurt to piggy-back on the publicity generated by the picture. This is a useful money-saving tip: Pay attention to upcoming movie releases and let Hollywood do the publicity for you.

The World's Most Expensive Christmas Card is a trademark of Atomic Antelope LTD.

Stirring Up Controversy

There is one final way to use the press to get noticed in the App Store, and that's to stir up an imagined controversy over your app. If there's one thing the press loves, it's conflict and argument. If you can convince the press that your app is in some way ushering in the downfall of society, or in some other way causing a lot of people to get angry, they will tend to seize on that controversy, amplify it, and generate a lot more angry people than were ever angry in the first place. Oddly, the more people who get angry, the more publicity your app gets, and the more it will sell. This phenomenon is extremely funny to watch in action, because in many cases nobody was angry to begin with. Just look at all the people who appeared to be angry over the videogame *Grand Theft Auto*, when only a tiny percentage of them had ever played it. You can see this kind of effect happening in news stories all over the place, and you can use it to publicize your app. I'm not going to give you specific examples, because I'll get in trouble with the newspapers and websites I've used this technique on. But I can give you an imaginary example of how you might create controversy over your app.

Imagine that you have made an iPad app that is a virtual cookery book. It holds 200 recipes for lots of popular dishes. The press is not interested in your app because there is no calendar event that it ties into neatly, and there is no celebrity endorsement—the only two things that usually get a newspaper editor interested in anything. What are you going to do to get press attention?

Well, let's think up some controversies that could surround your app. What if it means the death of traditional cookery books? Could you find a well-known cook to denounce your app and claim it will ruin the cookery book industry? The press might be interested in a story like that. Or, what if one of the recipes in your book is for dish that includes garden ants? Could you find someone who researches the nutritional benefits of eating insects and frame your press release around this? Is it ethical to eat insects? Probably; I don't know, but I'd be happy to read about it and a newspaper is more likely to print a story like this than they are to print a story that's purely about a developer launching a cookery app.

◀ *Source: Edmund Dulac illustration*

Right, now you know how to enter the iPad marketplace. You also know that the first step in building a killer app is not to build anything at all: First you must plan a marketing campaign. You also know how to save money by planning your app around a calendar or cultural event, or by joyriding a Hollywood movie publicity campaign. In the next chapter, I'll explain how to find inspiration for your killer app idea.

Chapter 3
Getting
Inspired

Picasso said, "Inspiration exists, but it has to find us working." Now you might be suspicious of Picasso because of those three years he refused to paint in any color except blue, but on this matter he makes an important point. You can't sit around waiting for a good idea to slap you on the forehead; you have to move about, engage in an act of creation. In this chapter I'm going to get you thinking about the kind of iPad software that will thrill and surprise your audience. But just reading this chapter is not enough; you need to take action based on my suggestions. Even if some of the app genres I'm covering here don't seem relevant to your specific project, you'll find it useful to read through every section in this chapter regardless. The design advice contained here is not specific to any particular app category and applies across all software you create for the iPad.

You might be surprised how often you find yourself inspired by app designs that, on the surface, appear completely different to the one you're designing. As you learned in Chapter 2, seeking direct inspiration from the App Store is not the best way to come up with an original killer app idea, but it is nevertheless extremely useful to get a sense of what is already out there because new ideas often spring from the merging of old ones. Keep half an eye on new apps because these will give you a feel for the iPad's general capabilities and the technologies that you can use. Designing for the iPad is all about opening your mind to new ideas, and some of these ideas may come from observing where existing apps fail, or adopting existing technologies and shaping them into new forms.

Grasping the Core Uses of the iPad

Nobody knows what the core uses of the iPad are yet. Lots of people are happy to take a pretty good guess, but the core uses of the iPad will eventually match the uses of the desktop computer, and then some.

Earlier we looked at how the iPad has eroded the barrier between users and software — the iPad hardware seems to literally become the software, taking on the properties of the virtual devices that are programmed to fit on its screen. This is because the iPad is a direct-manipulation device—you can actually touch objects on the iPad, and the device appears to physically "become" any number of other devices.

When the iPad looks like an electronic keyboard, it has actually become an electronic keyboard for all practical purposes. The same situation occurs when the iPad is used as a television, or when it becomes a Sat Nav system, or one of many other thousands of things it can morph into. The iPad is unique because, on a tactile level, it undergoes a digital transubstantiation into the hardware the software is simulating. As a result, its uses are enormously varied, and those uses go well beyond the traditional computing model.

What follows are some loose definitions of what are currently thought to be the core uses of the iPad. Yet there are hundreds of other ways of using the device that nobody has dreamt up yet. If you're working for a client, the likelihood is that their app will fall into one of these categories—clients tend not to be terribly imaginative. But if you are working on your own, be aware that the best app you can make will probably not fit neatly into one of these genres; it's more likely to be an unpredictable combination of them, or something else entirely.

TIP

*One useful starting point for developing a new iPad app is to consider a mash-up of existing services. Mash-ups have created some of the more interesting technologies of the last few years. To create a mash-up, begin with the simple premise: "What if I mixed X with Y?" For example, what if you mashed **MySpace** with **Flickr**? That's the thought process that led to the creation of Facebook. What if you mashed Twitter with a copy of **Cosmopolitan** magazine? You might end up with something that looks very much like **Flipboard**—a brilliant iPad app that takes your Twitter feed and uses it to publish a virtual magazine featuring your friends. What if you mashed **BBC News** with **Scrabble**? I don't know, but I'd be interested in finding out. Playing about with mash-ups is a great way to get you thinking about fresh iPad app ideas.*

The iPad as a Video Entertainment Device

Apple has the video market for the iPad catered for very well. Not only does iTunes serve films to iPad owners, but every iPad comes with a YouTube application that satisfies most users looking for video content. Your challenge in creating a video-based app for the iPad is in imagining something that is new and compelling not already served by iTunes or YouTube. This is not meant to discourage you from trying. There is plenty of room to make money in this area, but it's important to be aware that the obvious video applications for the iPad already exist. Your challenge is to come up with something that turns heads.

Flixster is a good example of an app that thinks laterally about the video category and avoids replicating features of apps that are bundled with the iPad. *Flixster* is a clever mash-up of three existing ideas: movie review websites, movie listings websites, and movie trailer websites. Within the *Flixster* app you can look up a movie, check the reviews and the trailers, check show times, and book a ticket. Although these things are already possible on the web, *Flixster* is far more elegant and complete than any web-based solution and is location-aware—it can tell you exactly what's currently showing near your iPad.

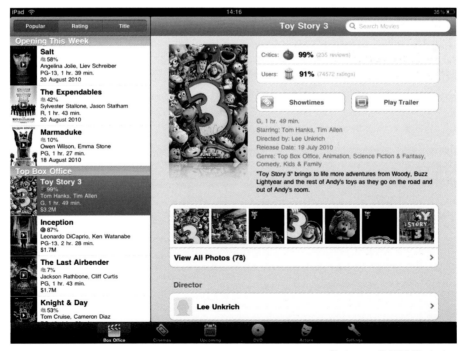

www.flixster.com © 2010 Flixster Inc.

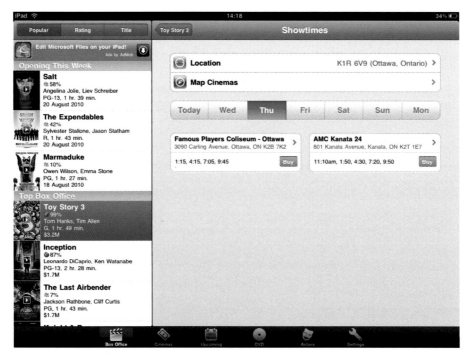

www.flixster.com © 2010 Flixster Inc.

The BBC has also produced an interesting video app for the iPad. It allows users to browse specific news categories and quickly view news footage. I recommend downloading it from the App Store and having a play. Although the *BBC News* app is fairly polished, it does illustrate one pitfall that many content providers are likely to struggle with on the iPad—the BBC app really doesn't do much more than rearrange the content from the BBC website. When you design your apps, be very careful that you are not reproducing content that is already best served by an exiting website. Having said this, what will probably happen in the case of many apps from major broadcasters is that their initial offerings will evolve into more substantial software that does eventually justify its status as a discrete app. However, unless you are extremely fortunate, you will not have the luxury of a big brand to finance your experiments. As indie developers, we have to get it right the first time or we often won't have any money left to give it another shot.

A more impressive video player interface is the offering from ABC. Their player offers a very clear and visually rich scheduling guide and has been carefully designed not to overload the viewer with options. It's immediately obvious how to interact with the player, and shows are selected with the minimum of taps.

www.abc.com © 2010 The Walt Disney Company.

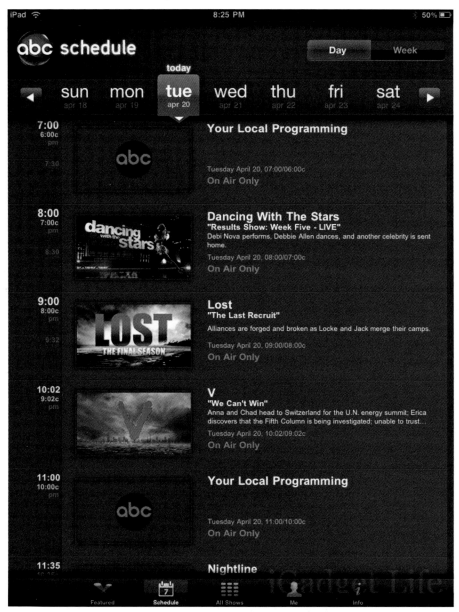

www.abc.com © 2010 The Walt Disney Company.

ABC has wholeheartedly embraced the iPad look and feel, and its app has the appearance of an extremely slick package. Be aware that users will have a visual-emotional response to your app before they touch it, and the more positive that response, the better they will feel about purchasing it. Although it's critical to back up a strong look with effective programming and good UI flow, you'll be surprised how much of an impression the appearance of your app has on a user.

Less successful is the *Netflix* app for the iPad which, while functional, does not appear to match the look and feel of the iPad UI guidelines. Graphically, *Netflix* feels a little forced on the iPad platform at the moment.

More interesting than these apps from the big broadcasters are the innovative efforts of smaller developers to bring video to the iPad. *Air Video*, for example, is one video app that elegantly solves the problem of mixed video formats, some of which are tricky to convert to a file the iPad will play. *Air Video* converts video formats like AVI and DivX on your desktop computer, converts them in real-time and then streams them to your iPad. *Air Video* is a good example of a well-executed concept coupled with a solid UI. It's also a free download from the App Store, and it's worth taking a look at what the developers have achieved.

www.netflix.com © 2010 Netflix Inc.

These apps will begin to give you an idea of the iPad's basic video functionality. The iPad can stream hosted video, and can store video locally. It can display high definition content and, because of its long battery life, users can watch video for a whole working day without charging the device. Interestingly, the iPad can also output video to a television screen or projector, using a VGA adaptor. However, as a developer, you must specifically enable this option in your app. Unlike a traditional laptop, the iPad does not permit video mirroring unless the app developer specifically coded a provision for this—blame DRM for this strange decision on Apple's part. This support for external video is extremely interesting, and few apps have really explored the possibilities for presentation here. Everything from digital presentation software, like Apple's Keynote, to full-blown VJ (Video Jockey) systems can be built for the iPad.

Imagining Games for the iPad

The siren call of the games category on the iPad will lure many developers onto the rocks, while others it propels to unimaginable riches. The profits to be made here are extraordinary for the lucky few who can stick it out in the most fiercely competitive category on the App Store. If you're a games developer there are several advantages to the iPad as entertainment platform, but perhaps the most appealing, in these early days, is that the iPad market is currently smaller than the iPhone market—so there's much more chance of getting your game noticed.

Many of the early titles from iPad game developers have been simple adaptations of their iPhone titles. Game designers are at an advantage over the developers of most other apps because a number of games do not suffer from usability problems when scaled. Consider a racing game, for example. To adapt this game for the iPad, the control mechanism (tilting the device to steer the car on screen) remains fundamentally the same on the iPhone and iPad. Although the iPad screen is significantly bigger, there are few on-screen controls, making it easier to address the scaling issues discussed in Chapter 1. You can see this in action in games like *Real Racing HD*.

www.realracinghd.com © 2010 Firemint Inc.

www.realracinghd.com © 2010 Firemint Inc.

Games are also an oddity in the world of apps because users do not expect UI consistency from title to title. This is because the game experience is not about "getting things done," but more about "having fun." The UI can therefore be more playful and idiosyncratic. Videogamers, unlike users of a word processor or email app, tend to accept that a game has a unique universe with its own rules and control system. This is because the user's main objective in a game app (to have fun) is not guided by a pressing external objective outside the app (to write and print a letter, or to calculate business expenses).

This is not to say that apps outside the games category cannot be playful and unique with their UI design, but users tend to come to some app categories—most notably productivity apps—with an expectation that they will recognize common features in the workspace you have designed for them. They expect that the word processor you have built them will in some way resemble the last word processor they used. For example, it will use a flashing cursor to indicate your place in the text, and it will have a Font menu.

If your app doesn't share some common features with other apps in the same category, you have impacted the user's productivity, forced him to learn new conventions, and made your app a more difficult sell. Perhaps, in the long term, you will have improved the user's productivity with a superior interface, but this will not be his first impression.

In the world of games, however, nobody expects *Tetris* to resemble *Pac-Man*, or *Little Big Planet* to resemble *Sonic the Hedgehog*. For many gamers, learning the control system is part of the fun of playing the game. This doesn't mean players will excuse a bad control system on the iPad, it just means that you don't have to pay too much attention to the UI conventions in your competitor's games—users are much more forgiving of innovative approaches in this genre. Look at *Zen Bound* for example. This iPad app doesn't resemble any user interface I've ever seen, but the result is spectacular. It uses an extraordinary control system that allows you to tie up objects on the screen. *Zen Bound* uses accelerometer data to work out exactly how you are holding the iPad. The lite version of the app is free to download, so it's definitely worth taking a look at if you had any doubts about the iPad shaking up the videogame industry.

The iPad is more interesting in this regard than conventional games consoles because designers can go one step beyond the popular motion control systems used in devices like the Nintendo Wii. As with a games console, the iPad's accelerometer provides a data feed that allows games to react to the iPad's orientation and direction of movement. But unlike today's game consoles, the iPad is both the display and the controller. It's this combination of features that allows games like *Multipong* and *Labyrinth* to exist. Both these titles use the iPad's unique features to their advantage. In the case of *Multipong*, the designers have used multi-touch recognition to allow up to four players and, in the case of *Labyrinth*, the game responds directly to the orientation of the iPad.

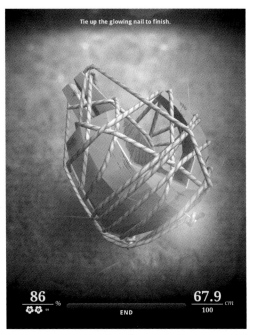

www.zenbound.com © 2010 Secret Exit Ltd.

www.zenbound.com © 2010 Secret Exit Ltd.

www.zenbound.com © 2010 Secret Exit Ltd.

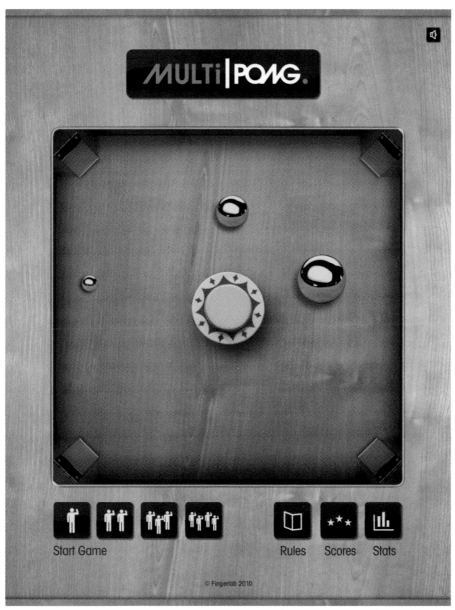

www.multipong.com © 2010 FingerLab Inc.

www.multipong.com © 2010 FingerLab Inc.

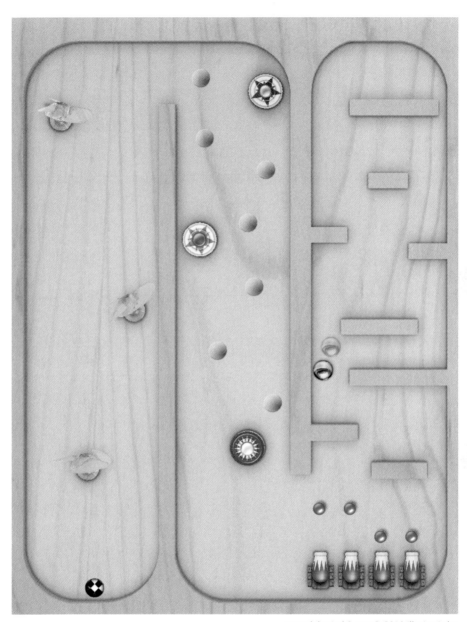

www.labyrinth2.com © 2010 Illusion Labs.

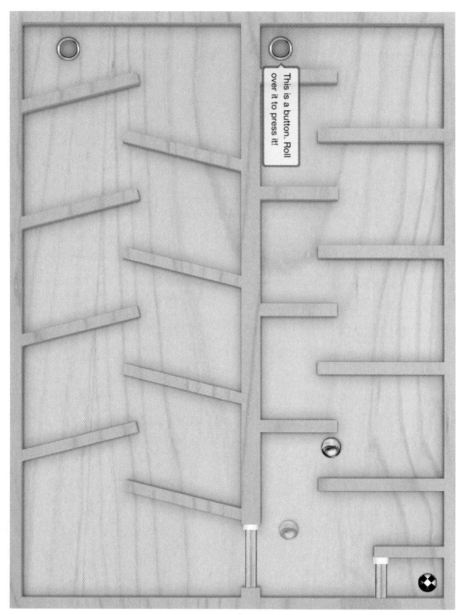

www.labyrinth2.com © 2010 Illusion Labs.

The iPad is unique because you hold it in your hands while watching the results of your movements on the same device. This allows for some unique game universes, but also presents some serious limitations you need to be aware of. One important limitation is that games cannot rely on too much accelerometer movement, or the display becomes difficult for the players to focus on. For example, a driving game that requires the players to make rapid movements of more than 30 degrees off-horizon, risks a situation where the players cannot concentrate properly on what it happening on the screen—it's all a blur. This rule applies across genres that use the iPad's accelerometer, and as a designer you must either restrict the range of possible motion, or the speed at which the motion occurs.

With these limitations in mind, there is an enormous range of possibilities for iPad games that are compelling and original, using gameplay elements that have never been imagined before. Early titles, like *Labyrinth*, have adapted a pre-existing game concept (the handheld puzzle game) and used the iPad's dimensions and accelerometer features to great effect. Other titles, like *Multipong*, have extended these ideas even further to create an addictive multiplayer game that really has no counterpart in the physical world.

By far the most extraordinary gaming success story on the iPad so far is *Cut the Rope HD*. This app is the perfect illustration of how simple, well thought-out concepts are the strongest sell for the iPad platform. *Cut the Rope* presents a series of increasingly tricky puzzles in which the gamer must cut ropes to deliver a tasty candy to a cute green creature, the "Om Nom." The rope physics in the game are extremely realistic and it's a very addictive casual gaming experience. As a result, ZeptoLab have sold millions of copies. Aside from the beautiful physics system underlying the game, ZeptoLab took the psychology of the gameplay very seriously indeed—as should you.

PocketGamer.biz asked ZeptoLab CTO Efim Voinov why the game was so compelling. Instead of going on about the graphics and features of the game, Voinov explained, "we also wanted to exploit the parental instinct of the players [with the Om Nom], because feeding a little baby is one of the warmest experiences the parents get. So, we felt that the emotional motivation for the player to complete the level would work best, not to mention that chewing action itself has some weird power of emitting the cuteness." So, you see, ZeptoLab wasn't just thinking about the game, they were thinking about the human psychology of the *players* and what would appeal to them.

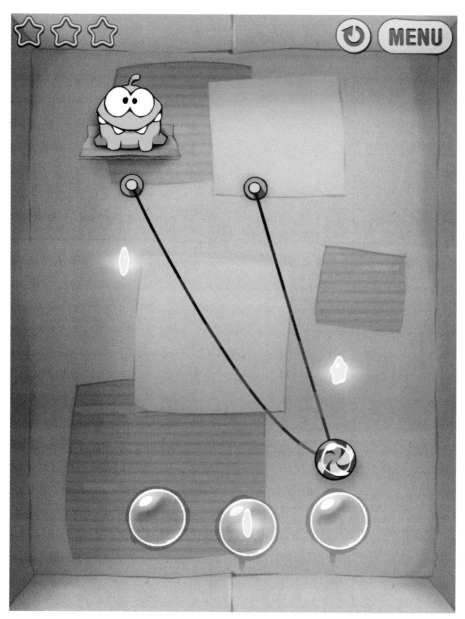

www.zeptolab.com © 2010 Chillingo.

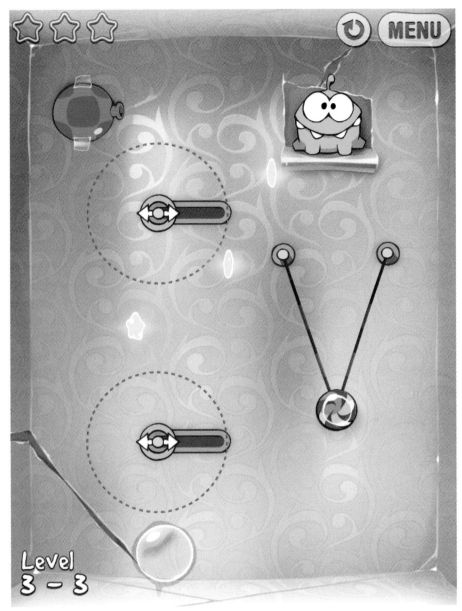

www.zeptolab.com © 2010 Chillingo.

As game designers begin to get to grips with the unusual control interfaces offered by the iPad, we will begin to see more games that evolve directly from the feature set of the iPad itself. Although it's still useful for you to consider adapting real-world physical games for the iPad (ball-based puzzle games being one obvious example), the most innovative titles will not rely on the existence of any real-world counterpart outside the iPad.

www.bigbucketsoftware.com © 2010 Big Bucket Software.

www.bigbucketsoftware.com © 2010 Big Bucket Software.

Take a look at games like *The Incident*, pictured here, which is a good demonstration of the surreal stuff iPad developers are now coming out with. This app takes the look and feel of an ancient 8-bit videogame and transplants it into the 21st century world of an accelerometer-equipped iPad. It's a neat demonstration of how, as developers, we can reuse elements of old videogame culture and give them a new twist for the device. *Super Mega Worm*, pictured here, is also worth looking at if you want another great example of an 8-bit revival game on the iPad. The rather horrific level of violence in the title is completely offset by the blocky pixilation of the graphics and glorious coin-op arcade aesthetic.

www.deceasedpixel.com © 2010 Deceased Pixel LLC.

www.deceasedpixel.com © 2010 Deceased Pixel LLC.

If you want to design a best-selling game for the iPad, you'll have to think very hard about how to use the accelerometer and touchscreen to your full advantage. You'll read about this in more depth in Chapter 8.

TIP

Educational Possibilities for the iPad

I'll let you into a big secret about the educational market for the iPad: It's huge! There are 76.6 million children in education in the United States alone. What's very interesting is that many of the educators I've talked to about the iPad are overwhelmingly enthusiastic about using the device in an educational setting, but have no idea how they should be using it yet. The market is wide open for innovation.

I've spent a lot of time in schools watching kids interact with the iPad—there's something about the touchscreen direct-manipulation interface that children really get. I think it's because they tend to find extraordinary pleasure in spatial interactions—moving objects around and exploring the world. The iPad is uniquely placed to engage them. It allows students to physically touch the educational materials they're presented with.

There are two big concerns over iPad use in schools, so I'll deal with these before you take a look at example applications for the iPad. The first concern is the expense of the iPad device itself. It can be reasonably argued that the iPad is a very expensive educational tool and will be made available only to the richest students. I agree that this is true at the moment, but as the iPad (and other tablet computers like it) assume a wider role in the classroom, the cost of iPads will begin to offset the cost of other equipment in the classroom. Expensive projector screens, interactive whiteboards, and the money involved in maintaining a school desktop computer network may be superseded by iPads and other tablets. If you also factor in the cost of classroom materials that the iPad can simulate—textbooks, drawing paper, and diaries—you can begin to see where I'm going with this. The iPad may eventually pay for itself in savings. There is now every indication that the cost of tablets will fall dramatically. Educators in India are already developing tablets for a very low cost. As the tablet market expands, your position as a developer in the early days of the iPad will mean you can take advantage of the tablet-computing explosion.

A tablet-based educational system might seem like a whimsical vision of the future, but it will quickly become affordable. As for any practical concerns over the tablet form-factor, don't forget that the education system was tablet-based many hundreds of years before the iPad—a curious full-circle in the evolution of form that apps like *MathBoard* pay homage to.

Educators often have another concern over the use of iPads in the classroom. They wonder how the iPad will change teachers and the students they teach. Although, as a developer, your first concern is probably economic (will schools buy this app?), the educational market carries some hefty ethical responsibilities. You owe it to your users to consider exactly when and how the iPad benefits a classroom, and when it does not.

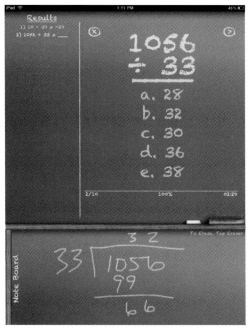

www.palasoftware.com © 2010 palasoftware Inc.

There is always the risk that devices like the iPad attempt to solve problems that do not exist. For example, consider the social aspects of iPad use in a classroom. Would it benefit students if they were all staring at iPads on their desks when a topic was being discussed, or is the social exchange where a teacher discusses a topic with a class and writes on a blackboard more effective for learning?

I'm not offering any easy answers to these questions at this point. I'll return to them later. However, in the educational genre of apps, more than any other, it's important to consider not just whether you can create an educational app for a certain task, but also whether you should. In some cases, like the excellent *Elements* app, the end result is resounding proof of the idea, but don't automatically assume that interactive is better.

www.palasoftware.com © 2010 palasoftware Inc.

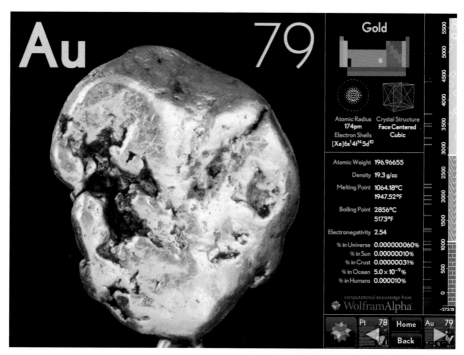

Au 79

Gold

Atomic Radius 174pm
Electron Shells [Xe]6s^{1}4f^{14}5d^{10}

Crystal Structure Face Centered Cubic

Atomic Weight 196.96655
Density 19.3 g/cc
Melting Point 1064.18°C
1947.52°F
Boiling Point 2856°C
5173°F
Electronegativity 2.54

% in Universe 0.000000060%
% in Sun 0.00000010%
% in Crust 0.00000031%
% in Ocean 5.0 × 10^{-9}%
% in Humans 0.000010%

computational knowledge from
WolframAlpha

Pt 78 | Home | Au 79
Back

www.touchpress.com © 2010 Touch Press Inc.

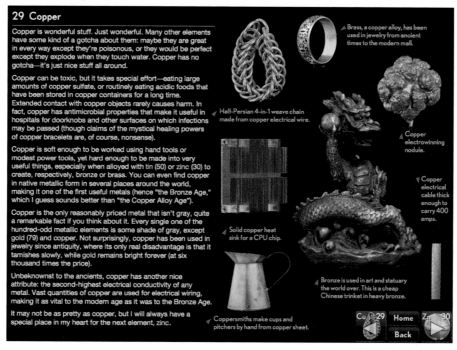

29 Copper

Copper is wonderful stuff. Just wonderful. Many other elements have some kind of a gotcha about them: maybe they are great in every way except they're poisonous, or they would be perfect except they explode when they touch water. Copper has no gotcha—it's just nice stuff all around.

Copper can be toxic, but it takes special effort—eating large amounts of copper sulfate, or routinely eating acidic foods that have been stored in copper containers for a long time. Extended contact with copper objects rarely causes harm. In fact, copper has antimicrobial properties that make it useful in hospitals for doorknobs and other surfaces on which infections may be passed (though claims of the mystical healing powers of copper bracelets are, of course, nonsense).

Copper is soft enough to be worked using hand tools or modest power tools, yet hard enough to be made into very useful things, especially when alloyed with tin (50) or zinc (30) to create, respectively, bronze or brass. You can even find copper in native metallic form in several places around the world, making it one of the first useful metals (hence "the Bronze Age," which I guess sounds better than "the Copper Alloy Age").

Copper is the only reasonably priced metal that isn't gray, quite a remarkable fact if you think about it. Every single one of the hundred-odd metallic elements is some shade of gray, except gold (79) and copper. Not surprisingly, copper has been used in jewelry since antiquity, where its only real disadvantage is that it tarnishes slowly, while gold remains bright forever (at six thousand times the price).

Unbeknownst to the ancients, copper has another nice attribute: the second-highest electrical conductivity of any metal. Vast quantities of copper are used for electrical wiring, making it as vital to the modern age as it was to the Bronze Age.

It may not be as pretty as copper, but I will always have a special place in my heart for the next element, zinc.

Brass, a copper alloy, has been used in jewelry from ancient times to the modern mall.

Half-Persian 4-in-1 weave chain made from copper electrical wire.

Copper electrowinning nodule.

Copper electrical cable thick enough to carry 400 amps.

Solid copper heat sink for a CPU chip.

Bronze is used in art and statuary the world over. This is a cheap Chinese trinket in heavy bronze.

Coppersmiths make cups and pitchers by hand from copper sheet.

Cu 29 | Home | Zn 30
Back

www.touchpress.com © 2010 Touch Press Inc.

Finally, be aware of the weight advantages to the iPad, and its flexibility in delivering interactive textbook, or traditional, static textbooks. The iPad may be more cumbersome than a single text book, but as a student begins to attend classes, and collects increasing numbers of bulky books, the weight can soon add up. This is especially true of university students, and fortunately this is also the educational group most likely to have the means to purchase iPads—making them a great target for your app designs.

The iPad also allows textbook publishers to push live updates to their apps, modifying information in their books as new studies and theories are announced. iPad textbooks are also an appealing proposition because they can contain interactive parts, including video, audio, and physical simulations. The iPad is particularly useful in presenting educational material with an interactive element. Take a look at how much more interesting a learning app is when instruction accompanies a practical element in the app TabToolkit, which teaches music.

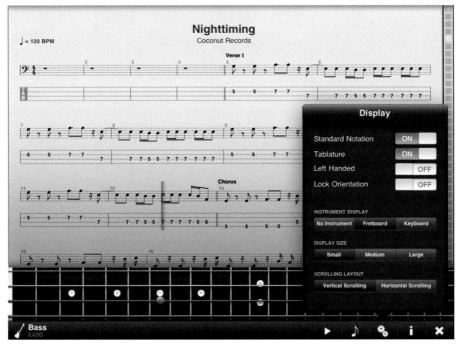

www.tabtoolkit.com © 2010 Agile Partners Inc.

www.tabtoolkit.com © 2010 Agile Partners Inc.

Using the iPad for Content Creation

Content creation is a pretty broad category, but I've picked that phrase intentionally to make an important point. A lot of criticism has been leveled at the iPad by developers and journalists who view it, and Apple, as being in the business of content consumption, not content creation. Some critics think the iPad will be used foremost to passively view video content supplied by Apple through iTunes, and to browse websites. Again, this is one of the many assumptions about the iPad that you, as the developer of a killer app, will have to ignore. The iPad is perfectly capable of "lean-back, feet-up" computing, but this is far from all is it capable of. There is some confusion among developers over the iPad's role as a device for drawing, writing, producing music, and other expressive forms. I want to clear this confusion up before you go any further: The iPad is one of the most advanced content-creation devices ever built.

The iPad is already better suited to advanced content creation than a desktop computer because, as I discussed in Chapter 1, it allows direct-manipulation; the user touches the objects on-screen directly, not by using a mouse or keyboard. In many traditional arts, whether it's a painting (brush on canvas) or playing music (fingers on the strings of a guitar), the person behind the creative work has a tactile involvement in its production. The same is uniquely true on the iPad. This has naturally inspired software simulations of real-life instruments like *Air Harp*, which simulates a harp, and *AmpliTube*, which simulates guitar effects and amplifier cabs.

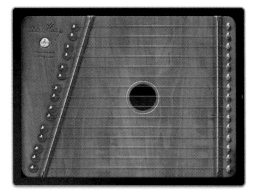

www.air-harp.com © 2010 touchGrove LLC.

www.amplitube.com © 2010 IK Multimedia Production Srl.

At the moment, many of the finger-to-screen interactions used in iPad apps are still quite crude. This is because many app designers are still locked into the old paradigms of desktop computing.

Remember that, until this point in computing history, most user interfaces were designed for use with a mouse and keyboard. It's hard for us, as designers, to break free from the conventions that sprung up around these older input devices, and we don't always recognize that we are falling into the old way of doing things. There is also a tendency towards real-world parallels in the iPad interface designs from many apps so far. Consider the look of the *Mixr* app, which looks very much like a traditional pair of record decks.

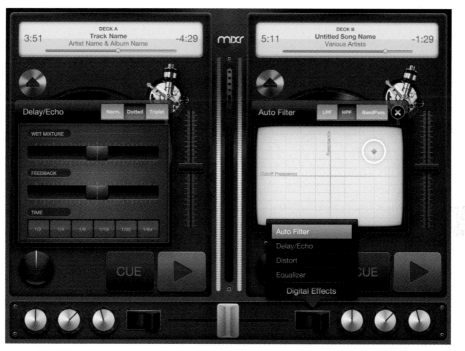

www.ipadmixr.com © 2010 Noe Ruiz and Ben Stahlhood II

Although reasonably effective, it attempts to shoehorn an existing analogue control system into the digital realm. What might be a more exciting avenue of approach is to reconsider the basic user interface of a musical device, like the record decks, break it down to its core purpose—in this case, to mix between tracks—and then invent a new interface that achieves this purpose without relying on legacy metaphors—in this case, the old analogue record decks. For one example of what I'm getting at here, take a look at *PatternMusic,* which completely departs from an interface that has any traditional parallel, but at the same time makes the experience of creating music infinitely more suited to the iPad's specific feature set.

To make full use of the iPad, you'll need to build content-creation apps from the ground up that embrace touch gesturing, and you'll have to let go of the old conventions. You'll need to consciously censor your impulse to build systems designed for a mouse—because this is inevitably what your instincts will compel you to do—until it becomes second-nature for you to create great direct-manipulation UIs. Build user interfaces that bring fingers directly in contact with the medium your creative user is working in. Many art apps already take advantage of the intimacy of contact between a user and the screen. Take *SketchBook Pro*, which is a showcase of great interface design on the iPad.

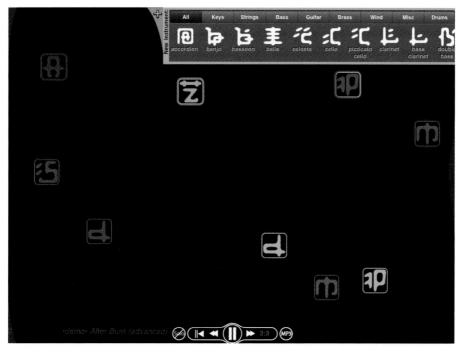

Tap brush icon to open the brush editor

Touchez l'icône du pinceau pour ouvrir l'Editeur de pinceaux
Tocca l'icona del pennello per aprire la galeria pennelli
Tocar el icono del pincel para abrir el Editor de Pinceles
Tippen Sie auf das "Pinsel-Symbol um den Pinseleditor zu öffnen
轻触画刷图标用于打开画刷编辑器
브러시 에디터를 열으시려면 브러시 아이콘을 가볍게 두드리십시요
ブラシエディタを開くためには、ブラシ アイコンを軽くたたきます。

News   Help   Prefs   About

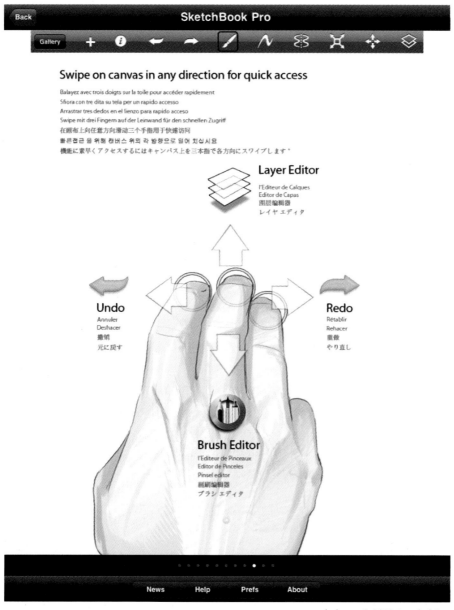

Some great examples of content-creation apps already exist on the iPad. Apple's *Pages* is a showcase for what can be achieved with the platform. Here you can touch objects, scale them, move them, and rotate them using gestures—there is also a whole range of sophisticated controls for editing objects in situ using only your fingers and simple movements. *Pages* is an excellent case study for interface design on the iPad, and you'll take a look at it in much more detail in Chapter 8.

www.apple.com © 2010 Apple Inc.

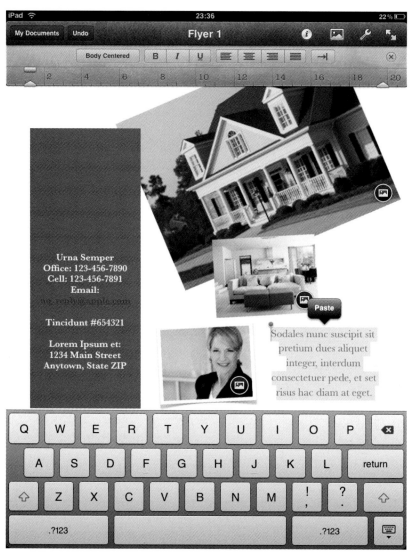

www.apple.com © 2010 Apple Inc.

Distributing Newspapers and Magazines

Lot of publishing giants—Rupert Murdoch most memorably—seemed to think that the iPad would save the newspaper and magazine industry. Although some publishers have found early success by launching digital editions of their magazines for the iPad, even these publishers have quickly discovered that simply being on the iPad is not enough to guarantee long-term sales.

Wired stands out as a good example of why such publishing ventures should not be entered into lightly, and I hope they'll forgive me for using their magazine as a great example of how not to deliver digital print to the iPad.

Wired ran into all kinds of trouble developing a magazine app for iPad—in fact their situation became so wretched at one point that Adobe was forced to develop an entirely new publishing platform for the magazine, just so that *Wired* could publish on the iPad.

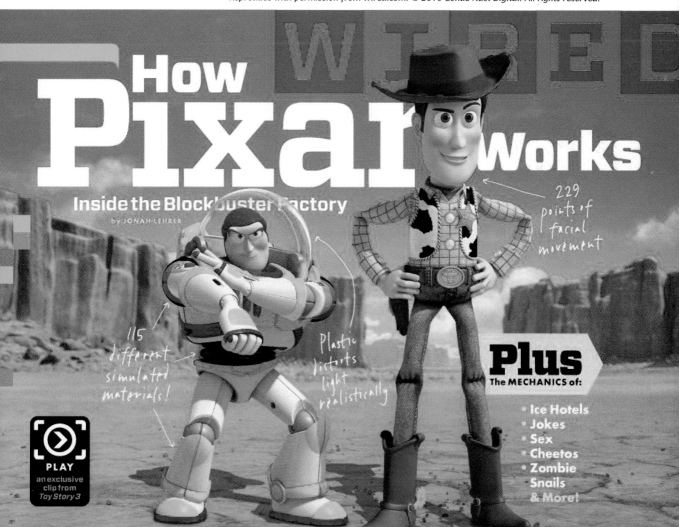

Wired's first mistake was to design their prototype magazine in Adobe Flash, hoping that Apple would allow Flash applications on the iPad—Apple did not allow Flash on the iPhone, so this was quite some gamble and did not pay off. Apple has since relaxed its rules on apps that are cross-compiled from Flash, but the problem was compounded by the fact that *Wired's* app weighed in at 527MB (megabytes), making it impractical to download over anything but the fastest Internet connections. It also made it much too big for anyone to build up a sensible collection of magazines on their iPad. The entry-level 16GB iPad would be capable of storing just a few months of magazines if they were all around the size of the *Wired* app—and that's assuming the iPad wasn't also filled with videos, photos, and music.

Other publishers followed suit, although some of them chose the more sensible option of allowing content to be downloaded into the app, as needed, from the Internet. However, as the novelty of iPad publishing wears off, many users are now asking themselves whether the iPad edition of their favorite magazine is in any way superior to the web-sites of those magazines. In almost every case, the answer is no. The immediate, open, and universal qualities of the Internet are hard to beat for magazine publishing. If you boil it down, the argument for a stand-alone iPad magazine app is purely a financial one. It is easier to charge money for an app than access to a website. However, this makes the app magazine format advantageous only from the perspective of the publisher. The consumer would be better served by a website. CSS is more than capable of creating the typographical layouts shown in iPad magazine apps, and segregating topical content from the Internet is a step backwards that consumers are already beginning to tire of.

Unlike the other app categories I've discussed, you might have noticed that I'm not brimming with enthusiasm for the newspaper and magazine category on the iPad app store. This is because the publishing industry will quickly come to an understanding that there is already a much more efficient and flexible means of publishing to the iPad and it already exists. It is called a website.

Essentially, the publishing industry is trying, and failing, to repackage their existing websites in an iPad format that is now becoming painfully reminiscent of the interactive CD-ROMs of the 1990s. At the moment most publisher's focus is not on content, but mainly on showing off new technology, whooping, "ooh! look at this!" Once the novelty of this showboating has worn off, both readers and editors are likely to return to the web, where publishing is much more effective, less flashy, and wider-reaching. In the meantime, feel free to sell iPad publishing solutions to your clients, just don't expect much thanks for it in a few years from now.

Of course, there are exceptions to the point I'm making here. News aggregators—software that collects news from various sources and displays it in new ways—could be a very profitable app category on the iPad. Already, software like *Pulse Reader* and *Flipboard* are using the iPad as an extremely effective way of navigating through news and information from many sources. But, critically, these apps are filters for the primary news source: The Internet.

There *is* certainly lots of money to be made selling apps that filter web-based content. However, it's unlikely that there is any long-term future in the Murdoch-endorsed model of taking web-based content from a single-source and repackaging it as a branded app. Single-source news was a compromise made over a hundred years ago because of the inherent nature of the printed newspaper. Today there is no need for a single entity to gather and transmit the world's news in its entirety, nor are many consumers interested in paying for news delivered in this traditional in-house format. The iPad won't save the newspaper and magazine industries; instead it may, ironically, erode the boundaries between discrete news sources, allowing users to customize their experience of the news while largely ignoring the branded source of that news.

The new wave of iPad news-reader apps, like *Flipboard* in particular, let users organize their consumption around topics that interest them—sports, finance, or even the antics of specific celebrities. It also allows them to hook into Twitter or Facebook feeds and transform the lives of their friends into custom designed magazines that appear to have been crafted by a private publishing house dedicated to them personally. These extraordinary automatic magazine creation tools are unlike anything you've seen before, and you must download *Flipboard*, which is free, to get a sense of how much potential there is in this field.

You can see in the screenshots here what happens when you point *Flipboard* at the Atomic Antelope Twitter feed. The app automatically generates a magazine based on the content of the tweets I've put up over the last few months. It gets even more bizarre and engaging if you point *Flipboard* at one of your friend's Twitter feeds, or at Facebook. I'll discuss *Flipboard* in more detail in Chapter 9.

www.flipboard.com Reproduced with permission from Flipboard.

www.flipboard.com Reproduced with permission from Flipboard.

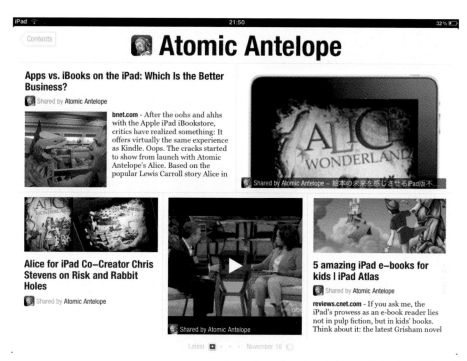

www.flipboard.com Reproduced with permission from Flipboard.

In this sense, the iPad poses a huge threat to traditional publishing models, but not to primary news sources. The iPad is an excellent device for new meta-web software—apps that farm content from many sources on the Internet and turn it into a new product—that have the most to gain from this iPad platform. In the end, far from saving any single magazine brand, the iPad, and news aggregation software like the superb *Flipboard* app, may actually do more to denigrate publishing brands, perhaps to the point of irrelevance. Although news-gathering sources will still be critical to the sourcing of information, the distribution system is ultimately unlikely to belong to any brand. Don't tell Murdoch, though.

Books on the iPad

Books have a natural home on the iPad. Fiction titles in particular are generally more typographically rigid than a newspaper or magazine, and a typical eBook title might weigh in at only a few megabytes. Books benefit from discrete pagination—in children's books, for example, text and illustrations are strongly tied to each other on the same page. Contrast this with a newspaper, which tends to lead with a photo, flowing text beneath arbitrarily to fit around other articles. A newspaper is typographically flexible, and it easily finds a home on the web where scrolling is horizontal. A book, however, is more suited to a tablet, where scrolling is replaced with swiping vertically and pages are broken into distinct units. A book is also a more prolonged and intimate reading experience than a news story. Users react differently to a book format, and issues like hyphenation, tracking and kerning, font choice, and layout become much more important.

How much of this is down to traditional and convention is difficult to know. Books have remained largely unchanged since the illuminations of monks. Compare the number of books you have read on the Internet to the number of news stories you have read on the Internet. Have you ever read a book on the Internet? I haven't. Some people can manage it, but for most it's a tiring and strange experience.

Current affairs and features lend themselves well to the vertical-scrolling of the Internet and perhaps that's where they should stay. However, the printed book—especially the fiction book—finds a more comfortable home on the iPad. If you want to be the next hot iPad eBook developer, you should focus your efforts to build a killer app right here, in the world of popular fiction.

I'm going to take a very detailed look at creating books for the iPad in Chapter 9, where I'll run you through the nuts and bolts of putting together a seriously killer iPad title.

TIP

*Don't group brainstorm! Psychologists have found that individuals working on their own come up with ideas that are far better than any group's effort. Brainstorming sessions create what researchers call an "illusion of group productivity." It gets worse though, a study by researchers at Texas A&M University, and published in **Applied Cognitive Psychology,** built on previous studies to demonstrate that not only are brainstorming sessions less effective than working alone, they actually block creativity because they encourage fixation and a conformity of ideas. So, your best approach to the dreaded brainstorming meeting is to let everyone have their say—their sense that they are contributing—and then thank them all for their time. Now go away, think up your own ideas, and present them back to the group, praising them enthusiastically on the results of "their" brainstorming session.*

Part II
Planning Your Killer App

In my app design studio, the planning stage for apps begins with a straightforward conversation between the lead illustrator and me. We'll both have a few ideas for different apps. We argue over these for a few hours, rubbishing the other's ideas in subtle, barely detectable ways. Then, eventually one of us will give in and we'll start considering the commercial potential of the apps that survived the first debate.

This is a fairly messy way to go about figuring out what app to develop, but it's significantly better than the alternative option, which is to brainstorm app ideas with a crowd of "creative" people in a boardroom. Sadly, this is the way your clients are likely to approach this kind of thing. For some reason, men in suits have a strange obsession with "brainstorming" ideas, despite the fact that numerous psychological studies have demonstrated that this is actually counterproductive to generating good ideas. It might not chime with your democratic ideals, but the businesses that flourish creatively tend to be those that are driven by a benign dictator. A single-minded, often partly insane, highly driven ego-maniac with a head full of talent and a burning desire to create something great. Committees are fine for organizing a town fete, but if you want to make an app that blows people away, get dictatorial.

Chapter 4
Working with Clients

Clients are the lifeblood for most app developers. This is because it's much easier to convince The *Turbo Cheese Corporation* to give you $60,000 to make a branded game app for them than it is to sell $60,000 of said game app on the App Store. Selling apps on the App Store is hard, but selling the app dream to clients is easier. Once clients have signed up to you, the money is guaranteed—usually. However, you will be amazed by exactly how frustrating and soulless it can be working with many clients. For example, take a look at the sort of extraordinary documents that agencies are currently sending out to iPad developers. This is from a recent request for proposal (RFP) I was sent by one of the biggest ad agencies in the world. Incidentally, you will find that clients like to use pointless acronyms like RFP; it makes them feel clever:

> "The objective of this project is to create an iPad book application. This application is a *digital tactic within [the company's] broader holiday campaign, with a target submission date to the iTunes Store by [two weeks from today]*"

This is a perfect example of the madness that is going on in iPad app development. Here a well-respected ad agency expects a worthwhile iPad book app to be produced in just two weeks. They also call the app "a digital tactic." Already some alarm bells should be going off. Who uses this kind of language? What is a "digital tactic?" I still can't figure it out. In reply, I responded:

"Hi,
We had a think about this, but it sounds awful.
"The application is a digital tactic?"
We're not interested in this kind of thing; we want to make kids dance in the street with
their iPads held aloft in the moonlight.
Get in touch with me when you guys start really dreaming and believing again. We'd love
to work on something good.
Chris,
Director, Atomic Antelope"

We're at a strange point where many companies want a presence on the App Store, but most don't have the slightest clue why they want to be on it, or what service their app will provide. They see that Nike has an app, and that their rivals across the street have an app, and they want an app too. I've spoken to numerous companies whose thoughts on app design have literally gone no further than "we want one." This puts iPad developers in an interesting position. Your clients will rely on you to do more than build software to their specifications—they probably want you to dream up a purpose for their company's app. When you meet with a corporation to discuss their plans for an app, it's not just your programming and design services that will be questioned. Clients will often look to you for advice on a very basic level: They want to know what their iPad app should do.

Explaining the iPad Proposition

The person in the corporation you end up pitching to may never have touched an iPad. I can't tell you the number of times that a senior manager has instructed one of his under-lings to meet me and I've quickly discovered that they have no idea what an app is. This might sound like a total disaster, but use these situations to your advantage.

I've discussed how the iPad is great at engaging newcomers—it seems to draw people in almost instantly. I owned an iPad before the UK launch and could create crowds in London restaurants by pulling out the iPad and using it. Strangers would ask if they could touch it. This is not rational behavior, but for one reason or another, the iPad has this peculiar power to attract attention, it seems like a visitor from the near future. You can use this mechanism of attraction to excite clients who have not seen the iPad before. In fact, in any meeting I would recommend that you quickly assess which of your clients has never seen an iPad before and focus your pitch on them. They will be the ones who will be talking to everyone about your presentation for the rest of the day. Consider them your free advertising.

TIP

The iPad is difficult to explain in words—hence all the misunderstandings in the press about what it was—but it is very easy to demonstrate, people get it straight away. If you are asked to explain to clients what the iPad can do and what they might use it for, it's a pretty good idea to keep your mouth shut. Instead, turn the iPad on and demo a few apps.

Pitching iPad App Ideas to Clients

When you are pitching app ideas to clients, you are not a programmer. You are not a designer. You are a storyteller. Remember that and you'll win the pitch. If you forget for a moment that you're telling a story, you'll bore and bewilder your audience with information they do not need.

The best way to pitch an iPad app is to imagine that your audience is a group of children. I do not mean that you should patronize them (children are generally very smart), but you should make sure that the language you use is clear and digestible. Keep it clear, do not assume your client has technical knowledge, and concentrate on the experiences of the user. You'll find that lots of software developers hide behind jargon and technical ideas that could easily be explained in normal English. Instead they retreat behind phrases like "back end systems," "push data," and "interstitial ads." All this may sound very reasonable and normal to a developer, but to any normal person it is complete and utter nonsense. You might as well shriek in Latin and throw a glass of water at the wall if you're going to talk to clients like that.

TIP

Clients will often nod even when they don't have the slightest idea what you are going on about. Nobody in the room will want to admit that you are describing things they do not understand, but when you leave, you're unlikely to win the business you wanted. Keep things simple and engaging.

One final piece of advice I have for pitching to clients is this: Keep asking questions. Find out everything you can about your client—their business, their hobbies and interests, and who they are. This might seem like a lot of irrelevant information, but it serves to do two things. First, it endears the client to you, because everyone's favorite subject is themselves. But, also, it gives your brain a lot of information to churn over and forge into ideas for apps that may appeal to your client. If your client runs an accountancy firm, you may be at a complete loss as to what kind of iPad app to pitch. However, if you discover that your client is a keen golfer, you'll probably have a lot of success pitching a branded golf game to his accountancy company.

Adapting Existing Flash Apps

I'll go out on a limb here: Flash is dead to you. Don't go near his corpse or you'll fall ill too. Of course you can cross-compile from Flash to Objective C (the programming language of the iPad), but you're creating a mess for yourself. Apple has flip-flopped all over Flash. One moment it wasn't an acceptable development platform, the next it was. The basic truth of the matter is, it's not worth the hurt. The only rational excuse for not coding in Objective C is that your programmer doesn't know how to code it. Objective C will be faster, more efficient, and App-Store-future-proof. If you find yourself in the position of having to adapt an existing Flash app for use on the iPad, the most sensible option is to strip the graphical assets from the original Flash app and write a new version in Objective C. I know companies who had to rewrite projects from scratch, just weeks before launch, because they chose to use Flash.

In a few years Flash will likely be a distant memory. The world's most profitable phone, and the world's most popular tablet computer, don't use Flash at all. The Internet is also rapidly transitioning from Flash to more accessible video and animation formats that don't rely on any one vendor.

There was a big bust up between Apple and Adobe over the absence of Flash on the iPad and iPhone, and the upshot is that Flash has been subjugated on all Apple platforms. The newest MacBooks don't even ship with Flash anymore. Apple's reasons are pretty sound. To date, Adobe has been unable to demonstrate Flash working particularly well on any mobile platform, and the Mac version of Flash has always been an inefficient, power-draining horror.

You can read the arguments about this decision all over the web, but iOS developers will probably end up in a mess if they try to deliver cross-platform apps using Flash as a development tool. The best advice, if you have the option, is to stay clear of Flash altogether.

Agreeing on Designs

Most of your discussions with clients will involve talking about design. Clients have a blind spot when it comes to what goes on behind the scenes of the app—the gritty job of programming holds little appeal for them—but you'll notice they're always pretty keen to offer their views on how the app looks.

Whenever corporations work with artists there are always tensions. It's your job, as a developer, to negotiate carefully with the client so that they feel like their input is respected without damaging the usability of the app. Sometimes it might seem easier to just give into all the whims of your client—if they want pink text on a fluorescent green background, so be it, they're paying for it. But unfortunately, your reputation is at stake, and your client may even come back and blame you if it fails in the App Store.

TIP

When dealing with clients, your job is 5% designer and 95% negotiator. I used to work with a designer who now lays out one of the best-selling magazines in the world. He let me into a trick he used with publishers when he was pitching front cover designs. He noticed that every time he mocked up an amazing and innovative cover, the magazine's publisher would ask for this and that to be changed until the cover began to look the same as every other magazine cover—a shadow of his intentions. So, he devised a very clever way of giving the publisher what she wanted—a sense of control over the product—without compromising the design. The next time he went into a cover meeting, he took along several awful designs, which he showed to the publisher. Then, at the last minute, he would pull out the great design he'd been working on. As a result, the publisher would invariably pick the great design without debate. Rejecting the other designs had given her the sense of control over the process she required. Whenever you pitch designs to a client, it might be worth throwing in a few bad designs to give your client something to reject. Remember, the devil finds work for idle hands! Without the bad designs to give the illusion of control, you might find your client starts redesigning your work in the boardroom.

A Word on Revenue Sharing

Many clients will be keen to share revenue with you instead of paying upfront. They'll have read all the newspaper stories about the app gold rush, and many of them will have the skewed impression that the App Store is a podgy little cow, eager to disgorge money if only you can be bothered to suckle on its teat. They will offer you a share of imagined riches if only you give them your time and expertise for free. "Look," they say, "You'll make a lot more money if we split the profits."

My advice? Don't do it.

The problem with revenue sharing is that the risk is all yours. If the app doesn't sell, your client loses nothing, but you could spend months working on a project and end up not getting paid. Luckily, you're not a web designer—you don't constantly run up against the boss's 16 year-old son who claims he can design a corporate website in return for a pack of chewing gum—you're working in a niche industry. The boss's son is, thankfully, unlikely to be able to program Objective C and market an iPad app. For this reason, an iPad developer's skill set is valuable. Don't give it away for free.

*Don't accept a revenue share as your only payment. There are obviously a few exceptions, depending on the scale of the offering. If you are offered 20% of a new Harry Potter app, or 15% of everything sold through a Levis' app, you may have to think twice. But in almost every case where you're offered **only** a revenue share it usually means one thing: Your client is not convinced enough of their app's success to offer you any real money. They don't believe in their brand, the project, or you. This is not a good position to design apps from.*

Chapter 5

Working on an Independent iPad App

Small independent studios are the most interesting places to be right now. Either by design or accident, Apple has given birth to an extraordinary cottage industry of small development teams working on successful apps that might otherwise struggle to get made inside larger companies. As part of a small development team—often as small as just two people—you'll have huge advantages over your larger competitors. Not only do you avoid the horrors of design-by-committee, popular in big corporations, but also your overheads are lower, meaning you can profit on a number of smaller, moderately successful apps.

Apple has done more to put bedroom developers on a competitive footing with the likes of EA or Sega than anything else in the recent history of computing. These are exciting times for indie teams with an appetite for innovation. Of course, the biggest advantage to indie development is that you can really have fun pushing new boundaries, and nobody in an office on the top floor is going to shut you down, or take the credit.

Designing in a Team

In my experience, the best iPad development teams are like the best rally car driving teams: no larger than two people. My team on *Alice for the iPad* consisted of one designer (me) and one programmer. We were lucky because our core skills did not overlap. This avoided a lot of arguments. However, we both had a good understanding of the other person's field from a non-technical standpoint. It's best to work with a programmer who knows how to use Photoshop and it will also make development easier if your designers know their way around Xcode (the programming software Apple provides to iPad developers).

 Being in an indie development team is like being in an indie band. If everyone in the band wants to be the lead singer, you're heading for disaster. Make sure that the team you build is made up of people who actually want to do the task you're setting for them.

It's almost unheard of for a good programmer to also be a good graphic designer, and vice versa—I would argue these career choices are philosophically quite different. Both careers are artistic, and neither is superior, but if you're attempting to fulfill both roles as a single individual, you are either supernaturally talented (which is, of course, possible), or more likely you are kidding yourself. If you want to make an app that sells, make a serious assessment of your skills, and team up.

Agreeing on Roles

If you've followed the advice in the previous section, agreeing on roles should be easy. The raw process of building an app has two parts: The mechanical and the aesthetic—the programming behind the app, and the way it looks to the users. In a two-person team, one person should concentrate on each of these roles.

However, these roles are intertwined. To build great apps, the programmer needs to work closely with the designer from the very beginning of the development process. What tends to happen in bigger companies is that a graphics department spends weeks playing about with designs, a committee of managers approves these designs, and then it's all handed over to a programming team to "make it work." The result of this is that the final app is a shadow of what it might have been if the programming team had been given input at the planning stages.

Working Internationally

It might surprise you to learn that the team behind *Alice for the iPad* never held a meeting less than 5,000 miles apart. Yes, the top children's book at the launch of the iPad was, from start to finish, designed, and programmed on different continents. I designed the graphics from my home in London, England and the programmer worked from his home in Seattle, Washington.

How did we manage this remarkable feat? We used *Skype*.

Video calling is cheap and easy, and doesn't interfere with the development process. If anything, it makes it easier because you can select team members from anywhere in the world. Because of this technology, you don't have to restrict yourself to teaming up with a programmer or designer who you physically meet to develop projects.

Motivating Yourself

Woody Allen famously wrote, "80 percent of success is showing up." I often think about this quote when beginning new iPad design projects. What I think Woody Allen means is that most people just don't even try to find success, so their failure is certain. It's extremely tempting to dismiss the idea of actually doing anything. "I won't succeed," you think to yourself. "This won't sell." "Maybe I should pick a better desktop wallpaper photo first." All these kinds of thoughts will prevent you from showing up.

The simple act of sitting in front of a sketchpad and moving your pencil across the paper is showing up. Opening Photoshop and tweaking an iPad interface design is showing up. Testing the current build of your app in Xcode is showing up.

Show up enough and you'll eventually be in a position where you have a great app in the store. The hard part usually isn't finding the time to work on your app; it's resisting the temptation to do something else instead.

Different designers have different methods of motivating themselves to continue working on a project, but perhaps the most useful piece of motivating advice for an iPad development team is this: Make sure you pick a project you love. Because by the end of the project, all the love you had for the idea will have been put through a thresher. The blood, sweat, and tears that go into your app will demand a pretty big heart. If you make sure your app is worth loving, then when things are tough you'll still want to see it through.

TIP

For whatever reason, creative endeavors make humans very nervous, especially if the field is new to us. You will feel a natural resistance to making your first iPad app, but you should fight through this feeling. Remember, even Van Gogh didn't have any confidence in his abilities, but that didn't stop him creating masterpieces. Of course, he then cut his ear off and shot himself. But still.

Keeping in Touch with the iPad Community

The iPad development community is, in my experience, knowledgeable and generous. Numerous forums exist where you can discuss design or code problems you're having and get first-hand advice from experts all over the world.

Many of the technologies you'll be using to develop iPad apps are extremely new. So new, in fact, that you may well be the first person attempting to use Xcode to create software for a certain task. This often means that there is a very small group of programmers who can offer you advice. Luckily, because of the wonders of the Internet, you can talk to these people directly.

Although the language used to code iPad apps, Objective C, is a relatively mature language, many of the features included in Apple's implementation of this language for the iPad are brand new. There are also frameworks, like Cocos2d (a library of pre-built graphics routines that make iPad programming easier), that have a strong but comparatively small following of programmers. These frameworks have dedicated forums available in which to discuss special techniques for their use. Unless you're a freakish genius, you will need to turn to them when you have a question about the latest technologies.

Chapter 6
Life as an Apple Developer

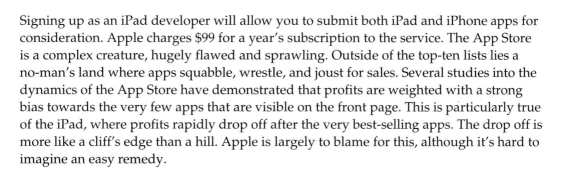

Signing up as an iPad developer will allow you to submit both iPad and iPhone apps for consideration. Apple charges $99 for a year's subscription to the service. The App Store is a complex creature, hugely flawed and sprawling. Outside of the top-ten lists lies a no-man's land where apps squabble, wrestle, and joust for sales. Several studies into the dynamics of the App Store have demonstrated that profits are weighted with a strong bias towards the very few apps that are visible on the front page. This is particularly true of the iPad, where profits rapidly drop off after the very best-selling apps. The drop off is more like a cliff's edge than a hill. Apple is largely to blame for this, although it's hard to imagine an easy remedy.

The problem is that the front page of the App Store only has room for a certain number of apps in the charts and apps on promotion. And, because the majority of users find apps simply by browsing the App Store—often just the front page—99% of iPad apps are almost entirely invisible on the store. The only option at the moment is to grin and bear it.

If your app does not instantly hit the front page, or one of the category top tens, the marketing plan discussed in Chapter 1 is all the more important. Realistically, no app will hit the front page without a marketing plan.

TIP

Accept the App Store for what it is: an easy way to collect payment for your app once you have attracted customers to it. Do not expect the App Store to do the selling for you—it probably won't. The App Store is like a warehouse the size of Texas, with a shopkeeper outside. But the shopkeeper has only ten products on display, no signs promoting the rest of the contents of the warehouse, and no enjoyable way to search through it. How is anyone going to know to ask for your product?

Communicating with Apple

Communicating with Apple requires a simple act of understanding on your part: Apple rarely communicates directly with independent developers. The company has built a very successful business based on a code of silence and wrapped in an aura of mystery. This carries through to their approach toward creatives working on apps. Although this behavior is clearly part of their corporate psyche, there is also a practical reason why Apple will not talk to you directly—there are simply so many developers and apps active on the App Store that it would be impossible to sell memberships for $99 and at the same time fund the staff to take care of every query from every developer.

Although you will eventually get an answer to any questions you pose to Apple, it could take a very long time indeed—sometimes upwards of a month. Then, even when you do get a reply, you might simply be asked if you still need an answer to your question at this point, because so much time has passed since you asked it! You'll save yourself a lot of anguish if you accept, before beginning an iPad project, that your development team lives in a world controlled by a benevolent but invisible corporate deity. If you need help, get it from manuals, forums, and your peers. Apple isn't talking. Having said this, sometimes Apple will surprise you and respond very promptly. It's hard to know what to expect, and my recent experiences with Apple suggest that they're improving.

TIP

If your app is rejected, there may be no choice but to negotiate with the reviewers by email, but in almost every other situation, save yourself the trouble and find an answer to your problem elsewhere.

There is, of course, one scenario in which Apple do become chatty. That's when you have a hit app on your hands. When your app hits the big time, Apple's approach changes, but only slightly. You are likely to be asked for graphics Apple can use to promote your app. Sometimes these graphics are used on billboard posters, or more likely on small banners inside the App Store. You will save yourself some time beforehand if you foresee this possibility and have your app graphics available as scalable vector files. But, in most cases, it will be easy enough to redraw them as vectors if Apple wants to promote your app in print.

Working in a Small Team

Working on an app with other people can be an extremely rewarding process. As explained in Chapter 5, the most creative combination is often a two-person app team. Here, one team member takes charge of graphics, and the other codes the software. Any more than two people working on an app and the situation gets infinitely more complex. Of course, some apps might be simply impossible to build without the hours that a larger team can put in, but I would advise against large teams for several reasons.

Firstly, if you have a large-team project, it's incredibly likely that you are building an iPad software solution that is unnecessarily complex. It's unlikely that your app is focused on a single function that it performs with excellence.

Many of the most successful iPad and iPhone apps have been created by tiny teams of dedicated individuals. Although a large team can power through projects, you risk a loss of focus. Of course, a carefully managed project can overcome this risk, but it's important to realize that you can build a very successful iPad app with only two people, and in rare cases, just one.

The App Store is uniquely equipped to allow the individual craftsperson to sell their work directly to the public. It's a shame not to take advantage of this.

Understanding Apple

I know, I know. If you wanted a potted history of Apple you would have bought a Steve Jobs biography, but bear with me here, because once you've got Apple figured out, you're half-way to understanding the customers for your iPad app. It's also important to absorb the philosophies of the company that is 100% responsible for your iPad app income, and your chances of promotion in the App Store.

The story of Apple sounds like something dreamt up by Hollywood scriptwriters, with exciting plot twists and a classic story structure. Amazingly though, it's true.

Steve Jobs founded Apple in a garage in California, together with his friend Steve Wozniak. Together they built the Apple I and Apple II computers, before Jobs took on the task of creating the Macintosh.

Photograph © Matt Yohe

As the driving force behind the Mac, Jobs was largely responsible for the invention of the modern desktop computer and the popularization of a windowed operating system. But, in 1995, Jobs found himself locked in a vicious power-struggle with then Apple CEO John Sculley, with the result that, only a year after launching the Macintosh, Jobs was fired from Apple.

Like any good protagonist in an epic tale, Jobs wandered in the wilderness for years before returning, like a prodigal son, to save Apple from certain doom, restoring the company to health with first the iPod, then the iPhone, and finally the iPad—although to be honest it wasn't exactly a wilderness. Jobs had spent his time founding NeXT computers and designing a computer operating system that he sold back to Apple, and which became Mac OSX and, in part, the iPad's iOS.

Apple has been extremely successful since Jobs returned, and as a result the company is shaped around his vision. Luckily, Jobs seems to have a knack for profitable visions.

Confusingly, Apple has constructed an image around itself that suggests its users are young hipsters, throwing paint at canvases, dancing in the streets and never far from a skateboard or a coffee shop. However, the exciting reality of the situation for you, as an iPad developer, is that Apple's audience actually crosses all demographics and personality types. Don't think you have to build apps for stoned web designers who ride around Soho on fixed-gear bikes. Don't be distracted by the aspirational marketing that surrounds Apple; your customers will come from all walks of life.

Apple's approach to software and hardware design has always been extremely humanistic—a rare quality in a technology industry that often likes to bewilder consumers with indecipherable product names and encourages spec-sheet fetishism. Apple's designers keep things simple, focus on doing specific tasks well, and above all else, concentrate on usability, not specs.

What Apple Wants

Apple's core interest is selling more iPads. Secondary to that is an interest in selling apps. The best apps, and the ones that will garner you real interest and promotion from Apple, are the apps that meet both of these two criteria. The kind of apps that not only sell themselves, but also sell the platform they were designed for, are what the industry calls *killer apps*. For the Macintosh, one killer app was Photoshop.

Photoshop sold Macs. Millions of them.

For the Nintendo, one killer app was *Super Mario*. For Sega, *Sonic* was a killer app, and for Sony's PlayStation, games like *Grand Theft Auto* and *Tekken* were killer apps. For RIM's Blackberry phone, one killer app was Microsoft Outlook. A killer app sells the platform and itself. If people want to buy an iPad because of your app, you have hit the jackpot. Apple is going to be all over you. Apple wants you to make apps that will sell iPads. This is the core intent of the App Store, and should be at the forefront of your mind when designing an app.

Learning to Accept Apple's Silence

The situation could be better, but there's not much point in joining the hoards of complainers outside Apple's gates. The App Store appears to operate a lot like Willy Wonka's Chocolate Factory: No one ever goes in and no one ever comes out. Until you produce an outlandishly successful app, Apple will keep absolutely mute. I've personally had situations where I've kicked up a fuss in the global media about Apple's policies in the App Store, but it didn't make a bit of difference. Apple knows the power of silence, and uses it well.

TIP

Before you start building your iPad app, reach a sense of internal peace over the fact that you will be creating software to be approved or rejected by a mostly silent gatekeeper. There are obviously risks involved—you never know for sure how the gatekeeper will react to your creation—but it's all part of the thrill of the gold rush.

Chapter 7
Organizing Your Workflow

Your iPad project will need a clear workflow. An iPad development workflow determines the order in which an idea is turned into code and graphics and then deployed to the iPad. An iPad development workflow is not always a logical chronology of events. For example, it may make sense for some graphics to be built before the code is written, or the opposite may be true. There may also be situations in which one task relies on the completion of another task, or conversely where a task can be completed as a discrete item—like, for example, registering the app name on the App Store.

When you think about the way in which your workflow should be organized, consider what needs to happen before other tasks can be completed. Plan ahead to make efficient use of time. You don't want to be in a situation where the illustrator is sitting around waiting because the programmer hasn't decided which graphics framework to use. Structure the order of your workflow with other team members' workflows in mind.

TIP

As soon as you have struck on a name for your app, consider registering it. You don't have to actually write a single line of code prior to registering the name of your app. My company spent months developing an app, but when it came to registering the app's name, we couldn't. Someone else had already registered the name but without any corresponding app in the App Store. Worse still, unlike domain names, we had no way of contacting the person who had registered the name. It turns out that squatters have moved into the App Store. They're worse than domain name squatters though, because you can't even enter into nego-tiations with them. You don't know who they are, or where they are. Some of them take advantage of the fact that a developer can pretend to submit an app, but abandon their submission at the last moment, avoiding the need to actually create an applica-tion, but keeping hold of the app's name. Luckily, registered app names for which a developer doesn't publish a corresponding app expire after 90 days. At his point they return to the pool for everyone to use. It's a pretty fair system, but can be frustrating if your app name is taken and you have to play a waiting game.

Planning Your App

The best way to plan your app is to use a storyboard. Storyboarding is an ancient prac-tice, but is still the best way to communicate the functionality of an app. A *storyboard* is a series of static drawings that show the progression of events through time—or, put even more simply, a kind of comic strip showing how your iPad app should look and behave as a user interacts with it. A solid storyboard will provide an invaluable reference point for the programmer(s) and designer(s) to check progress against.

The other key tool you'll need is a big wall, some paper, and marker pens. More or less wallpaper the wall of your office with your paper, and then use the marker pens to draw a huge schedule across the paper. Not only will this give you an unavoidable daily reminder of your commitment to an iPad project, but you'll get the extremely satisfying pleasure of crossing off tasks as they are complete. Your wall should begin to look some-thing like the wall in this picture.

Collaborating with Designers and Programmers

It's not the most romantic gesture imaginable, but before you begin collaborating on an iPad project, you must draw up a business contract between yourself and those you are collaborating with. Through hard-won experience I have learned that the most amicable collaborations have the potential to turn sour and, without documentation, proving your part-ownership of the app you're working on will be near impossible. Imagine the worst possible circumstances that could occur, and make sure that your contract anticipates this.

Image by Yandle (www.flickr.com/photos/yandle/). (Licensed under Creative Commons.)

The likelihood is that your iPad development team will run smoothly and everybody involved will be happy with the outcome. However, you'll eventually run into all kinds of legal complications if you simply assume this will always be the case. What commonly happens is that, as humans, we're not very good at predicting long-term risks. Your instinct will be to trust everyone you're working with, because at the beginning of a project everyone is filled with optimism and excitement. It's hard to foresee anything going wrong. However, when the project is a huge success, attitudes can change. Just look at all the lawsuits filed by past collaborators against Mark Zuckerberg, the creator of *Facebook*.

Using Sketches to Communicate iPad App Designs

As much as the media tries to convince us that there is a digital revolution going on, I still haven't found a more effective means of communicating an idea than picking up a pencil and a piece of paper and drawing. These two basic tools have been marginalized by a generation brought up on Photoshop, but nothing beats a good old hand-drawn sketch.

It's possible that you, as a designer or programmer, may not have good sketching skills—drawing tends not to be taught as a core part of all design and programming courses, but it should. Although you can get by with using computer-based illustrative techniques, your apps will benefit enormously if you can sketch out ideas.

If you're hopeless at drawing, fear not. There are many excellent guides to drawing well even if you consider your current technique unsalvageable. It's not a starting point that many iPad design manuals will recommend, but I can't think of a better move for an iPad app designer than to get hold of a copy of the book, *Drawing on the Right Side of the Brain*, by Betty Edwards, and follow the instructions inside.

Here again, you need to fight against the logical fallacy of designing for the iPad; the assumption that to create great apps you need to study other great apps. In fact, the better choice is to study art and design itself, and to get to grips with the traditional techniques of hand-drawing.

In the same way that the iPad brings us one layer closer to the computer, by removing the abstraction of keyboard and mouse, the pencil brings the human brain closer to the paper. Using Photoshop, Illustrator, or any other graphics package will abstract your connection to what you're creating, and slow you down. The best app designs are made with pencil and paper first, and then Photoshop.

Using Google Docs for Project Coordination

Google Docs is one of the most useful collaborative tools I've come across. And it's free.

If you haven't used Google Docs before, you might assume that it's a simple alternative to the Microsoft Word suite and, in a sense, it is this. But it's also a lot more. My team found that Google Docs was invaluable during the design and development of *Alice for the iPad* because it allows for collaborative editing of a single spreadsheet or text document. A document can be shared between several people. Any one person in a team can edit it, and the changes are updated instantly in everyone's copy of that document.

There are alternatives to Google Docs that also work well, but I'm going to focus on Google Docs because it is likely to be most developer's first choice of collaborative tool. You may also decide on a different use of the Google Docs system, but I'll let you know the most effective working setup I've organized using this free tool.

If you don't already have an account, begin by signing up to Google. Next, open up the Google Docs section of the Google website and create a new spreadsheet document. This document will now serve as the central reference point for your whole team, allowing everyone to see what tasks have been completed, what tasks are yet to be done, and the current status of pending tasks. This document is henceforth your king, your touchstone, your Don Vito Corleone. Acknowledge its power.

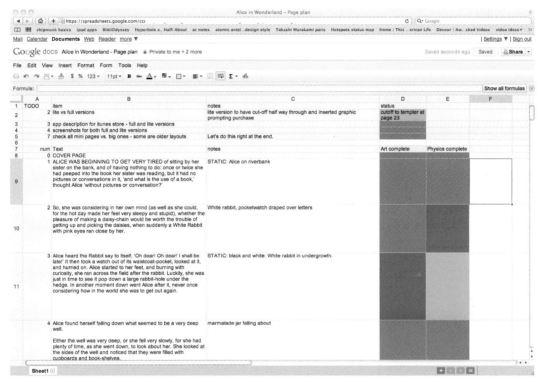

Google Docs © 2010 Google (docs.google.com)

Now, begin by listing the app's central components vertically down the left side of the spreadsheet. The various pages in the book are listed along the length of the spreadsheet, and the production work involved in completing those pages is listed along the width. In the case of a physics-enabled book, each page involves typography, backgrounds, physics, and sound effects. As the programmer or designer completes parts of the production work required for each page, they change the highlight color of that spreadsheet cell to indicate work completed. The programmer(s) and designer(s) can also write notes to each other in the cells, which are then updated automatically in everyone's copy of the document.

This project-management system is surprisingly effective, and it just goes to show that you don't need to buy complex and expensive software to organize a fairly elaborate iPad development project.

Good Working Practices

How you work will depend on whether developing iPad apps is your main job, or something you work on in the evenings and at weekends. Many hobbyist developers find time to work on apps in their spare time, slowly building confidence in their skills until the point where they can make it their full-time job.

Alternatively, working as a bigger team brings its own rewards. For a start, socializing with other humans makes it harder to go insane. But, it's also worth bearing in mind that, despite the appeal of having a centralized office, it is increasingly less important to work in a traditional building. There are many successful app design teams who work in different countries, across time zones, and with no formal office space. This also saves considerably on overhead costs.

As for the gritty work of sitting down and developing your app, it's best to keep your focus on completing the list of tasks you've outlined in your shared Google Docs and on the large planner you've papered across your wall. The sheer size of many projects is daunting to begin with, and when viewed as a whole might appear insurmountable. The trick is to break everything down into smaller, achievable goals on a day-to-day basis.

Ultimately, how you organize your workflow is up to you. I'm not a big fan of prescription, and you may find that you're capable of planning and directing an iPad app using the back of an envelope and your brain. Humans are very resourceful, and I confess that I have run creative projects mostly in my head. If you're part of a larger company, this will completely freak out everyone around you and you'll be branded a lunatic. Even if you can coordinate things without any formal documents, it helps to have them around to convince the wider world of your mental stability.

Now you've got a solid idea about how to formally plan your app, in the next chapter I'm going to show you how to take full advantage of the iPad's most prominent feature: The touchscreen.

Part III

Designing for Touchscreen Interfaces

The iPad is different from every other mass-market computer that went before because you can touch the screen directly. In its raw form, an iPad is a large, accurate video display that reacts to fingers, with a very tightly packed mass of extremely clever hardware and software hidden behind it. This apparently simple evolution in the way users control a computer system in reality changes everything. In this section, I'm going to show you why the iPad is unlike any computer you've designed for in the past, and I'm going to show you tricks you can use to elevate yourself above the thousands of other app developers who haven't grasped that interacting with the iPad bears no relation to interacting with a computer mouse.

The human finger, together with the touchscreen, radically alters user interface design and presents problems for designers that are not only tough to overcome but often hard to spot in the first place. In this section, you'll learn techniques like how to avoid having the users' hands obscure vital parts of the screen, how to strip your app down until it shines, and why children tend to make the best software testers.

Chapter 8
Delighting the Users of Your App

If you want your iPad app to sell its way into the App Store top ten, make sure it delights people. Programmers rarely use words like delight. They're more likely to talk about functionality, features, and options. Although these qualities are all important parts of an app, the most compelling reason for iPad owners to buy and recommend your app is if they enjoy using it. Delight is a tricky butterfly to pin down, but in this chapter, you'll take a look at the ways you can move beyond a mere list of features, and towards a user experience that places your app miles above the competition.

Understanding the iPad's Strengths

The first step in designing for the iPad is to work backwards. Rather than thinking simply, "What software can I make for the iPad?" ask, "What iPad features can I take advantage of in software?" It's a small difference in the thought process, but a critical one. A common mistake is putting your primary focus on the features of the software when, in fact, the focus should be on both the software *and* the device.

The iPad has a unique feature set—outlined in Chapter 1—and the more of these unique features you take advantage of, the more desirable your app will become. Again, it seems obvious when laid out in these terms, but so many app designers fail to use the full feature set of the iPad in their apps. The starting point for doing this is to write a list of the iPad's capabilities and check that your app exploits as many of these features as possible. Here is my list.

Inputs:

- Touch (single and multi-finger)
- Drag
- Shake
- Tilt
- Spin
- Rotate
- Voice (the iPad has a built-in microphone)
- Audio (via the dock connector)

Outputs:

- Video (internal and external)
- Audio
- Data (via the dock connector, or WiFi)

When I'm giving talks to the industry about designing interactive iPad apps, especially designing books, I usually give the very simple advice that designers need to ask themselves: "Can I touch it? Can I tilt it? Can I shake it?" If an app meets these three criteria on the iPad, at the very least, it is on the right track. If it doesn't, it's almost certainly time to go back to the drawing board.

TIP

Whatever kind of app you're making, you'll need to ask yourself questions about how your app takes advantage of the iPad hardware. If you don't have a unique and exclusive purpose on the iPad platform, it will be much harder to get public interest and press coverage, and consequently much harder to sell your app.

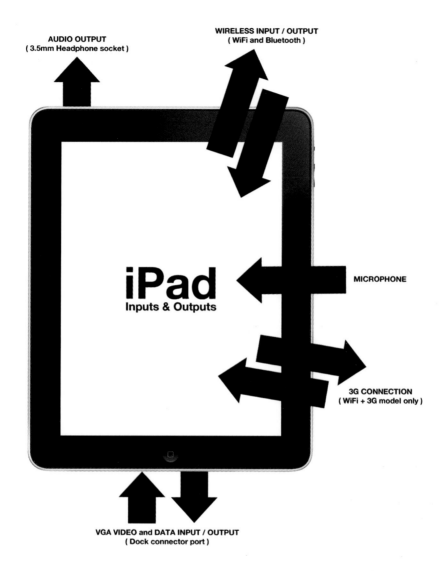

Losing Your Fear of Stripping Down

I have some very straightforward advice for all iPad app designers: Strip down the features of your iPad app, strip them down again, and then strip down the remnants until you have a gleaming engine focused on one exceptional task. Computers are quickly moving away from the 20th century model of software design. Desktop software applications had become a sprawling mess of menus and buttons with endless obscure features and peculiar behaviors available to its users. But good iPad software is nothing like this. Good iPad software is modular, elegant, and focused.

It's one thing reading this and nodding, and another thing to actually have the determination and sheer guts to strip features out of your app. Every instinct in your body will tell you you're crazy not making this option, or that option, available to the users. Fight that fear. Programmers are especially troubled by the concept of stripping down a feature set, and will campaign relentlessly to stuff every available option into the app. This is not an act of sabotage, but instead the simple consequence of being a programmer. When you live and work in a computer software environment that allows absolute control over every tiny bit of the computing experience, it's bound to make you feel like the same opportunities should be available to the users of your app. This logic is quite reasonable, but flawed. Although you might assume that the more features and options you provide in your app, the more the users will thank you, this is far from the reality. Remember: You are not representative of the users of your app.

The Feature Fallacy

Interface experts have a term for the false logic where a software designer assumes that adding features improves functionality. They call it "feature creep" or "software bloat." It's not uncommon to discover that the majority of users would not miss 80% of the features in any given piece of desktop software—they simply don't use most of it. Look at the gargantuan mess of menus and buttons in Microsoft Word, Adobe Photoshop, or 3D Studio Max, as just a few examples of software that has found it necessary to cater to increasingly niche sections of its audience. How many of the menu options do you personally use in these apps?

On a desktop computer, feature creep is frustrating, but not fatal. Screen space on a desktop computer is not at a premium and users are accustomed to ignoring vast swathes of options they never use in menu systems. As a result, a lot of desktop software gets away with some degree of feature creep. However, the iPad has a much smaller screen than the average desktop system, and the touchscreen paradigm is extremely intolerant of multiple buttons and deep-nested menus. The iPad does not forgive feature creep.

The decision to pare down your feature set will be immediately apparent in the quality of the user interface you design. The fewer options you provide, the more breathing room there is to design an effective and slick UI around these features.

TIP *If you absolutely must add a complex range of features to your iPad app, consider holding them back for future revisions. First impressions are critical on the App Store, and it's better to release a polished first edition with a basic UI, than to risk confusing the early adopters of your software. You can always add more options later, after observing how users are reacting to your app. You'll also find it's easier to deal with criticism from the first wave of users—and rest assured, there will be criticism, lots of it. It's easier to respond to a critical reaction to a small feature set, and refine that first, than to burst onto the scene with an app that is so elaborate and feature-rich that users bombard you with thousands of tiny requests for changes to your monster.*

Interface design experts have discovered that the more features you stuff into an interface, the more you alienate the bulk of your audience. The majority of your app users will use the smallest number of the features it offers. Nobody has ever made a really successful iOS app without stripping options and interface controls down to an elegant minimum. Sophistication and complexity are two very different qualities. An extremely clean and refined UI can provide the front end for a very sophisticated application.

WATCH OUT! *Don't confuse complexity with power. Strip your iPad app down.*

Planning for Fingers

At first, you may think fingers look clumsy in comparison to a mouse pointer. However, while they may appear to lack the pinpoint accuracy of a mouse, fingers are infinitely more versatile. The trick to designing for fingers is to think outside the traditional paradigms of desktop computing interfaces. Imagine the last 25 years of microcomputer technology had never existed. Now begin. Easy, right?

Fingers Allow Direct-Manipulation

The relationship between the motions made by the user's hand and objects on the iPad screen is direct and literal. There are strong parallels between iPad gestures and the way objects are moved about in real life. Direction, distance, and speed are all determined by your fingers, in intimate contact with the screen, with no intermediary input device. This makes the iPad pretty unique.

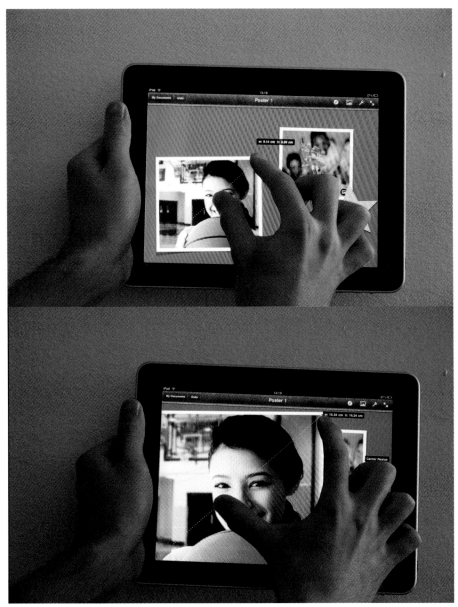

Apple Inc. © 2010

Fingers Get There Faster

Touchscreens immediately resolve a problem that mouse-based desktop computer systems have struggled with for years: They allow you to interact with the user interface in a *spatially absolute* way. This means that you can select an object onscreen very quickly because the object's position, within the frame of the iPad, is fixed in space relative to your finger. You know exactly where the button you want to press is, and you know where your finger is. This contrasts with a mouse-based UI where object and pointer are *spatially relative*; selected in relation to the current position of the mouse cursor. In a spatially relative input system, you don't immediately know for sure where the object you're aiming for is (the button to click) in relation to the object you're aiming at it with (the mouse pointer). I've heard the process of using a mouse best described by a beginner as "like trying to ring a doorbell with a broomstick."

In order to click a button on a traditional desktop computer, you need to first establish where the mouse pointer is, and then move the pointer accurately, relative to its starting position, to the point where you want it to be—a significantly complex operation that may seem second nature to you, but confounds many users and, whether you're aware of it or not, slows all mouse users down. Touchscreens elegantly avoid this problem.

Note in the figure that the distance from a hypothetical mouse pointer (A) to target (B) is spatially relative. This is because the mouse pointer can originate its movement from any position on the screen. The distance and positioning are also relative to the arbitrary starting position of the pointer, and related to the physical position of the mouse on the desk.

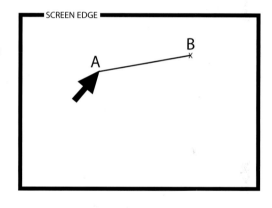

However, the distance from target (B) to the edges of the screen is spatially absolute. This means that, unlike a computer mouse system, the touchscreen system allows users to touch the target directly without first establishing its position relative to an intermediary (the mouse pointer). Target B's position is known, fixed, and quickly touchable in such a system.

It's worth noting that desktop computers do have an alternative to the mouse, which is much more effective and uses the faster *spatially absolute* method: The graphics tablet and stylus.

You Always Have a Finger with You

It's easy to overlook, but you always have a finger available. You don't have to hunt around in your pockets for a stylus, or reach for a mouse and keyboard. The iPad works with a common human finger and does not rely on any specialized input device (not to insult the finger of course, which is an enormously complex and clever biological input device).

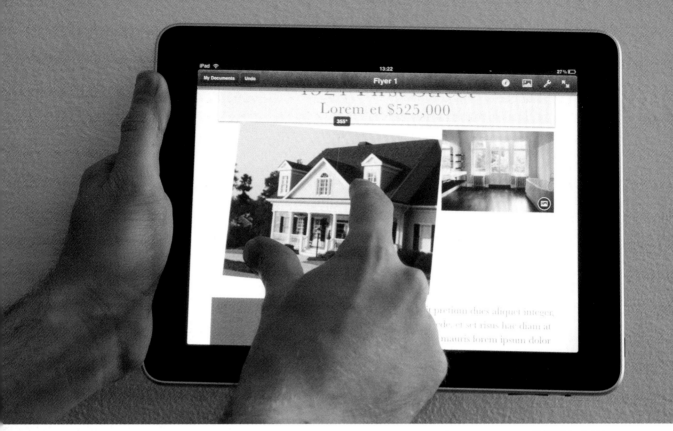

This makes maintenance much easier, and makes the iPad ideal for situations where there is high finger traffic for the device—an information system in a mall, for example.

NOTE

Fingers are pretty incredible at communicating complex information. You only have to look at sign language to realize that human hands can shape themselves into many exceptionally detailed forms.

Enterprising developers have determined that the iPad reliably detects 11 simultaneous finger touches; this range gives you enormous scope to allow all kinds of advanced finger-object interactions in your apps. Apple's in-house effort at a next generation word processor, *Pages*, is a good example of the kind of new gestures that a touchscreen makes possible. Users can scale, rotate, crop, and edit objects with a series of different finger gestures. Some of these gestures are already beginning to form a kind of gesture dictionary. Rotating objects, for example and as shown in the images, appears to have been standardized in a form where the user takes one finger and places it on the origin of rotation.

The user then simultaneously places another finger on the screen and moves this concentrically around the first finger to rotate the object.

This is just the beginning of a new gestural syntax. These motions will develop over the next few years and, bizarrely enough, we may end up using the kind of elaborate input semaphore made famous in the movie *Minority Report*.

Apple has already filed patents for a *multi-touch gesture dictionary*, which includes numerous standardized gestures for scaling and rotating objects, swiping pages, and controlling other interface elements. But more interesting still is Apple's patent for *gesture learning*, which suggests that the company is developing a detailed sign language for touchscreens, as shown in the images. This new sign language is particularly interesting because it gives you, as a developer, an important clue about how you might use gestures in your app. However, the danger, at the moment, is that you could end up overcomplicating your app by forcing your users to learn a series of non-standard gestures.

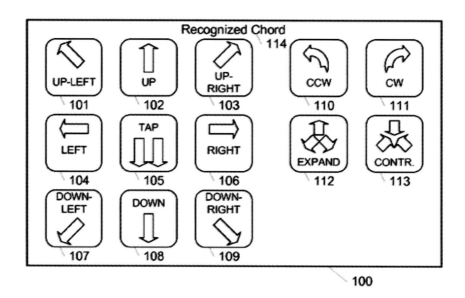

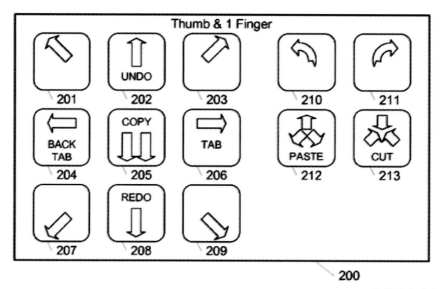

You may decide to lead the charge into new territory and establish conventions. And you might find that a new gesture-based interface on an old software idea will give you the killer app you're after.

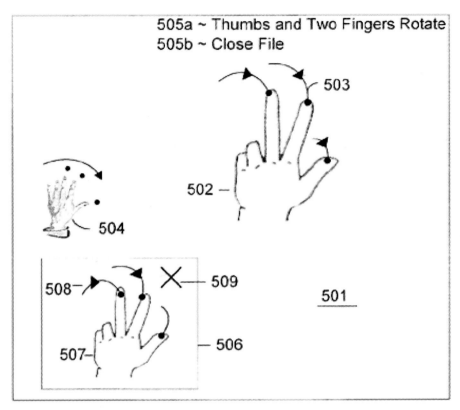

505a ~ Thumbs and Two Fingers Rotate
505b ~ Close File

Apple's *gesture learning* patent breaks multi-touch interaction down into two parts. The first part describes the number of fingers, and other parts of your hand, you place on the iPad screen. This positioning Apple calls the "chord." The second part describes the movement made by the chord—did you move your thumb and forefinger closer together, or away from each other? Did you move your hand up or down the screen? Together these two parts make up the "gesture."

*Before you rush out to build the computer system from **Minority Report,** let's not get carried away. The big problem with introducing an elaborate sign language for touch interaction is not a technical one. You could quite easily build an iPad app today that responded to hundreds of different gestures. The real problem is convincing users to spend the time and effort needed to adopt a new input method.*

The current gestural repertoire of the iPad is, given the enormous scope of what is possible, extremely conservative—and for good reason. Users simply will not learn a new input method unless you give them an exceptionally compelling reason to do so. Although the limited adoption of Dvorak keyboards is one commonly cited example of this effect in action, the more relevant example here is Palm's *Graffiti*, a stylus-input system used in a now-discontinued series of PDAs.

Graffiti used a shorthand system that massively improved handwriting recognition, but required users to learn a slightly new way of writing the alphabet. The system's inventor, Jeff Hawkins, argued that since it took weeks or months to learn how to type, people would be happy to spend 15 minutes learning the *Graffiti* input system. Unfortunately, I don't know anyone today who uses Hawkins' system—many people simply were not prepared to invest the time in learning it. Users tend to have very short-term goals, and the long-term advantages of learning a detailed gesture system does not motivate the vast majority of users who want to send that email *now*, or check their friend's blog *now*. Future rewards are a tough sell.

As touchscreen devices become increasingly popular over their desktop counterparts, we may see a transition from basic dragging and pinching to the full-scale gesturing anticipated by Apple. For now, it's important to be aware that these gestures are possible, and to consider engaging ways of carefully introducing them to first-timers—Apple suggests that building them into a rewarding game system might be a good approach.

It's still early days, and how we eventually get to a standardized gestural syntax is up to app developers like you. It's worth taking a look at some of the gestures listed in the Apple patent application to get a feel for the kinds of touch interactions that are possible on the iPad.

Exploring New Semantics

Semantics, as meant here, is the study of the relationship between signs, words, or symbols and what those words and symbols actually represent. For example, the relationship between

the word "fork" and the multi-pronged metal object you chomp your spaghetti from is a semantic relationship. The letters F, O, R, and K do not bear any actual relationship to the object they describe—we've just chosen them, as a culture, to describe that object. When you see the word "fork," you get a picture of the relevant piece of cutlery in your brain. The word "fork" is called a *signifier* and the image that provokes in your mind is the "signified."

My reason for explaining this is not to provoke a weird existential crisis in you, but instead I mention it because that this slightly bewildering concept of semantics is very important in all user interface design. Especially in touchscreen app design. Objects in a user interface are manipulated using graphical signifiers that manipulate the signified object, but do not necessarily literally picture the change.

TRADTIONAL USER INTERFACE SEMIOTICS

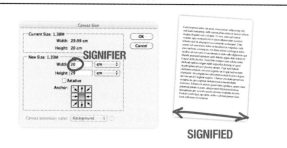

iPad USER INTERFACE SEMIOTICS

Software shown on iPad reproduced with permission of Jason K. Smith.
© 2010 Colordodge Labs Inc.

Up until this point in computing history, interfaces have tended to represent settings as numeric values that are input using a keyboard, or adjusted with a slider. For example, if you want to change the font size in a traditional word processor, you would most likely type the font size into the relevant box, or select it from a list of numbers in a drop-down menu. Both these methods are standardized metaphors for what you're actually trying to do: increase the font size.

© 2010 Apple Inc.

On the iPad, a more effective method of increasing the font size might be to tap the relevant portion of text and then pinch outwards with the fingers to enlarge it to the desired size. In this example, you're removing a layer of abstraction between what the user wants to achieve and the controls they're using to achieve that aim. Because the iPad is a touch-based system, the best app designers will very carefully consider every single signifier in the app.

Again, the problems of UI design dogma will likely be a problem for you here. All of us, as designers, have been heavily exposed to the old WIMP paradigms, and they've lodged deep in our minds. Approaching the iPad from a fresh perspective is very tricky, but you should ask yourself whether the controls you've included in your app are the best for that purpose. Touch interaction is much more effective when a setting is represented with a well thought out metaphor.

It's easy to pinpoint the major metaphors that have now changed—swipe instead of scroll, pinch instead of locating the zoom function in a menu. But there are hundreds of less obvious ways you can improve your app by looking closely at every single control and asking yourself: Is there a better way to do this with a touchscreen?

A simple rule of thumb is that if your iPad app is using a control method that has a direct parallel in traditional desktop PC software, it is very likely not making best use of iPad's touchscreen. It would be an extraordinary coincidence if the same control system that works well with a mouse also worked well with a touch-based input system.

Typography on the iPad

The first typographic quirk you'll notice is that pixels on the iPad are probably not the same size as pixels on your Mac's monitor. This presents a challenge because you will be designing for iPad-sized pixels using Mac-sized pixels—with the notable exception of the high-resolution screen available as a special order on the 15" MacBook Pro, which seems to almost exactly match the resolution of the iPad. In some ways, the larger pixels on most Mac screens are an advantage, because you can do detailed pixel-level work at a resolution above the final resolution—this makes good work look even sharper on the iPad's display. However, the resolution difference on most monitors adds an element of the unknown—until you've double-checked your designs on the iPad's screen, you can't be

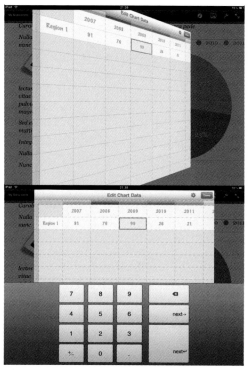

© 2010 Apple Inc.

sure that your design is actually legible. This is especially true of text, where a design that is perfectly legible on the screen of your Mac in Photoshop, might become less readable when transferred to the higher pixel density of the iPad's display. Two known solutions exist to check your iPad typography for legibility. You can print your designs at exactly iPad screen size and determine legibility that way, or the more eco-friendly, and frankly more conclusive, method is to regularly send design updates to your iPad and check the design in-situ.

The sharpness of the iPad's display comes as a shock to many designers, especially those dealing with text rendering on the device. Text on the iPad is crisp, but at close range does suffer from visible pixilation, especially with high-contrast color combinations.

With *Alice for the iPad*, I had to go through many, many revisions of the text onscreen before finding a legible format. Some book designers offer users the option to scale the text in an app—this is the case in *iBooks*, for example.

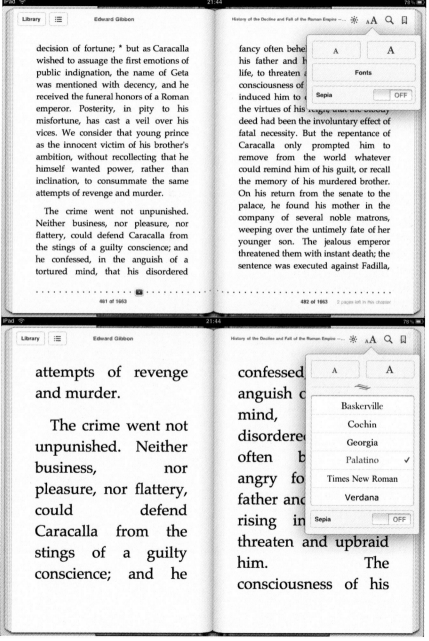

© 2010 Apple Inc.

But in other cases you may want very strict control of the text in relation to graphical objects, in which case you may need to define a font size that users cannot change, but which is legible to the majority of your audience. This is a challenge faced by traditional book publishers every day, but on the iPad it's a trickier proposition owing to the special nature of backlit pixels and the unpredictable effects of pixel density on typography. Although the iPad has a higher pixel density than a regular computer monitor, it is not as resolute as the iPhone—which is another good reason why designing for the iPad is a different experience from designing for its smaller counterpart. The iPad is also commonly held much closer to the face than a traditional monitor and users will subconsciously scrutinize the legibility of text in your iPad apps. The iPad has a number of fonts available by default. Although there are ways of using fonts other than these in your apps, these are a good starting point, especially if you want to build your app quickly or don't have any strong preference for fonts outside of the built-in range.

BodoniSvtyTwoITCTT-Book
BodoniSvtyTwoITCTT-BookIta
BodoniSvtyTwoOSITCTT-Book
BodoniSvtyTwoOSITCTT-BookIt
BodoniSvtyTwoOSITCTT-Bold
BodoniSvtyTwoSCITCTT-Book

BradleyHandITCTT-Bold
Chalkduster
Cochin-BoldItalic

Font sizes that might work on the iPhone or your computer monitor may not achieve the same level of legibility on the iPad. In most cases, text is legible at comparable point sizes, but it's always worth comparing different treatments because, as I discovered with Alice, there is a big difference between text on the iPad merely being *readable*, and text on the iPad actually being a *pleasure to read*. Achieving the latter takes more time, but you're more likely to have a killer app on your hands if you take the time and effort to produce beautiful typography.

The worst mistake you can make is to assume that the typographical rules of the desktop computing world translate to the iPad; in many cases they do not. Keep checking your text designs on the device itself and play about with new forms until you're happy with the results.

As with any typographical design work, the color of the text and the background will also affect legibility on the iPad. The iPad's display is naturally capable of high contrasts, meaning that you may find that combining certain colors that work on a computer monitor results in a design that is too harsh on the iPad. Placing black text on a plain white background on the iPad does appear starker than on many computer displays—it also draws attention to the edges of letters. You may find that opting for lighter color: darker color combinations result in more legible text than do extremes. You could also try experimenting with light grey backgrounds for black text, and subtle paper grains; these substantially take the edge off the harshness of simple black-on-white typography. If there's an overall message for typographers on the iPad, it's this: Experiment.

I'll return to the issue of typography in Chapter 10, where you'll learn exactly how I decided on fonts and typographic layouts in Alice for the iPad.

TIP

Understanding iPad Ergonomics

The first official Apple videos of the iPad showed the device being used in casual situations—the living room, the bedroom, and the kitchen, and Apple's advertising campaigns have tended to emphasize the feet-up, iPad-on-lap style of gripping the device. Ergonomics experts were quick to point out that this pattern of use would quickly fatigue the users because our bodies often feel uncomfortable holding a feet-above-hips position like this for any length of time.

As an iPad owner, you've probably noticed that your grip pattern on the iPad changes depending on which application you're using, and where you're using the iPad. Personally I have found myself adopting all kinds of new and strange grip patterns on the iPad. Although I'm not always conscious of it, I do sometimes observe myself and others shifting about and resting the iPad on my knees, thighs, tabletops, and the arms of chairs, depending on the length of time I've been using the device, and the location I'm using it in. For most purposes, there are two main grip situations for iPad use. The first situation is when the user is sitting down and the second is when the user is standing up.

TILT OF HEAD

LINE OF SIGHT

ANGLE OF ARMS

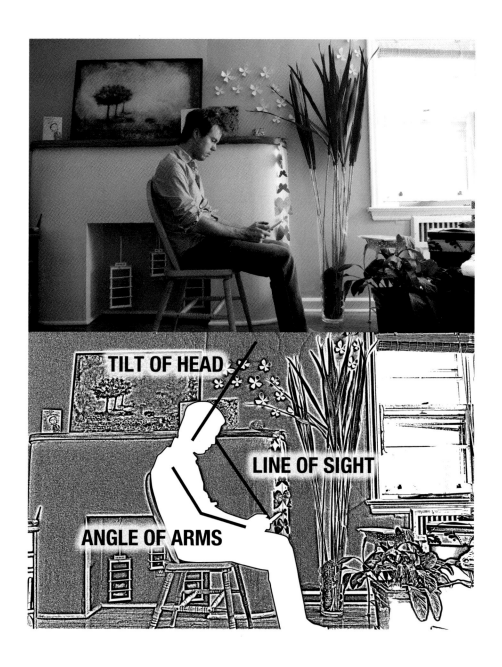

I'll examine these two modes of use in some detail, because the ergonomics of these grip patterns will, to some extent, help you to design a good interface for your iPad app. A standing user, for example a warehouse employee working on a stocktaking task, will have considerably different interface requirements than a casual user watching a movie at home on her sofa.

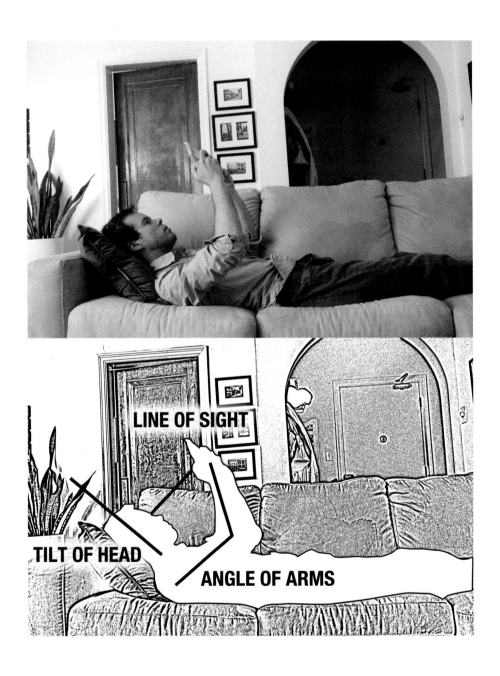

First, you'll take a look at the needs of a seated user, in a casual setting. When the iPad is used by a seated user, the most common grip pattern seems to be to rest the iPad on the thighs, balancing the iPad between the legs, making both hands available to tap and type on the device, using the palms for added support. Some users will, as in the Apple adverts, choose a seating position where it is possible to raise their feet from the floor, using a coffee table or similar, to increase the angle of the thighs, tilting the iPad upwards to create 60-90 degrees between the line of sight and the iPad's screen. Others will lean over the device to create the same effect. In this situation, the user finds it reasonably easy to tap any part of the screen—both hands are free to manipulate objects and a full-range of ten-finger multi-touch gestures are available to the software designer. Whether left- or right-handed, the user will not risk destabilizing their grip on the iPad no matter where controls are placed; however you will need to be conscious, as a designer, of where the user's hands move when they are manipulating on-screen controls.

TIP

It's not all good news for fingers and hands. They do have a frustrating habit of obscuring the object they are manipulating. Unlike a mouse pointer, which is a small and unobtrusive collection of pixels cutting a quiet wake across the expanse of millions of other pixels, the human finger is a bulbous sausage of flesh, blocking out huge portions of the touchscreen. Perhaps thousands of pixels in one fell swoop. You need to be aware of how your interface design forces the human hand to move across and obscure the screen—the human hand is not a mouse.

Because the rest of the hand sits below the fingers, the fingertips tend to delineate the point below which the screen is partially obscured. This has significant repercussions for iPad app designers, because it requires constant vigilance to make sure that the controls that affect an object onscreen are placed below that object, not above. Controls that change the whole interface, and not a specific object to be referred to onscreen, can sit above. Of course, this is a generalized rule, and only in testing your interface design will you be able to establish exceptions, or discover new methods of working around obstructions caused by the hand(s).

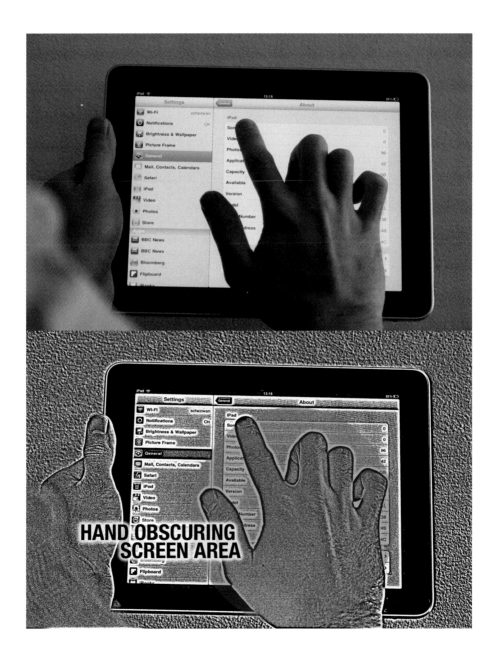

HAND OBSCURING
SCREEN AREA

Other interesting new observations apply to the iPad too. A right-handed user is more likely to obscure the iPad when operating controls on the left side of the screen, and for left-handers the opposite is true.

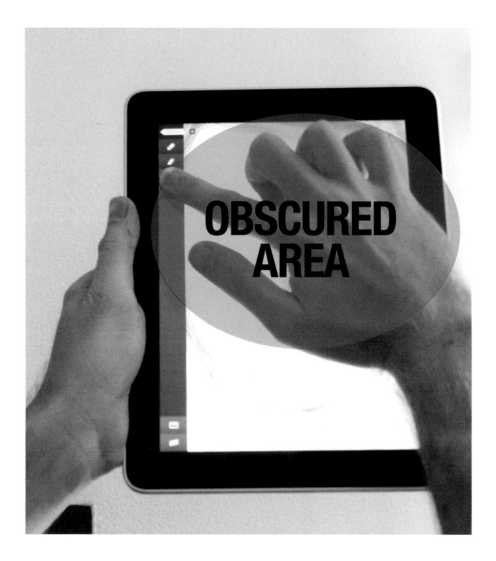

Also, more of the screen will be obscured by the user's hand and wrist in portrait mode than in landscape mode, and reach patterns are significantly altered. Unless a user repositions his grip, you should prioritize UI elements so that the most-used functions are in the easiest-to-reach areas, if there is a lot of keyboard work involved during operation of the app. You can see in these diagrams how UI design might be organized based on how easily users can reach across the screen in various grip stances.

Using the iPad in a standing position is a more curious, and far more challenging, situation. You'll need to be careful about exactly how you place controls, and also take into account the different requirements of left-handed versus right-handed users. In many cases, an app that is designed to be used standing up may benefit from the option to "flip" the user interface, so that controls are optimized for both sets of users.

In a standing position, the weaker spot for interaction is the point farthest away from the hand gripping the iPad. In the case of a right-handed person, gripping the iPad with her left hand and tapping with the right, the weakest point on the screen will be the far-right edge.

It is here that the law of levers places the most stress on the hand gripping the iPad. Although with moderate use, the effect is barely noticeable, during prolonged use (stock-taking tasks, for example), this could become fatiguing. As a result, it may be best to place popular controls on the left side of the screen, but paradoxically, this is also the side of the screen that will cause the most obscuring as the hand passes across. The compromise might be to put the most frequently used buttons in the lower-left corner, where grip is strongest, and the risk of obscuring content is lowest. Other controls could then be arranged in order of frequency of use from left to right and lower to upper portions of the iPad's display. You could also have the option to flip them for left and right-handed users if you think your app will often be used by people standing up. All these are broad guidelines, designed to provoke your own experiments—the rules are still unwritten.

It's still early days for the iPad, and the ergonomics of the device are likely to shift over time. There are also the interesting possibilities offered by embedding the iPad into existing hardware—a car dashboard, for example, where ergonomic considerations will change drastically. The most powerful tool you have at your disposal in these situations is observation: Watch how your users respond to the interfaces you create and consider new ways of arranging content to fit their behavior. These quirks, and the difficulty in discovering them, brings you onto a critical part of good app design: prototyping your designs.

The Importance of Prototyping

Prototyping your designs might seem like an unnecessary step—more like the kind of thing that a big car company is likely to do than an indie iPad developer outfit. But I am regularly surprised by how much time can be saved by creating rough prototypes of an iPad app, even before the user interface is added or considered. It's often very tempting to rush ahead and hope that deficiencies in the software can be fixed at the testing stage, but what if your app idea is more fundamentally flawed? This is not a discovery you want to make after many hours have been invested in its development. The alternative to prototyping is to hope for the best, and wait until the app is finished. Sometimes you will get away with this gamble, but every now and again you will fail spectacularly. I know, because I've been there.

When I came to design *Alice for the iPad*, I'd already had the experience of working extensively on several iPhone projects. One of them, in particular, met several technical hurdles we could have avoided if we'd stopped to consider prototyping earlier in the design process. Around a year before Alice came out, and before anyone outside Apple had dreamt of the iPad, we began work on a game called *Twitch Origins*. This was designed to be the first true four-player game for the iPhone, allowing a group of players to battle against each other using the same phone. However, we quickly discovered that the iPhone, at that time, could not accurately detect four simultaneous touches from different people's fingers.

It seemed defeatist to give up at that point, and we were determined that we could find a solution to the problem—in fact, we *had* to find a solution to the problem because we had already invested several months of development time into the project. This is not a situation you want to be in. We should have established, before any graphics and substantial coding was done, whether the basic premise of the app—being able to detect four individual's fingers simultaneously—was possible. Luck would have it that we did eventually discover a solution to the problem (if you're curious the solution is to avoid placing any active contact point on the same lateral coordinate as any other). However, it could very easily have been the case that the iPhone screen was not capable of this interaction, and months of work may have been wasted. Looking back on the experience, it seems horribly obvious that prototyping the concept should have been an early priority. But, as so many developers do, we made some dangerous assumptions about what the hardware could handle, but later discovered unexpected behavior that very nearly derailed the entire project. The problem with *Twitch Origins* was fairly serious: If the iPhone could not handle four players, our game concept was sunk. However, in most cases you are likely to find that, if you fail to prototype your concepts, they won't fail as obviously as this. Instead they'll simply work suboptimally, which is perhaps worse, because you'll be tempted to settle for this and keep slogging though to the end of the project.

Let's take a quick look at what I mean by prototyping your iPad app. First, you should sketch out all your designs by hand, as discussed in Chapter 1. This immediately sidesteps all the abstractions of

Photoshop, where you're likely to end up mistakenly designing an interface for use with a mouse. Secondly, you should hold these designs in your hand at iPad scale—either by attaching them to cardboard cut out to match the size of the iPad, or by photographing your sketches and transferring them into the iPad's Photo app, where you can preview interface placement on the iPad's screen.

App designers typically get to the stage of standing back and brutally assessing their apps only after they are almost ready for submission to the App Store, but by this time you've invested so much time in designing it that rationally reappraising the app is incredibly difficult. Even experienced iPad app designers find it very hard to let go of bad work; this is because we often assess the value of our own work in terms of the raw number of hours we put into it. While this cold, managerial approach to valuing work might be passable in some industries, in the app design world, nobody cares how much time and energy you put into making your app; they only care about whether the end product is any good. This is exactly the reason that I suggest prototyping, because it is the only way to avoid this issue altogether. It allows you to stop a bad app idea in its tracks before any emotional attachment to it has set in and blinded you and your team.

These two steps should take no more than a few hours to complete, and at this point you will be able to make a fairly clear assessment of whether your app will work properly from a crude, non-functioning perspective. Play-act interactions with the app—does the system you've devised make sense? Are you still excited by the concept? Remember, you will have to live with this project for weeks, if not months.

Once you take a good look at the sketched version of your app, you will need to assess the mechanics behind it—is this app possible to build programmatically? The only person who is able to decide this for certain is your programmer. If you are the programmer, you will probably know your own abilities, and can ask members of online forums for their advice if you're unsure about a novel use that has never been attempted.

The final stage is to build a functioning mock-up of the app, or those vital parts of the app that are critical to its functioning and have not been tried on the iPad platform. At this stage the graphics will be incredibly rough and basic. The intention is simply to prove, conclusively, that the project you're about to embark on is within the realms of possibility and an appealing use of the iPad. This functioning mock-up should be installed on an iPad and explored at length by you, the programmer, and other members of your team. This is the point of no return. It may be hard to let ideas go, even at this early stage, but good ideas are often the result of dismissing a lot of bad ones. Don't be afraid to stop and start again.

Make Decisions; Don't Offer Choices

Great design is not simply about what you put into your software, but what you leave out. The decision not to include certain options in your software—even options that may seem trivial to implement—is the key to building an iPad app that appeals to the majority of users. Remember, if you want to win the app gold rush, your target audience must be the *majority* of consumers. Make sure the features you include in your app appeal to this group of users, and that they will not be confused by half-finished ideas you've included just to satisfy a niche of spec-sheet nerds. To satisfy the majority of users, you need to make clear decisions about what your app will do, and how the user interface will work. Making definitive choices at the design stage focuses you on creating elegant software. Offering choices, especially multiple ways of achieving the same result, is often the outcome of a sloppy design process. I'll give you some examples of what I mean.

When Apple first launched the iPhone, there was an outcry from a niche of technical users who could not understand the absence of a copy-and-paste function on the device. It would be hard to argue that it was not within Apple's engineering ability to include some kind of copy-and-paste feature on the first iPhone OS, but they chose not to include it. The reason?

At the time, Apple didn't feel like they had worked out a way to make the copy-and-paste feature accessible to the majority of their users. Notice the word *majority*. So, instead of including a half-hearted copy-and-paste, Apple chose to leave it out rather than confuse the majority of users. Steve Jobs has since specifically referred to the copy-and-paste feature as one that Apple held back on, waiting until the company felt it had got it right. Compare the way the iPhone handles copy-and-paste to the terrible implementation other SmartPhones were using at the time, and you get the feeling that he was probably right. The point here is not to applaud Apple, but to demonstrate that sometimes you have to make difficult decisions not to include a feature against the bald demands of your users. In the case of copy-and-paste, the feature was eventually included on the iPhone, and works very well.

There are other choices you might be tempted to offer users of your apps, such as the option to customize the user interface. Again, this is likely to end in messy software. It is up to you to decide the most efficient way for the majority of users to interact with your iPad app; it's not for them to decide. This may sound like arrogance, but it is quite the opposite. By making good choices at the design stage you free the users from having to make those choices when they use your iPad app. The users are supposed to be getting on with the business of completing a task, not figuring out the best way to accomplish that task in the software. There is, of course, a niche of user who delights in exploring obscure menus and working around the confusing trail of buttons and settings that complete a task—in fact, for some people this is what computers *are*—but the core of your audience on the iPad wants clarity in the app's interface. A philosophy of simplicity is especially important when designing iPad apps because the size of the display and the nature of touchscreen interaction leave little room for mistakes. Providing too many choices, or the wrong choices, is an abdication of your responsibility as a designer. It is your responsibility to make choices so that your users don't have to.

Make sure your iPad app doesn't offer too many choices, settings, or options, especially as an interim step in performing a defined task. People are often paralyzed by choice. The psychologist Barry Swartz has done some excellent research into this subject, analyzing sales data collected by a pensions company. This revealed a curious trend. The data demonstrated that for every ten extra pension plan options presented to workers, participation in the pension scheme dropped by 2%. In other words, an

increase in your choice of pension plans would, bizarrely, cause a reduction in your participation in any scheme. This meant that 10% fewer people would participate if there were 50 options than had there been just five options. Swartz believes, and I agree with him, that adding options increases confusion and reduces satisfaction. Although we live in a culture where choice is king, we tend to be happier when options are fewer, and when these few options have been carefully chosen for us and best meet the demands of the majority. In iPad app design, you will find that the most satisfying interactions you can provide for your users are those that offer the least choice, but maximum usefulness.

There are many paradoxes in the idea that offering choice benefits a user. In fact, making decisions can slow users down so considerably that they would often benefit more from simply not having to make the decision. Many choices in software leave users bewildered—Did I make the right menu selection? What about this other option? The more menu options you put between your users and a task they want to accomplish, the longer they will take to complete that task, and the less satisfying the user experience will be. By giving the user more choices, paradoxically, you have actually limited them.

TIP

*Interestingly, legend has it that Palm computers used to have a "tap counter"—a person who would count the number of taps the user of a handheld computer had to make on the screen with a stylus to accomplish any given task. If the user had to make more than three taps, the software was sent back to the designers who were instructed to redesign the menu to allow the task to be completed in fewer than three taps. This is a useful starting point for designing iPad software; however, also bear in mind that simply expanding the content of menus to reduce the number of taps, or in the case of the iPad, **touches,** is just as bewildering to the user as increasing the number of subsequent menus. Perhaps a more suitable starting point might be: No more than three touches, and no more than three options in any one menu. Of course, this is not a definitive rule and circumstances vary, but you will need to think about minimizing the complexity of your interface in these kinds of ways if you want to build a killer app.*

An experience I had while designing the sound on *Alice for the iPad* will give you another example of a situation in which it was necessary to make a design *decision* rather than offering a *choice*. In one of the early builds of *Alice*, we had music playing in the background throughout the app, but I quickly discovered that because the music didn't change with the flow of the *Alice in Wonderland* story, it often jarred against the events being described on the page. It was like watching a film with the same song on loop. When Alice is peacefully sleeping by the riverbank, there is quite a different sense of dramatic urgency than when Alice is falling down the rabbit hole, or being attacked by cards. Clearly no one piece of music would suit all situations. Sadly, recording different music for every scene was not an option for us if we wanted to bring the app out in time for the launch of the iPad. I had a decision to make: Either I left in the music, with an option for the users to turn it off or we could remove the music entirely. It might appear like the correct decision in this case is to give the users the choice of having the music or not, regardless of whether it would eventually annoy them—that's what current thinking tends to be in western society: give choices. However, what I decided to do was make a decision for the users: I decided the music would annoy them, so we left it out and made plans to record music for a future edition of the book. Your iPad apps will benefit from this kind of thought process and these simple, repeated acts of deciding not to add certain features when they are not 100% ready yet. I'll take a more detailed look at using sound in iPad apps in Chapter 11.

TIP

*Avoid confusing **beautiful** interfaces with **functional** interfaces. Functional interfaces are almost always beautiful, but beautiful interfaces are not always functional. This is a critical distinction, and you need to be conscious that your design choices offer elegant solutions both graphically and functionally. Apple has some critics who dismiss their computers as "pretty" and "superficial," and this is because good design will almost always look and feel elegant. However, the confusion arises because design that looks elegant is not automatically good design—Apple's critics have probably encountered this phenomenon a lot in their lives, and suspect Apple is guilty of the same sin—putting looks before functionality. Sometimes Apple is guilty of this, as illustrated here, but more often than most companies it is not. Don Norman, a brilliant scientist who looks at the emotion of design, has done research into the beauty of design and puts it far better than I can, "There are many designers, many design schools, who cannot distinguish prettiness from usefulness," says Norman. "Off they go, training their students to make things pleasant: façade design, one of my designer friends calls it (disdainfully, let me emphasize). True beauty in a product has to be more than skin deep, more than a façade. To be truly beautiful, wondrous, and pleasurable, the product has to fulfill a useful function, work well, and be usable and understandable. Good design means that beauty and usability are in balance. An object that is beautiful to the core is no better than one that is only pretty if they both lack usability."*

*EDITION29 ARCHITECTURE ISSUE 002

V23K16 / THE NETHERLANDS
LEIDEN

OPEN HOUSE
HOLLYWOOD

SURF HOUSE
LOS ANGELES

CASA PR34 / MEXICO
TECAMACHALCO

SLIT HOUSE / JAPAN
SHIGA

HEIDI HOUSE
TOKYO

S HOUSE / POLAND
WARSAW

XS HOUSE
BOSTON

HOUSE FOR THREE CHILDREN
OSAKA

BOX HOUSE / BRAZIL
SAO PAULO

PHOTOGRAPH OF MICHEL ROJKIND BY ULI HECKMANN
EDITION29 ARCHITECTURE ISSUE 002
CREDITS

ARCHITECTS **KLEIN DYTHAM ARCHITECTURE** TOKYO
HEIDI HOUSE HOUSE
JAPAN

Reproduced with permission of Edition29 www.edition29.com. © 2010 Edition29 Inc.

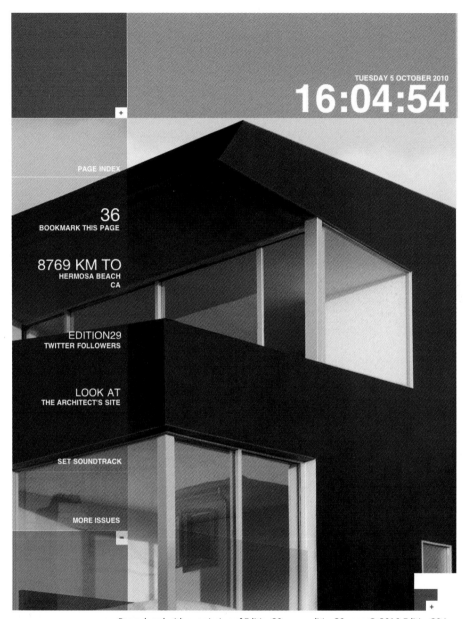

TUESDAY 5 OCTOBER 2010

16:04:54

PAGE INDEX

36
BOOKMARK THIS PAGE

8769 KM TO
HERMOSA BEACH
CA

EDITION29
TWITTER FOLLOWERS

LOOK AT
THE ARCHITECT'S SITE

SET SOUNDTRACK

MORE ISSUES

Reproduced with permission of Edition29 www.edition29.com. © 2010 Edition29 Inc.

Reproduced with permission of Edition29 www.edition29.com. © 2010 Edition29 Inc.

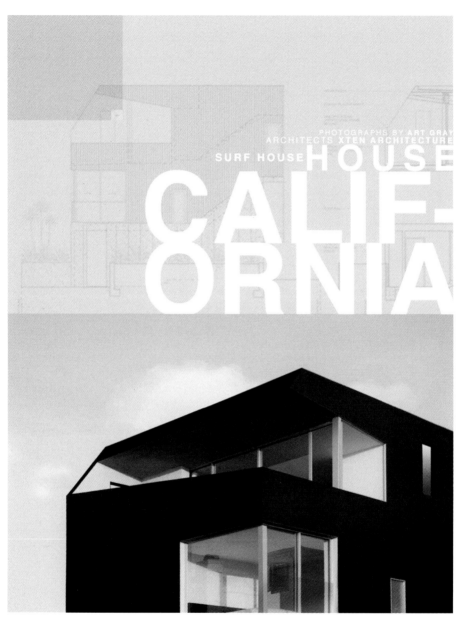

PHOTOGRAPHS BY ART GRAY
ARCHITECTS XTEN ARCHITECTURE
SURF HOUSE HOUSE
CALIF-
ORNIA

Reproduced with permission of Edition29 www.edition29.com. © 2010 Edition29 Inc.

TUESDAY 5 OCTOBER 2010

16:05:31

PAGE INDEX

24
BOOKMARK THIS PAGE

8743 KM TO
HOLLYWOOD HILLS
LOS ANGELES CA

EDITION29
TWITTER FOLLOWERS

LOOK AT
THE ARCHITECT'S SITE

SET SOUNDTRACK

MORE ISSUES

PLANS SHOWING PASSIVE VENTILATION

The User Is Always Right

Many programmers are inclined to blame user error for problems that are reported, but the same programmers are often reduced almost to tears when they are first-hand witnesses to a user struggling to achieve something with their software—the effect is very humbling, and very motivating. Observation is the key to understanding how users are interacting with your app, and it allows you to see what changes can be made to improve that interaction. Observation brings problems out of the abstract and into the concrete: You can literally *see* the users struggling. This is very different to responding to user criticism in forums and emails. Making alterations suggested by your more vocal customers could land you in trouble, as I'll explain in a moment. Instead, by far the most effective method of determining flaws in your user interface is to watch users operating your app. This way you receive first-hand, undeniable evidence of flaws in action.

NOTE

*In effect, **user error** does not exist—forget the term. Either your app design anticipates user error and avoids presenting situations where it is possible, or your app is at fault, not the user. I know it's hard to accept this. There is a history of a computer culture that often sneered at end users, blaming their incompetence for mistakes. But these same users are clearly capable of much more complex tasks than using an iPad app—holding conversations, maintaining a job, and so on. So, to assume that the user is at fault in the majority of cases, and not the software, is at best naive, and at worst arrogant.*

I'll give you one example of how I used this observational approach when designing *Alice for the iPad*, and also how simply *listening* to criticism, rather than *observing* behavior can lead to a huge misunderstanding of the problem. In the first release of *Alice for the iPad*, we allowed readers to turn the pages of the app only by tapping arrow buttons in the lower portion of the screen; however, we soon got complaints from some users, and from Apple themselves no less, that our app did not use the newly established gesture for page changing: the finger swipe. Although I had been aware that we weren't using this gesture, I had omitted it from the *Alice* app because I thought it would confuse the interface. I thought that arrows were clear, obvious, and unambiguous to any user, but page swipes required a degree of familiarity with the iPad technology.

Despite my reservations, we duly responded to this feedback—especially since some of it had come from Apple—and implemented finger swiping as a means to change the pages. As a result—you guessed it—disaster struck. We discovered that the bulk of users were now accidentally swiping to change page when what they actually wanted to do was move a physics-enabled object on the page.

© 2010 Apple Inc.

Although, on paper, the ability to swipe to change the page seemed like an obvious omission from the app, in reality including it made the app much harder to use, and frustrated more users than had originally been annoyed that they couldn't swipe to turn the page.

The problem here was two-fold. First we had implemented a change based on the criticisms of a small but vocal portion of the user group that did not reflect the needs of the majority of users. Second, we implemented this change without observing the effect it would have on the average user, the person-in-the-street. Instead we made the assumption that swipe-to-turn-page was an innately "good feature" in any context, and we also assumed that the average user would understand this feature.

This experience illustrates a wider point about good iPad app design, and software design in general. A feature that looks and sounds good on paper may fail to live up to expectations in reality, in fact it may actively sabotage the app you're designing. In the case of *Alice for the iPad*, we ultimately decided to re-program the navigation interface so that it defaults to the basic arrow navigation, and then provided an option to enable swipe-to-turn for users who were particularly aggrieved by its absence. The fiasco taught us an important lesson.

There is no substitute for observing your app in the hands of the users, especially the person-in-the-street. Do not make any assumptions about the way your app will be used, or assume that those using it will be familiar with conventions. Perhaps in a few years, as conventions become established, it will be possible to make more assumptions about how users will react to your app design, but for now the world of touchscreens is still very new to the majority of your customers.

The point of this chapter is not to discourage you from using swipe-to-turn-page—on the contrary it's a great gesture in certain contexts—but to help you be aware that small changes to the way a user interface functions can have significant and unanticipated effects on the end user. The way to avoid this is to observe their behavior, not just your own behavior.

Attention to Detail Is Everything

A sloppy design choice anywhere in your iPad app will compromise the app as a whole. When you design your app, every detail in it must be considered closely from the perspective of the end users. Don't settle for something that works "okay;" make sure it works to the best of your design and programming abilities. If any feature does not meet these criteria, leave it out entirely until it does. This is especially true of UI flow, where designers often make compromises because the metaphors used in prototype menu systems (the graphical way you choose to display information) distracts you from taking a really good look at the basic mechanics of how best to allow users to navigate your app. This may sound like a pretty abstract statement to a first-time iPad designer, so let's look at some examples of what I'm talking about here.

In the fourth release of *Alice for the iPad,* we decided to allow advanced users the option of swiping to turn pages, but we left this option off by default, for younger users and the inexperienced. "Oh," I hear you cry, "but swiping to turn pages is a basic gesture." This probably will be true a year from now, but today you'd be surprised how many people pick up an electronic book and need to be instructed on how to turn the page. The problem might be that the gesture is almost too intuitive—not something people are used to with computers. *Alice* originally shipped with arrows you could tap to turn the pages. Apple then suggested we change this to swipe (with the disastrous results I explained earlier) and so, in the fourth release, we decided the *Alice* app would default to the arrow-style navigation, but we would add an options screen so that advanced users could turn on swipe. This menu was designed to stay out of the way of casual users. To avoid some of the complications caused by offering users too much choice (described earlier in this chapter), we stowed these advanced options in a sub-section of the index screen. This was a place that would not confuse the majority of users, but would be accessible to the niche audience that wanted fine-control over the reading experience.

You will find many situations in your own iPad apps where you need to offer several options to your users and you may discover that even a very small range of options can be extraordinarily difficult to present in a clear UI flow—especially if you are not using stock UI components from the Apple library. The kind of menu we developed in *Alice* will be typical to many book apps, and elements of it will be present in all apps.

You can see from these prototype menu designs that there are several ways to achieve the same end, but which do you think is the most effective? Can you tell by just looking at the design, or would you need to test it? Also, consider the different ways of displaying the settings information. In some designs, users can toggle between different options,

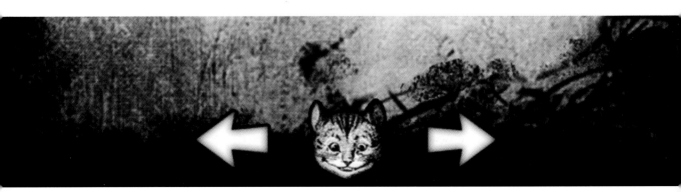

but do some toggles make more sense than others? You'll notice than in some of the designs, the options are grouped in different ways, also note that some of the designs do not fully continue the metaphor of the rolled scroll, whereas others do. Often with custom UI designs like this you will need to strike a balance between sustaining the original metaphor, in this case a rolled scroll, and providing the simplest most obvious way for users to access the controls they need and make the required changes.

Let's take a look at another simple menu option in Alice for the iPad: the ability to switch between full and abridged versions of the story. This binary choice is the common in apps of any genre: The UI prompts the user for a simple either/or decision—do you want to go this way? Or, do you want to go that way? Again, there are various solutions to this UI problem. Can you think of a better way to present this information? What if I had used a stock Apple UI component for clarity? Would that have helped, or would it have compromised the aesthetic of the app? Generally I believe that stock UI components should be used wherever possible, but in the case of this splash screen, I felt that the available menu choices were so obvious to the users that it was worth preserving the look and feel of the *Alice in Wonderland* world, rather than introduce 21st century iPad buttons. If your app is not trying to feign some long forgotten era, I strongly suggest that you use the stock UI components, at least as a starting point for your designs. Stock UI has the benefit of coming pre-tested by Apple's UI experts, and will also feel instantly familiar to the users of your app. Each case varies of course, and this is just a taster of one of many decisions you will have to make for your iPad app. The little details in your app really count because what is your app other than all these tiny interactions glued together?

NOTE *Every tiny detail counts. Did you realize that Apple designed the pulsing light on a Mac in sleep mode to perfectly match the rhythm of a human breathing? They chose this pace because it was "psychologically appealing" to consumers. A human respires at 12-20 breathes per minute. Take a look at the sleep LED on your Mac, it's pulsing around the same rate. Stare at it for long enough and you may find that your breathing changes to synchronize with the pulse of the LED. Freaky, hey? Now, **that** is attention to detail. Put this kind of effort into your iPad apps and you're on the right track.*

Using Reality in Your Apps

Apple recommend that your iPad apps be designed to look like physical objects, making them more inviting to touch. You can see this aesthetic in evidence in apps like *Calendar*, which resembles a real-life calendar with a leather background and metal eyelets holding the "paper" in place. But iPad designers are already divided over this use of real-world metaphors for iPad software equivalents. Although there is clearly a kitsch appeal to interface designs like this, and the *Calendar* app is pleasant to use, there is a risk for you, as a software designer, in literally translating pre-existing real world objects onto the iPad. Although the result will often look attractive and provide a reassuring familiarity for the first-time user, it is not always that case that the best way of organizing information in the amorphous, digital world of the iPad is to take the physical object that once did the same task and simply simulate it.

© 2010 Apple Inc.

Deciding if a current real-life object should be directly translated into a software simulation of that same object is a tricky decision. This growing trend can be seen most obviously, and perhaps least effectively, in Apple's *iBooks*. Here, books are arranged on a virtual bookcase, as if in the real world. However, unlike in the real world, this arrangement is totally impractical, and demonstrates a basic pitfall of blindly using real-world metaphor in your iPad apps. Where, in real life, bookcases allow you to quickly scan through the spines of, perhaps, thousands of available titles, and pulling one off the shelf to read, the iPad screen is just too small to allow this metaphor to work productively, nor are books arranged with their spines facing the user—for the obvious reason that they would be barely legible at this size. Instead of a useful indexing system for a range of book titles, *iBooks* ends up presenting the worst of both worlds, a simulation of reality that is infinitely worse than the reality it simulates.

© 2010 Apple Inc.

Luckily there is an alternative view in *iBooks* that allows titles to be browsed in a long, scrollable list. But it would have been more useful if Apple had devised a new indexing system that took advantage of the iPad's feature set, rather than shoehorning the existing "bookshelf" concept into the digital realm. You can see this literal adaptation of physical objects into digital equivalents is a popular theme throughout the App Store, and it may be some time before the bulk of designers gain enough confidence on the platform to experiment with new interface paradigms.

© Monotone Records Inc. TrixMix 2

© iKiosk. Visit http://www.bild.de

© iStudiez. Visit http://www.istudentpro.com

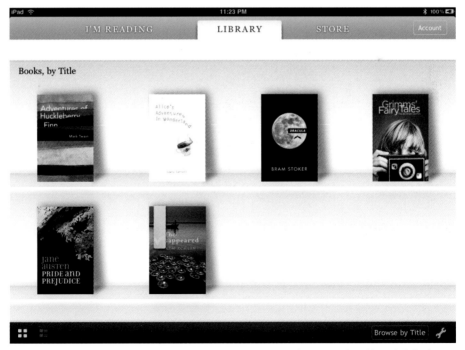

© Kobo Inc. Visit http://www.kobobooks.com

© Apple Inc.

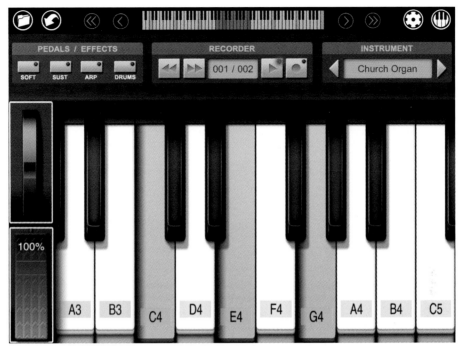

© MooCowMusic Inc. Pianist Pro. Visit http://moocowmusic.com

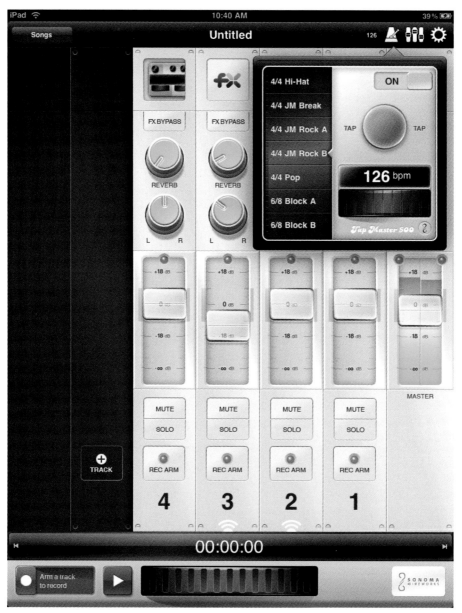

© Studiotrack. Visit www.sonomawireworks.com

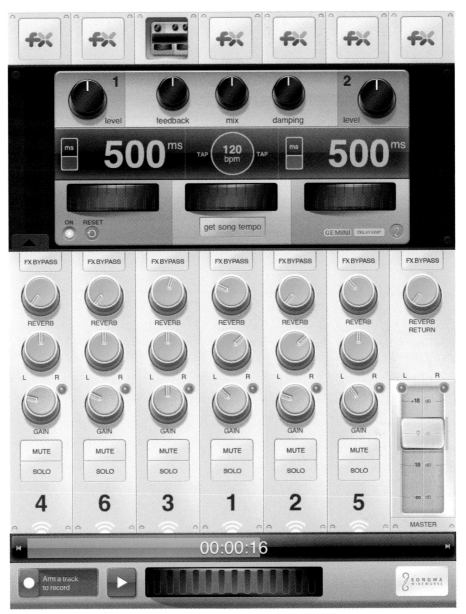

© Studiotrack. Visit www.sonomawireworks.com

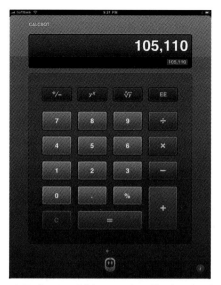

© Tapbots Inc. Calcbot. Visit http://tapbots.com/
software/calcbot

© Korg Inc. Visit www.korg.com

© Korg Inc. Visit www.korg.com

TIP

There are more interesting and more effective ways to organize information than literally taking the real-world objects that currently do the task and simulating them. Once the boundaries of the physical world are removed, things get a lot more exciting. Although at this early stage of iPad software development there is a tendency towards simulating reality, your app will eventually find a wider audience if you ignore real-world parallels and concentrate on the best way to display information in the digital world. Productivity trumps novelty in the end. However, you may find that the best solution lies halfway between reality and software: You can draw users into your app with an interface that look familiar and unthreatening, but don't limit yourself to only allowing interactions that are possible with the physical object—software can do much more.

Why Children Make the Best App Testers

If you've spent time around children, you'll have noticed their refreshing lack of concern about offending you. The average child has very little hesitation in telling you that you look weird, or asking why your voice is ridiculous. Perhaps you are lucky enough to be without a physical defect obvious to a child, in which case they will probably find some new and unexpected way of shocking you with their direct approach to the world. As we grow up, we're gradually conditioned to exist in a society that hides its real concerns behind a veneer of polite conversation, and by adulthood our masks are firmly tied. This is very useful information for an iPad app designer to know, because it suggests that it's almost impossible to trust the opinion of an adult—they will tend to say almost anything to avoid offending you. So, if you really want to know whether your app will be a global success, there is often no better litmus test than placing it in the hands of a precocious 12-year-old. If it were up to me, there would be a 12-year-old installed in every design studio in the country, a sort of child-pharaoh who would coldly assess the output of the designers.

Because of the way society is structured—new children are needed to eventually replace today's adults—there always tends to be a child to hand, whether its your friend's or your own. At some point in the design process, you would do well to enlist this child to try your app. It may be that, in some rare cases, your app is broadly inaccessible to a child—your iPad app might calculate tax returns and be unable to sustain the interest of a child. But even in these rare cases, I've found that a child is still quite capable of pointing out many glaring flaws with the design, flaws that are equally frustrating to adult users of the same app. You'll find that a smart, articulate kid is roughly equivalent to an averagely computer-savvy adult, only a lot more outspoken. In other words a child is the equivalent of the person-in-the-street discussed in Chapter 1, except a child is a lot more likely to give you a straight response to the flaws in your early designs.

I've spent a lot of time in schools demonstrating *Alice for the iPad* to children between 12 and 16 years old, and it is fascinating to see how savvy and critical they are towards modern software designs. This age demographic is "digital native"—they have no direct experience of a world before the Internet existed. To them these new technologies seem far less distant and alien than they do to much of the population currently.

TIP

Not only will you find children to be familiar with, and actively using, many of the latest technologies—from the iPad to Twitter—but they're also very quick to give you detailed emotional feedback on your software. This is exactly the kind of feedback that determines the success of your app, because design that elicits strong emotions is also design that sells.

Putting a Hand-Grenade in Your Cupcake

People often ask me, "what's the secret of making a hit iPad app?", to which I reply very seriously, "put a hand-grenade in your cupcake." The very last thing people expect to find inside a cupcake is a hand-grenade, and the moral of this story is to make sure your app, if you truly want it to be a global blockbuster, includes at least one devastating surprise—the hand-grenade in your cupcake. In *Alice*, it was the 250-year-old woodblock carvings, commissioned by an achingly famous long-dead author, springing to life. Nobody expected that to happen, a break from the status-quo most clearly evinced by Oprah Winfrey who, when playing with *Alice for the iPad* shrieked and pointed at the White Rabbit's watch. "Look, the clock! The clock moves!" It's this simple, profound emotional reaction to seeing something new, something challenging, odd, and fantastical that will really make your app shine. Now go bake some cupcakes and don't forget the secret ingredient.

Chapter 9
Designing Books and Magazines

If you're interested in making a book for the iPad, I've got a wealth of secrets to share with you about this genre of app. I designed the best-selling kid's book for the iPad, *Alice for the iPad*, Ben Roberts programmed it, and together we were at number one in the iPad book charts for most of the first month the iPad was released. Since then, I've been all over the world helping publishers and independent developers adapt books and magazines for the tablet format. I've noticed a few interesting things about many of the publishers I've talked to. The first is that they're deathly scared of committing resources to books on the iPad—at the moment most of them offer "revenue sharing," which is a euphemism for "you don't get paid unless we make money with this app"—hardly the most enthusiastic way to conduct new business.

There's a reason why they don't want to actually pay developers. Big publishers don't currently believe in the iPad format, they don't understand the iPad format and, conversely, most iPad developers don't understand book publishing. To an extent, I sympathize with big publishers. One of the biggest publishers in the world explained to me that they had contacted dozens of developers, asking these companies to give examples of how they could adapt one of the world's most famous children's books. In every case, the mock-ups provided by the developers looked terrible to the eyes of a seasoned book editor. You can imagine why.

Book publishing is very different from traditional app design, especially the kinds of apps we saw in the early days of the Apple iPhone. Books are not mechanistic and, in the case of children's books, they are tied to specific paper sizes, typeface choices, and numerous other typographical and tactile decisions—from the weight of the paper to the style of the binding—that have all been carefully thought through by the publisher and author. Given all these romantic choices that publishers are used to making when they print a book, you can begin to understand why the iPad freaks them out. It's a cold slab of glass and aluminum whose proportions cannot be physically altered; a lifeless window on a world of pixels. As a reading medium the iPad is, at first glance, pretty unwelcoming to these publishers. The iPad also seems to constrain the options available to publishers because the screen is equivalent to a fairly small paper size, substantially smaller than any paper format a publisher would traditionally use to print an illustrated book—although not far off a paperback.

While books made purely of text have already begun to evolve into an established format on the iPad—shaped by the typographic framework of Apple's iBooks app—the illustrated and interactive book formats have experienced a significantly more awkward birth. There is still no established paradigm for converting illustrated or animated books into an iPad format and most developers, like my company, *Atomic Antelope*, have chosen to publish books outside the iBooks store, where there are no preconceived restraints on what a book can or cannot do.

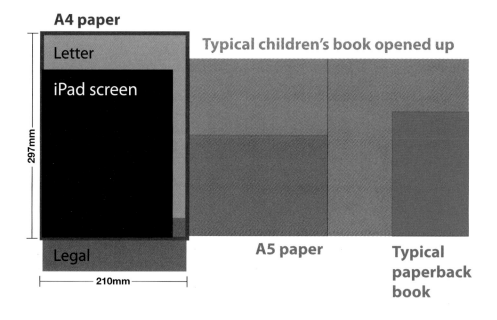

TIP

To learn more about whether you should publish your book in the iBooks store, or as a discrete app instead, take a look later in this chapter at the section entitled "To iBook or Not To iBook?".

Publishers are in a state of deep confusion over how illustrated books should be adapted for the iPad, and although *Alice for the iPad* has answered this question for them to some extent, it is still unknown how far this digital pop-up book metaphor can be pushed before the market is flooded with books in which graphic elements simply "wobble" and "tumble" when the iPad is shaken or tilted. We're already witnessing a painful stage where these ideas are re-applied to new content without significant thought over how the techniques benefit a story. There's likely to be a return to the 90s CD-ROM era where developers take respected titles from publishers and then shoehorn them into whatever pre-built mechanisms of interactivity they have at their disposal. For example, the concept of coloring-in book pages and completing jigsaw puzzles are two concepts worn thin by overuse in the "interactive" book genre, and I expect the same thing to happen to some degree with the techniques used in physics-enabled books like *Alice*. These techniques are extremely easy to reapply to new content and the temptation is to ignore the tricky stages of development—actually working out how to enhance a story. Instead many of your competitors are likely to blindly apply established transformations to new story elements.

© Steve Glinberg, 123 Color HD.

As an iPad book publisher, you should be careful not to over-use cookie-cutter physics code. The application of simple ideas, like graphic elements that respond to physical movements, could sustain an industry of indie book publishers, provided these techniques are used with taste and restraint. Applying them indiscriminately won't give you a killer app and does harm to the genre—you need to stop and think about how the graphic techniques you use complement the story. Pop-up books, the closest real-world analogue to the iPad's physics books, demonstrate that there is considerable longevity in paper-folding techniques, many of which can be adapted and enhanced for the iPad. If you use these techniques, use them wisely and with good taste.

Traditional publishers still can't seem to accept that the iPad is a new medium; it's not a device to shoe-horn existing books into and expect to somehow replicate the original experience. It's no more logical to expect a film adaptation of a book to resemble the original book than to expect an iPad app to capture the precise look and feel of the source text. Although purists will object, the aim of creating a book on the iPad is to create entertainment. There is no invisible god secretly judging you on how faithfully your iPad adaptation of a story matches the original material—in fact, this is an abysmally low aspiration for making books on the iPad platform. People won't buy your iPad app because it's faithful to a source text; they'll buy it because it's brilliant and entertaining. The iPad has significantly different properties than a traditional book, and it's a shame to reduce it to the lowest common denominator—the printed word. What I'm really looking forward to is the first traditional-printed adaptation of a book originally written specifically for the iPad, then we'll see which format is really the more constraining.

Deciding Whether an App Is Necessary

I need to get this fact out of the way early on: Most magazine apps are unnecessary. I touched on this in Chapter 2, but it deserves some more attention. If you're creating a magazine app for the iPad, you're in dangerous territory because, unless you're prepared to rely on the naivety of your audience, there should be some compelling reason for users to buy your magazine app rather than read the same content, using a web browser, in a format that is far richer and better suited to hyperlinking and embedded media. There is currently a trend for magazines to yell "me too!" and jump onto the App Store. Certainly there have been significant financial success stories—*The Guardian* and *The Times* both stand out as newspapers that did fairly well from the launch of their iPad apps, but the repackaging of website content into app form may not have much longevity on the iPad platform and is very unlikely to be a profitable exercise for any company without an established brand to trade on.

Source: Popular Mechanics. © 2010 Hearst Communication Inc.

Source: www.thetimes.co.uk. © Times Newspapers Limited, 2010.

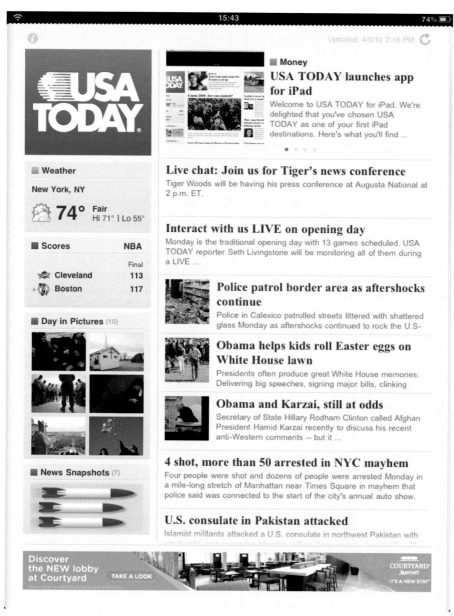

Source: www.usatoday.com

4 Melodies

Building on top of this substructure, Reznor and Ross spent two days recording ancillary melodies on a Moog Minimoog Voyager, an out-of-tune African marimba, a ukulele, and other instruments. "It seemed like a good collision of things, a nice blend of organic and electronic," Reznor says. They extracted and mixed in the best parts.

5 Vocals

Maandig recorded three verses into a mic connected to sound-processing software called Speakerphone. Reznor sang the verses again an octave lower. Because "The Believers" wasn't turning out to be a traditionally structured song, Reznor decided on a slow instrumental buildup to the first and second verses, another instrumental section, and then a sinister third verse to finish things off.

6 Polish

Once all the parts had been blended in ProTools, coproducer and longtime NIN collaborator Alan Moulder gave "The Believers" (5:36) its final layer of polish using the studio's mixing board. Moulder honed each musical element, mixed the track down to left and right channels, and sent it off to get mastered. Time from start to completion: seven and a half days.

PHOTOGRAPH BY **Bryce Duffy**

18.06 .... Rants

RE: Rise of the Machines

There are early adopters, late adopters, and now a third camp: reluctant adopters. Nearly three-quarters of the letters we received about the Apple iPad gave it a thumbs-down. Some were sarcastic: "The iPad is mankind's greatest invention since the wheel. One-handed typing and watching movies on a 9-inch screen are the best things anyone can expect of the future!" Others were just plain cynical: "This is another piece of Apple's self-promotion machine." But here's the thing. A few writers who despised and/or resented the glossy little number said they were going to hold their noses and buy it anyway. Somehow we're not surprised.

STEVEN LEVY

Getting There

PHOTOGRAPH BY **Jeff Mermelstein**

Tablets are here to stay—if they can grow cheaper, lighter, and more connected.

Since its release in early April, thousands of pundits have submitted reports on the iPad, and their upturned thumbs are getting sunburned. The hundreds of thousands of people who have bought one already realize that Apple's tablet is the first real step toward a new category of computing, nestled between the PC and the smartphone, enabling unique and just plain fun new activities. ¶ But a substantial class of doubters believes that the iPad is a luxury item, a transitory novelty that will fade as quickly as the hype. They're missing the point—this isn't just a flashy device but the long-awaited arrival of

Reproduced with permission of National Geographic. © 2010 National Geographic Society.

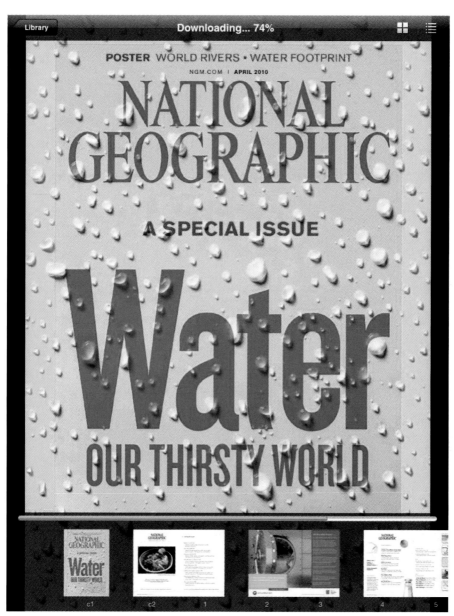

Reproduced with permission of National Geographic. © 2010 National Geographic Society.

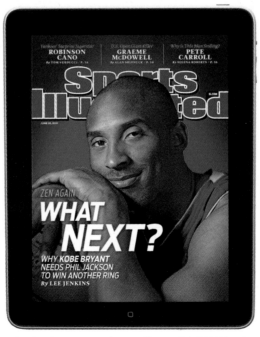

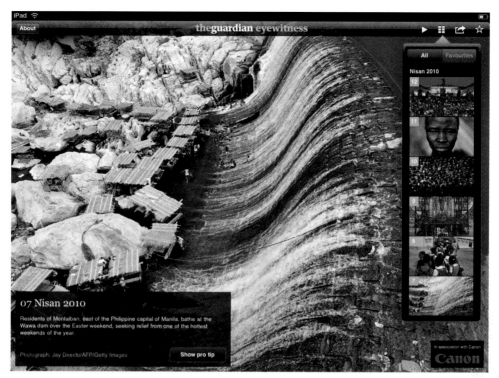

Reproduced with permission of The Guardian. © 2010 The Guardian Group.

Reproduced with permission of The Guardian. © 2010 The Guardian Group.

One of the main reasons why newspapers have found some success with branded iPad apps is that they can advertise their apps extensively, and at relatively low cost, in their own newspapers and magazines. The high sales figures for some branded website-alternative apps may simply be evidence that a traditional advertising blitz still works, rather than evidence that users have any particular desire to read web content rehashed into an app.

It's extremely important to consider why your branded iPad app is any better than your website, especially if you do not have the marketing clout to gloss over the issue. Just because this rehashing tactic worked for a few big brands, it doesn't mean that it will work for you, or that it was a good idea. The Internet was specifically designed to be platform agnostic, easy to update, and alive with content that can be linked between. Reinventing the Internet in app form as something half-book, half-website, but embracing the advantages of neither is a strange folly that only traditional publishers like the newspapers would have considered. Let's see where we are a year from now. I suspect much of this content will return to the Internet, accessed by a web browser, where it belongs.

To iBook or Not To iBook?

At the moment, the decision on whether to publish your book in the iBooks store is fairly straightforward. If you're publishing a book with many pages of text, no illustrations, and no interactivity (and I do not use these descriptions pejoratively), you are likely to be far better off publishing your material into the iBooks store. Publishing into iBooks avoids all the problems of inventing your own display format, page navigation system, and typographical controls. iBooks provides a shell within which your text can sit, automatically formatted for the iPad screen and navigated using controls that are identical between iBooks— thus making it easy for users to understand exactly how your text is explored. It's also the place that users expect to find these kinds of books. Producing a book for the iBooks store is also significantly less technically demanding. You can format books for the store without touching a line of code: the challenge is purely typographical. Rather than firing up Xcode, you can use InDesign or QuarkXPress to layout pages and output them directly to an iBook-compatible document.

Reproduced with permission of Apple Inc. © 2010 Apple Inc.

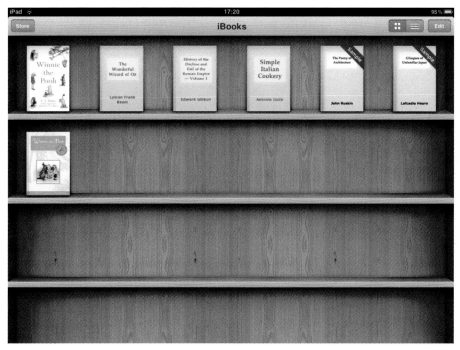

Reproduced with permission of Apple Inc. © 2010 Apple Inc.

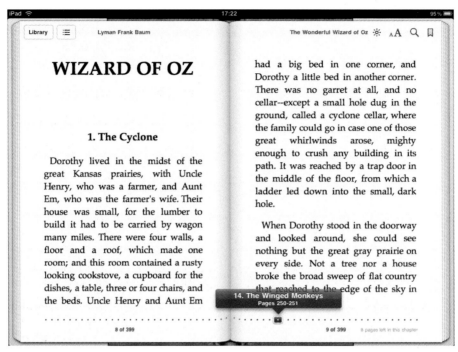

If, on the other hand, your book is rich in interactivity, multimedia, and animated typography, you will need to publish it into the Books section of the App Store itself.

TIP

The iBooks store and the App Store are completely separate entities—don't get them confused. Books that are purchased in the iBooks store sit on a virtual shelf inside iBooks, and are read using the standarized display system developed by Apple for iBooks. Books purchased from the App Store, by contrast, appear as discrete apps on your iPad—like any other app they have their own icon on the home screen and have access to the full range of the iPad's capabilities. The advantage of publishing your book as an app in the App Store is that you, as a designer, have complete control over every aspect of how the book looks and feels—your imagination is the limit. However, the disadvantage of publishing a discrete app in the Books section of the App Store is that you have to design and program everything by hand, from the method used to turn pages, to the way text is scaled on the screen. You'll essentially end up building your own eBook reader software, as well as designing the book—this can turn out to be a fair task. With iBooks, the reader software is provided, but you're limited to the smaller feature set of what Apple allows into its iBooks store.

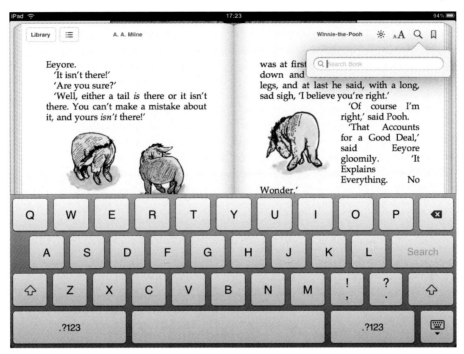

Making a Book App

I'm going to give you some of the best advice in the industry on building a hit book app for the iPad. Although a lot of self-professed experts out there will give you a list of complex rules and strategies for creating an iPad app, wouldn't it be nice if someone who'd actually written a hit app told you how to do it? The academic view of making a hit iPad app are all very interesting, but if these "experts" claim they can give you realistic advice on how to actually do it, why don't they personally have any apps in the top ten in the App Store?

I've seen how an iPad book grows from an idea to a global hit, and I've made a lot of money from the App Store in the process, so I'm not going to patronize you by breaking this all down into a contrived set of steps. I know that's just not how this stuff works in the real world. What I'm going to do instead is explain how I put together *Alice for the iPad*, why I think it worked, and how you can replicate the success of *Alice* in your own book app. I think you'll find that you can intuitively put these experiences to use in your own work.

Picking a Strong Source Text

My source story, *Alice's Adventures in Wonderland*, was written by Lewis Carroll in 1685 and illustrated by John Tenniel. I'm often asked why *Atomic Antelope* picked this particular book to adapt for the iPad. The truth is, there were many reasons. The first reason is that *Alice in Wonderland* is one of the best-known and best-selling children's books of all time. That meant that choosing *Alice* automatically gave access to millions of eager fans. Then there was the personal reason that I've always loved the *Alice in Wonderland* story, and really loving what you're working on is the most motivating force of all. There was also the practical advantage that the illustrations in the book were already perfectly suited to the physics effects I wanted to use in the app. Tenniel's original woodblock prints were outlined in thick ink and this creates a natural cut-out line to work from in Photoshop. The characters in *Alice* already have natural lines of segmentation between their body parts, so cutting them out and assigning physical properties to the components became a very natural process.

It's bizarre to think that Tenniel's artistic choices over 150 years ago made his illustrations more suitable for the Apple iPad in 2010. This leads to another reason I think Alice was such an effective book adaptation: it was charming.

Charm goes a fair way to selling apps and it certainly helped us that *Alice in Wonderland* was a well-loved book, close to the hearts of many readers. What also excited the people I spoke to about the app was that it used very old source material but applied the very latest in interactive digital techniques to the artwork in a way that kept the tone of the original book alive. Notice that I say "tone" of the book, and not the religious preservation of everything in the original book. If you're adapting a well known classic for the iPad, be aware that staying true to the tone is important, but details should be flexible. As you discovered earlier in this chapter, the iPad is not a book in the traditional sense, and nor should you treat it as one. While I was a fan of the source title, and knew the material well, I didn't treat it with such reverence that we were unable to have fun with the artwork. Of course, the world of Wonderland is inherently crazed and unexpected, so physics simulations worked unusually well with this material, but I believe what really draws readers into the world of *Alice for the iPad* is that their familiarity with the static artwork we based the story on makes it all the more unexpected and fascinating when those traditional artworks spring to life.

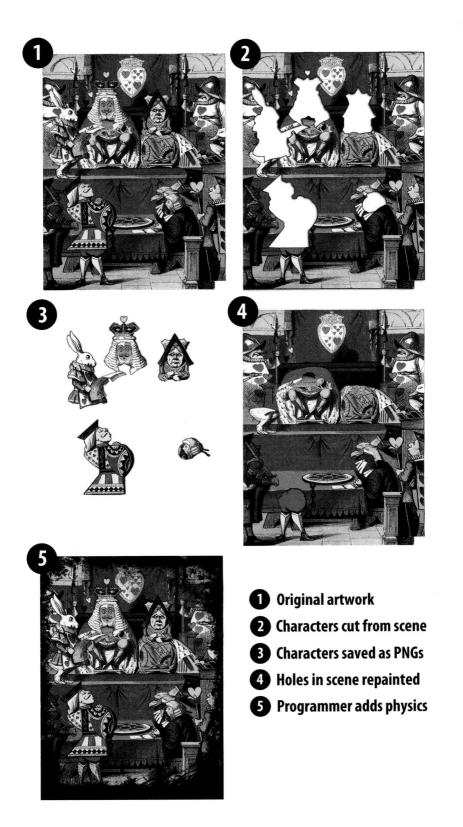

1. Original artwork
2. Characters cut from scene
3. Characters saved as PNGs
4. Holes in scene repainted
5. Programmer adds physics

Choosing Beautiful Illustrations

Had we used modern illustrations for *Alice* I think the effect would have been far less dramatic. People are used to cartoons moving, so artwork that looks like a cartoon will surprise no one when it moves. People are not used to paintings and illustrations springing to life—at least for now—so use this to your advantage if you're making an illustrated book, keep the surprises coming by subverting traditional artworks and bringing them to life to entertain new readers. There is a staggering wealth of gorgeous copyright-free art stretching back through the centuries, much of it untouched by modern designers. In our relentless pursuit of the new, most designers ignore the vast stores of amazing

source material that is available in libraries and museums across the country. Use this stuff to your advantage when you're building iPad books, and don't think for a moment that good art must be paid for on stock photo websites— the best stuff is not online, it's in old books and hanging on walls, and it's free to use. Although color photography is a relatively recent invention, color painting has been around for centuries and you'll be stunned at what you can find to repurpose in your apps.

"*You ought to be ashamed of yourself!*"

Phyllanthus speciosa
Jacq Coll vol.2.

NOTE

My most productive hours have been spent wandering around art galleries and noting down pre-1920s artists whose copyright-free work I can reuse on the iPad. What would those artists think, gazing back across the centuries? I think they'd be pleased to see their work reused and exposed to an entirely new audience.

Is It Reading or Is It Watching?

One of the most interesting paradoxes of iPad book design is that the more closely tailored your book is to the iPad's feature set (touch, tilt, and shake) the less of a "book" it is likely to be. Some traditionalists threw a small fit at *Alice for the iPad*, and questioned whether interactive books on the iPad would change reading from a quiet, reflective experience into a noisy, flashing interactive fairground. *The New York Times'* Verlyn Klinkenborg, said, "What will become of the readers we've been—quiet, thoughtful, patient, abstracted—in a world where interactive can be too tempting to ignore?" The worry seems to stem from the fear that children might end up watching books rather than reading them. Could the words become secondary to the images and motion, and perhaps so much so that the words go unread? It's a valid question, but I think it's predicated on the idea that the iPad will replace traditional books, while I believe it will in fact supplement them. Assuming I'm right, any fear of the iPad relegating words to second place is pointless; you could just as easily worry that paper pop-up books will overtake general fiction because they are easier to consume. It's an interesting topic though, and it's true there is a broader trend in the entertainment industry towards more challenging material being overtaken by digestible nonsense—the success of the *Transformers* movie franchise being a case in point. I mention this topic because I love literature, and I think—unfashionable though it might be to hold an ideology these days—that as digital publishers we owe it to our readers not to throw away decades of hard-earned experience. It's also important, if you claim to be publishing books, that there is some "book" left in the app you build.

How To Turn Pages and Build Indexes

The great iPad publishing debate rages on: Should you swipe to turn page, or should you scroll? A lot of designers have criticized Apple's use of swiping and page curls in the iBooks app because it seems like a crude affectation of the past, rather than an exciting way to push the book format forward. On the other hand, there is something very reassuring to new users about being able to turn pages on the iPad that look like they are pages in a traditional book. So, on the one hand, swiping and page curls are slightly kitsch, and a lot less effective than scrolling, but on the other hand users tend to quite enjoy the sensation that they are "completing" pages as they read them, rather than scrolling through a mass of text without clear delineation between pages, similar to the amorphous way they browse the web.

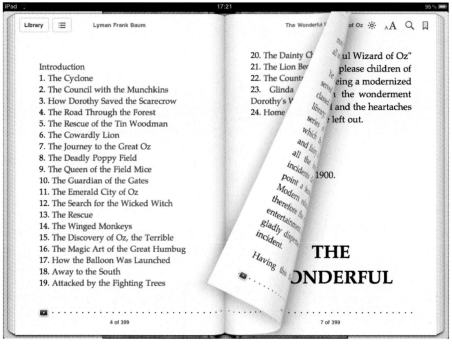

Reproduced with permission of Apple Inc. © 2010 Apple Inc.

IRAN CAN BE CONTAINED. *The path to follow? A course laid out half a century ago by a young Henry Kissinger, who argued that American chances of checking revolutionary powers such as the Soviet Union depended on our credible willingness to engage them in limited war.*

LIVING WITH A
NUCLEAR IRAN

By ROBERT D. KAPLAN

N 1957, A 34-year-old Harvard faculty member, Henry Kissinger, published a book, *Nuclear Weapons and Foreign Policy*, putting forth a counterintuitive proposition: that at the height of the Cold War, with the United States and the Soviet Union amassing enough hydrogen bombs for Armageddon, a messy, limited war featuring conventional forces and a tactical nuclear exchange or two was still possible, and the United States had to be prepared for such a conflict. Fresh in Kissinger's mind was the Korean War, which had concluded with a truce only four years earlier—"a war to which," as he wrote, "an all-out strategy seemed particularly unsuited." But President Dwight D. Eisenhower believed that any armed conflict with Moscow would accelerate into a thermonuclear holocaust, and he rejected outright this notion of "limited" nuclear war.

The absence of a nuclear exchange during the Cold War makes Eisenhower and what became the doctrine of mutual assured destruction look wise in hindsight. But more than half a century after *Nuclear Weapons and Foreign Policy* was

nuclear arsenals; some are stirred by religious zealotry; and only a few have robust bureaucratic control mechanisms to inhibit the use of these weapons. This conjunction of circumstances increases the prospect of limited nuclear war in this century. Kissinger long ago considered this problem in full, and the current nuclear impasse with Iran gives fresh reason to bring his book back into the debate.

Kissinger begins his study by challenging the idea that peace constitutes the "'normal' pattern of relations among states." Indeed, he describes a world that seems anything but peaceful:

On the ideological plane, the contemporary ferment is fed by the rapidity with which ideas can be communicated and

unchanged for centuries.

Continu his descri n of a world matches own,

Help   Quick Links

71   72   73   74   75   76   77   78   79

Readers remain overwhelmingly familiar with the traditional book format and still like the idea that "pages" exist, even if only virtually. In a few years I'm sure the simulated page curl will look extremely strange to us, but I've not seen a decent replacement for the metaphor. The Flipboard app uses an interesting open-door transition between pages that might become more popular, but my personal preference is a simple left-to-right swipe, without a page curl, that simply propels the completed page to the left of the screen and replaces it with the following page. The less attention you draw to page transitions, the less annoying they are likely to feel during extended use.

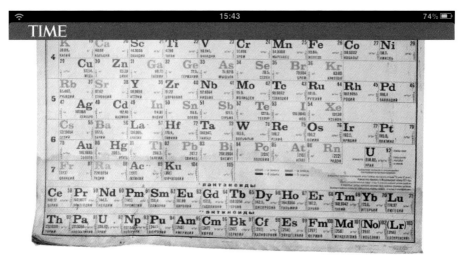

Old school *Russian chemistry professor Dmitri Mendeleev, right, organized the first modern periodic table in 1869*

Six atoms may seem minuscule—especially if they exist for only fractions of a second—but they can have huge implications. The recent announcement that Russian and American scientists finally managed to produce a tiny bit of element 117 by firing calcium atoms (element 20) at

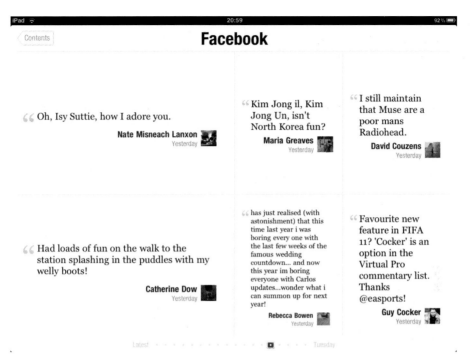

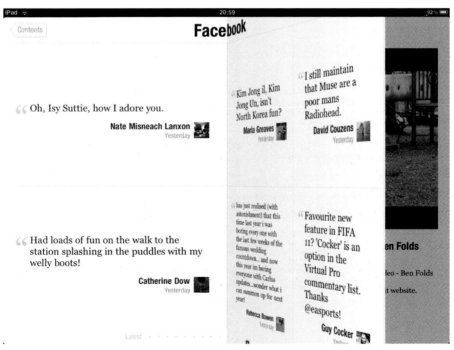

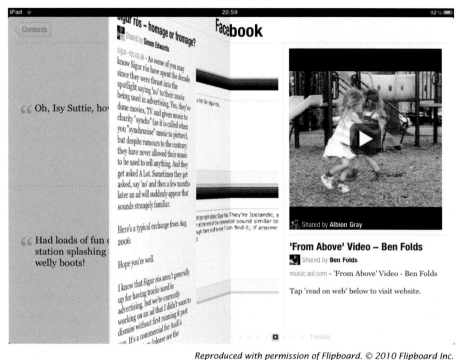

Reproduced with permission of Flipboard. © 2010 Flipboard Inc.

We are used to the discrete-page metaphor of the traditional book, where each page, or "screen" is a self-contained block of text with a purely chronological relationship to the page before and after it. But some designers have suggested alternatives to this structure. One suggestion is to treat the iPad as a window into a larger world, like a kind of hole through which you peek at a book that expands out from the current view and laterally across space. This format is best explained in the following diagram.

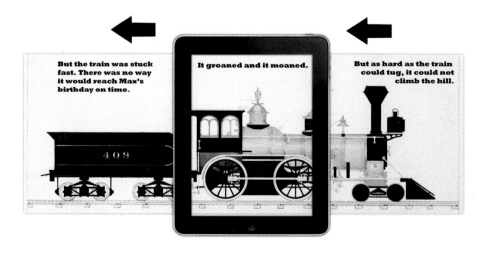

TIP

The ideas in this section show just a few ways that you can deal with book layout and typography on the iPad. Keep experimenting with new ideas and don't get stuck in the trap of purely trying to replicate the past in the digital realm. Traditional books only have pages that turn because of the physical limitations of the material we use to make them—paper—and the method used to bind this paper together. It's quite a leap of faith to let go of your preconceptions about what a book is, and how it is organized and presented, but leaving these ideas behind will help you engineer new and more effective methods of presenting literature on the iPad. Be brave!

Adapting an Existing Magazine

Luckily for you a lot of publishers have already had a go at adapting magazines for the iPad, so there's blood on the tiles to analyze. You'll notice that most of these publishers failed to create anything more compelling than their existing magazines and websites—although you'd have a hard time getting them to admit to this. A small number of publications have turned the momentum of their brand and the sheer loyalty of their existing readers into decent money on the iPad platform, creating the illusion of a vibrant market for digital magazines on a tablet, but can novelty sustain an entire industry? And what do you do if you're not already a world-famous magazine brand?

There is a big problem with creating a magazine app for the iPad, and I've touched on it before: Turning your magazine into an iPad app divorces it from everything that is great about the Internet. Where the Internet is rich with hyperlinks, easy to update with live news, easy to serve ads to, easy to embed multimedia in, and easy to serve content from, a discrete iPad app is often none of these things. Look at how *Wired* decided to stuff all its magazine content, regardless of whether it held interest for you as a reader, into a massive bloated beast of an app that would take over a week to download on many mobile iPad connections. Clearly the industry is a bit bewildered by the iPad and how it will be used to read content. It was confusing to watch as the magazine publishers took a collective step back ten years and decided that what we wanted all along wasn't the Internet at all, but glorified CD-ROMs with their magazine content shoehorned in.

The iPad magazine fiasco

544mb
WIRED MAGAZINE

2.8mb
GQ MAGAZINE

0.4mb
SMALL WEBSITE

250mb
3G DATA LIMIT

$20
A YEAR OF TIME MAGAZINE
PRINTED ON PAPER

$254
A YEAR OF TIME MAGAZINE
ON THE iPAD

$3.99
ONE ISSUE OF POPULAR
SCIENCE PRINTED ON PAPER

$4.99
ONE ISSUE OF POPULAR
SCIENCE ON THE iPAD

Time Magazine and Popular Science reproduced in this image with permission of Time and Bonnier Corporation Company respectively © 2010 Time Inc. and Bonnier Corporation Company.

Okay, so we've established that republishing magazine content as an iPad app is largely pointless, but let's take a look at some situations where it could be argued that a magazine app is the right way to go:

- You're creating extremely unique, touchable content for the iPad that cannot be coded in HTML. Content that is so innovative and compelling that the users will forgive all the compromises you've made in creating a discrete magazine app.

- The app you're designing integrates with a magazine website, downloads user-specific content, and allows it to be browsed offline—if the users are away from an Internet connection, say on a subway, they can read website content that has been selected to match their preferences.

- Somehow you figure out a way of presenting magazine content better than the web possibly can, in a way that I haven't anticipated.

Since the paper-magazine-adaptation genre is pretty much unique to the iPad, I think it's worth deconstructing what publishers have come up with so far: the good, the bad, and the ugly. It's interesting to see how the methods used to construct a paper magazine have crept onto the iPad without a huge amount of discussion about how well suited they are to the device, and touch interaction. Magazine publishers are naturally inclined to design content that can be published across mediums, and tend to stick to the lowest common denominator. You get the feeling that they have launched on the iPad with a fair degree of reservation, possibly anticipating that they might adapt this content for competing tablet devices that may not have the full functionality of the iPad.

Again, if you're not prepared to dive right into the iPad feature set and embrace everything on offer, it's generally a good idea to stick to the web, which is already the most platform-agnostic publishing option, and easily accessible on the iPad.

TIP

Keep an eye out for new magazine designs on the iPad. Although it seems likely that most titles will revert to the Internet once the novelty of discrete apps has worn off, you can expect to see a lots of interesting apps that aggregate content. The iPad isn't the saviour of the publishing industry but it could become to home to a load of exciting new magazine viewers that allow users to customize content from multiple sources. This is the kind of direction I suggest you take in your magazine designs for the iPad—forward.

Chapter 10
The Secrets of *Alice for the iPad*

Alice for the iPad was the first physics-enabled interactive digital pop-up book in the world. The techniques used to create the book have remained a secret, until now. I'm going to share them with you here. All I ask in return is that you make great books that delight and entertain your readers, that you follow the design advice in this book, and that you place storytelling above all other considerations. Don't just throw these techniques at any old material and expect to produce a hit app—the hard part is deciding *what* to do, not *how* to do it.

First, let's look at the basics of how *Alice* was created. Alice is based on a physics-simulation engine called Chipmunk Physics. This is a library of pre-programmed routines created by the geniuses at Howling Moon Software in Minnesota. This code takes a lot of the hard work out of designing books, games, and other apps that react to data from the *accelerometer* (the part of the iPad that detects how you are shaking or tilting the iPad). You give Chipmunk Physics certain bits of information about a scene—the locations of pivots, pins, and elastic bands— and the physics engine works out how things should move given the circumstances you've described in the code. Amazingly, Chipmunk Physics is free, and there's a vibrant developer community who can help you out with the code when you get stuck.

Behind each scene in *Alice for the iPad* is an invisible world of joints and springs that determine how the illustrations move. Although you can't see this hidden world of mechanisms, it's the magic that makes *Alice* work. Now, for the first time, I'm revealing how the animations in Alice were put together and explaining the ways you can adapt these techniques for use in your own iPad apps. But first, let's talk art.

Travelling Down the Rabbit Hole

Alice used source artwork from the original Lewis Carroll book, and there's a wealth of other public-domain titles that are ripe for adaptation. Building a physics-enabled book from source artwork involves three steps in Photoshop:

1. Separate the physics-objects from the backgrounds.

2. Redraw the background plates to fill in the holes.

3. Reintroduce the physics-objects and preview the movement of objects.

We were lucky with *Alice* because the source artwork came pre-drawn with nice thick outlines—this was the way John Tenniel created the original art. However, you will find that most source artwork on which copyright has expired will not have such distinct outlines and component parts. It's up to you as the designer to determine the best way to complement the aesthetic traditions of the illustrations you're working with. Alternatively, you can draw—or commission—new source artwork specifically for the iPad platform and with a view to separating the layers of art. Here you can see how the source artwork from the original *Alice in Wonderland* book was processed in Photoshop to produce a library of graphic assets ready for a programmer to pin to Chipmunk Physics objects. This is the same technique you will need to use for your own projects.

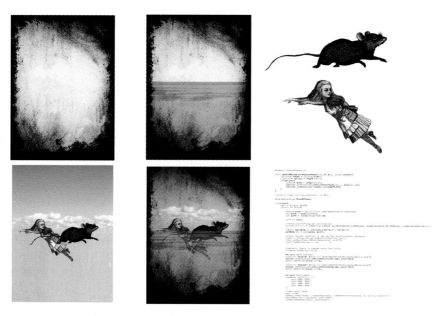

Reproduced with permission of Atomic Antelope LTD. © 2010 Atomic Antelope LTD.

Learning from *Alice*, Scene by Scene

Now that you know how to prepare artwork for a physics-enabled book, it's time to get deeper into the physics code behind *Alice*. The information in this section will be useful to both the designer(s) and programmer(s) on your project, but it is the programmer who will actually implement this code. I'm not going to deal with the procedures of creating a wrapper app for this Chipmunk Physics code—so, if you're new to iPad programming, you'll need to read the Apple guides that deal with creating an iPad app. This first step is to build the app framework that this code resides within, a topic that could fill a book many times this size. My focus here is specifically on Chipmunk Physics, and I assume a degree of familiarity with iPad app programming on your part.

TIP

Learning Cocoa Touch APIs and Objective-C memory management go beyond the scope of this chapter and are dealt with comprehensively in the official Apple documentation that comes with your developer license. Having said that, the Chipmunk process is not overly complicated and, even if you have no programming background whatsoever, you should be able to follow, at least in principle, the techniques described in this chapter fairly easily. Using this guide together with the Apple documentation and the more comprehensive Chipmunk Physics instructions at http://code.google.com/p/chipmunk-physics/ and you've got everything you need to create a hit iPad app.

First, I'm going to explain to you what Chipmunk Physics is and what it lets you do. Chipmunk Physics allows the iPad to easily manipulate 2D rigid bodies in a simulated physical world. Although this might sound wildly confusing at first glance, it basically means that it's a system that simulates how physical objects behave in real life—albeit a simulation of an imaginary real life that is flat or two-dimensional. There are four main components to the Chipmunk Physics word:

- Rigid bodies
- Collision shapes
- Constraints/joints
- Spaces

I'll run through each of these in turn so that you get a good feel for how the physics environment is set up.

WHAT THE READER SEES

THE HIDDEN PHYSICS WORLD

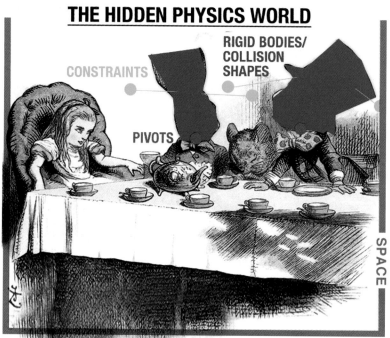

Reproduced with permission of Atomic Antelope LTD. © 2010 Atomic Antelope LTD.

Rigid Bodies

A rigid body describes the physical properties of an object. When you set up a rigid body in Chipmunk you define the mass of a specific object—its position in space, how it rotates, and the speed at which it moves. But a rigid body is not a shape. It does not have dimensions; it is simply a definition of physical properties that can then be attached to something called a collision shape—essentially the object that will hold these properties. Again, this might sound like the most bewildering thing you've ever heard, but it will quickly make sense when you begin to explore the system. Anything you don't understand yet should become clear as soon as you start using these techniques.

NOTE

At the moment, I'm avoiding demonstration of any code, because I don't want to scare off the graphic designers yet—these principles are useful to understand regardless of whether you are a programmer or a designer—you'll get to the code itself later in this chapter.

Alice heard the voice of the Duchess close to her ear. "You're thinking about something, my dear, and that makes you forget to talk."

Reproduced with permission of Atomic Antelope LTD. © 2010 Atomic Antelope LTD.

Collision Shapes

A collision shape is the physical form attached to a rigid body. When you attach shapes to a rigid body you give that body dimensions. More often than not, your object will be made up of multiple geometric shapes attached to a single body. For example, in the Caterpillar scene in *Alice for the iPad*, the mushrooms are each made out of two collision shapes—one for the cap of the mushroom, the other for the stalk. The vertexes (boundary outlines) of these two shapes are described in the code and then attached to the physical properties defined in the rigid body. Shapes also contain the surface properties of an object, including the friction and elasticity of that shape.

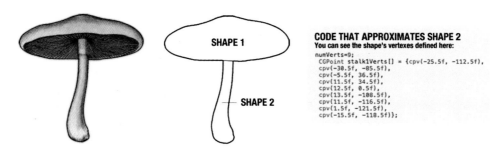

*It's worth pointing out at this stage that there is a world of difference between a collision shape and the actual graphics the end user sees on the iPad screen. The graphics you made in Photoshop are not colliding with each other. Instead, the invisible shapes, defined by the code, to which the graphics are attached, are colliding with each other. Did I blow your mind yet? Okay, so it's like a puppet show: The puppets (equivalent to the graphics) are stuck onto wooden poles and strings (equivalent to the collision shapes) that manipulate them. The puppets aren't moving, instead the invisible strings are moving them. In the same way, your visible graphics are not influencing the physics world, they are just attached behind the scenes to other, invisible shapes, and the physics world is influencing these shapes. This division sometimes confuses newcomers to the world of Chipmunk. Often your collision shape will match the physical dimensions of the graphics, also known as **sprites**, but sometimes they will bear little relation to each other. It all depends on the effects you want to create. This is what's great about sandbox systems like Chipmunk; there are no limits to what you can create other than the walls of your imagination.*

Constraints and Joints

Constraints and joints determine how rigid bodies are pinned, slide pointed, pivoted, or grooved in relation to each other. For example, in *Alice for the iPad*, Alice's arms are often pinned to her body so that they wobble slightly independently of her torso. And, in the Mad Hatter scene, the Hatter and the Hare are pinned at the lower portion of their heads and constraints are added to limit the movement to create a bobble-head look. Again, this kind of technique will become much more obvious when you take a closer look at the code later in this chapter.

Reproduced with permission of Atomic Antelope LTD. © 2010 Atomic Antelope LTD.

Spaces

Finally, you will need to set up the world your physics-objects inhabit. Spaces define the overall environment that your rigid bodies exist in, for example a space defines the gravity that influences your objects. It also provides a container for every rigid body that exists in a scene. You'll learn more about the parameters used to set up these environments when you take a closer look at code examples.

Now that I've covered the basics of how Chipmunk Physics works, you have a wonderful treat in store for you. Unlike other books where code samples and tutorials are taken from imaginary projects, I'm going to show you the actual, production code from *Alice for the iPad*. Yes, the actual code from the smash hit iPad app, the very same app that blazed its way through the store and beat Disney and Marvel to the top spot when the iPad launched. This is the code behind the app that Oprah Winfrey demonstrated to millions of people across the planet. Why am I doing this, you ask? Have I gone completely Michael Jackson? Well, yes, and no. The magic is in the implementation of this code—I am giving you the power to build, but the responsibility to create amazing art lies with you. Now come with me and let's walk around to the back of the puppet show and pull open the curtains.

Reproduced with permission of Atomic Antelope LTD. © 2010 Atomic Antelope LTD.

About These Code Samples

The first few scenes shown in this chapter include the full and complete code used in the *Alice for the iPad* app. However, to avoid repetition, the later scenes—from Bill the Lizard onwards—include information only on the main components of those scenes. All these code samples are to be used as a starting point for your own exploration into the brave new world of Chipmunk Physics. I have tailored this chapter both for designers seeking to understand the basic features available in a 2D physics world, and for programmers who want to see how this stuff is put together in a successful, commercial iPad application. Because these samples are so extensive, I'm not going to hold your hand through every twist and turn of the code—you'll have to do some work yourself to unravel some nuances of the demonstrations. I've found Chipmunk Physics extremely intuitive to work with, despite the fact that I am primarily a designer. You will also be able to get a good feel for what is being illustrated here, but I'm not going to patronize you.

To some degree, I'm throwing you in the deep end, but I think you'll learn far more from these commercial code samples that you would from a simple tutorial showing you how to make a ball drop down the screen and hit a box—the Internet is littered with these types of tutorials and I feel no compulsion to rehash those resources here. Although I do not dispute the value of learning these simple routines before embarking on a Chipmunk project, I realize that you bought this book to learn the good stuff, the serious hearty truth behind one of the iPad's best selling apps. There are plenty of online resources for the basic, non-commercial stuff.

So sit tight, and stay calm. The best way to approach the remainder of this chapter is to read through it with the latest Chipmunk documentation to hand, which is available at http://files.slembcke.net/chipmunk/release/ChipmunkLatest-Docs/. You will also need to download the latest version of Cocos2d from http://www.cocos2d-iphone.org/, which integrates the Chipmunk Physics engine.

Creating the Marmalade Jar Scene

This is one of the more basic physics setups in the book, and a great starting point for coming to grips with Chipmunk Physics. Although the physics system can seem fairly daunting to an absolute beginner, I'm convinced that anyone can learn it quickly and easily. It's surprisingly intuitive.

Alice found herself falling down what seemed to be a very deep well.

Either the well was very deep, or she fell very slowly, for she had plenty of time to look about her as she went down. She looked at the sides of the well, and noticed that they were filled with cupboards and book-shelves.

She took down a jar from one of the shelves as she passed. It was labeled "ORANGE MARMALADE". She did not like to drop the jar, so managed to put it into one of the cupboards as she fell past it.

"THUMP!"

Alice hit the ground.

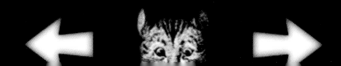

Alice found herself falling down what seemed to be a very deep well.

Either the well was very deep, or she fell very slowly, for she had plenty of time, as she went down, to look about her. She looked at the sides of the well and noticed that they were filled with cupboards and book-shelves.

She took down a jar from one of the shelves as she passed. It was labeled "ORANGE MARMALADE. She did not like to drop the jar, so managed to put it into one of the cupboards as she fell past it.

THUMP!

Alice hit the ground.

Reproduced with permission of Atomic Antelope LTD. © 2010 Atomic Antelope LTD.

NOTE

One final note before you begin. Where the lines of code in these examples have exceeded the width of the page, I have indented the following line to indicate that the code should in fact be one continuous line. For example, although this line is split, it should be entered as a single line of code:

```
wallShape = cpSegmentShapeNew(zeroBody, cpv(0,size.height),
                              cpv(size.width,size.height), 5);
```

Now that I've set up the basics, let's start by creating a file called Falling.h (when we were programming *Alice* "Falling" is what we called the scene with the marmalade jar).

This file will be used to import the code library resources that this scene requires. Almost all the scenes in *Alice* use this exact same .h file. The file imports the code libraries that the page needs to function: Foundation.h, cocos2d.h (the cocos2d libraries you downloaded from the cocos2d website), Chipmunk.h (the Chipmunk Physics libraries), Constants.h (the file *Alice* stores its configuration data in), and PhysicsContent.h. Here are the full contents of the Falling.h file for the Marmalade Jar (Falling) scene:

```
#import "cocos2d.h"
#import "chipmunk.h"
#import "Constants.h"
#import "PhysicsContent.h"

@interface Falling : PhysicsContent {

}

@end
```

After you've defined all the resources that the scene requires in Falling.h, you need to create another file called Falling.m. This file begins by importing the Falling.h libraries:

```
#import "Falling.h"

@implementation Falling

-(id)init{
    if((self = [super init])) {CGSize size = [[CCDirector sharedDirector]
    winSize];
```

Now you can begin to define the rigid body properties of the marmalade jar:

```
cpBody *zeroBody = cpBodyNew(INFINITY, INFINITY);
        zeroBody->p = cpvzero;
```

Almost all of the pages in *Alice* are fenced in by invisible walls, as defined in the code. These walls create boundaries at the edges of the book's pages, in this case to prevent the marmalade jar from slipping off the page and disappearing forever into some unknown abyss. You can create walls around a scene as follows:

```
cpShape *wallShape = cpSegmentShapeNew(zeroBody, cpv(0,0), cpv(0,size.
    height), 5);
        wallShape->e = 0.5;
        wallShape->u = 1.0;
        cpSpaceAddStaticShape(space, wallShape);
        wallShape = cpSegmentShapeNew(zeroBody,
                    cpv(0,size.height), cpv(size.width,size.height), 5);
        wallShape->e = 0.5;
        wallShape->u = 1.0;
        cpSpaceAddStaticShape(space, wallShape);
        wallShape = cpSegmentShapeNew(zeroBody,
                    cpv(size.width,size.height), cpv(size.width,0), 5);
        wallShape->e = 0.5;
        wallShape->u = 1.0;
```

```
    cpSpaceAddStaticShape(space, wallShape);
    wallShape = cpSegmentShapeNew(zeroBody, cpv(size.width,0),
            cpv(0,0), 5);
    wallShape->e = 0.5;
    wallShape->u = 1.0;
    cpSpaceAddStaticShape(space, wallShape);
```

Now you import the graphical sprite for the marmalade jar. This is the graphics file you've created in *Photoshop* that will be attached to the physics world:

```
CCSprite *marmalade= [CCSprite spriteWithFile:@"marmalade.png"];
    [marmalade setPosition:CGPointMake(550, 700)];
    [self addChild:marmalade z:-1];
```

You must also define the jar's shape in vertexes so that the physics world knows its size and shape. Remember, Chipmunk Physics can't see sprites; it can only see the shapes and rigid bodies that you attach the sprites to:

```
cpVect marmaladeVerts[] = {
        cpv(-marmalade.contentSize.width/2,-marmalade.contentSize.
            height/2),
        cpv(-marmalade.contentSize.width/2, marmalade.contentSize.
            height/2),
        cpv( marmalade.contentSize.width/2, marmalade.contentSize.
            height/2),
        cpv( marmalade.contentSize.width/2,-marmalade.contentSize.
            height/2),
    };
```

Next, you need to define the physical properties of the marmalade jar, its *rigid body:*

```
cpFloat mass = 5;
    cpBody *marmaladeBody = cpBodyNew(mass, cpMomentForPoly
                            (mass, 4, marmaladeVerts, cpvzero));
    marmaladeBody->p = cpv(570, 700);
     cpSpaceAddBody(space, marmaladeBody);
```

And finally, you tell Chipmunk Physics to use the vertexes you defined earlier to give the object a shape in the virtual physics world. You then close the file:

```
cpShape *shape = cpPolyShapeNew(marmaladeBody, 4, marmaladeVerts,
                cpvzero);
    shape->e = 0.3; shape->u = 1.0;
    shape->data=marmalade;
    cpSpaceAddShape(space, shape);


    }
  return self;
}

-(void)dealloc{
    [super dealloc];
}

@end
```

SO

she was considering in her own mind (as well as she could, for the hot day made her feel very sleepy and stupid), whether the pleasure of making a daisy-chain would be worth the trouble of getting up and picking the daisies, when suddenly a White Rabbit with pink eyes ran close by her.

Creating the Pocket Watch Scene

SO

she was considering in her own mind (as well as she could, for the hot day made her feel very sleepy and stupid), whether the pleasure of making a daisy-chain would be worth the trouble of getting up and picking the daisies, when suddenly a White Rabbit with pink eyes ran close by her.

Reproduced with permission of Atomic Antelope LTD. © 2010 Atomic Antelope LTD.

First you make a PocketWatch.h file here, importing the relevant cocos2d and Chipmunk resources the scene requires. The .h file for this particular scene is slightly different from the others in *Alice*:

```
#import <Foundation/Foundation.h>
#import "cocos2d.h"
```

```
#import "chipmunk.h"
#import "Constants.h"
#import "PhysicsContent.h"

@interface PocketWatch : PhysicsContent {
    //chipmunk objects
    cpBody *pinBody;
    cpBody *segmentBodyA;
    cpBody *watchBody;

    CGPoint pinPoint;

    int numLinks;
    int segHeight;
    int bodySize;
}

-(void)setupChipmunk;
-(void)addWatch;
-(void)addWatchString;

@end
```

Now you create a file called PocketWatch.m and import this setup in the first line of this new file:

```
#import "PocketWatch.h"
```

And define the space:

```
@implementation PocketWatch

-(id)init{
    if((self = [super init])) {
        pinPoint = CGPointMake(170, 485);

        [self setupChipmunk];
        [self addWatch];

        GRAVITY_MULTIPLER = 3500;

    }
    return self;
}
```

Next, you add a string to the space:

```
-(void)setupChipmunk{

    segHeight=10;
    bodySize=10;
    numLinks=14;
```

And *pin* the string so that it has a fixed point to dangle from:

```
pinBody = cpBodyNew(INFINITY, INFINITY);
    pinBody->p = pinPoint;
int numVerts = 9;
    CGPoint lowerVerts[] = {cpv(-285.0f, -43.0f),
        cpv(-281.0f, 40.0f),
        cpv(-264.0f, 41.0f),
        cpv(-42.0f, 37.0f),
        cpv(-64.0f, -5.0f),
        cpv(-93.0f, -30.0f),
        cpv(-120.0f, -47.0f),
        cpv(-176.0f, -62.0f),
        cpv(-227.0f, -59.0f)};

    cpShape *sLowerShape = cpPolyShapeNew(pinBody, numVerts, lowerVerts,
        cpv(215,28));
    sLowerShape->layers = 1;
    cpSpaceAddStaticShape(space, sLowerShape);

    numVerts = 14;
    CGPoint upperVerts[] = {cpv(-221.0f, 122.0f),
        cpv(-255.0f, 135.0f),
        cpv(-280.0f, 158.0f),
        cpv(-295.0f, 198.0f),
        cpv(-295.0f, 237.0f),
        cpv(-282.0f, 271.0f),
        cpv(-258.0f, 300.0f),
        cpv(-213.0f, 323.0f),
        cpv(-178.0f, 329.0f),
        cpv(-132.0f, 328.0f),
        cpv(-90.0f, 319.0f),
        cpv(-70.0f, 313.0f),
        cpv(-74.0f, 236.0f),
        cpv(-80.0f, 147.0f)};

    cpShape *sUpperShape = cpPolyShapeNew(pinBody, numVerts, upperVerts,
        cpv(215,28));
    sUpperShape->layers = 1;
    cpSpaceAddStaticShape(space, sUpperShape);

    cpShape *oShape = cpCircleShapeNew(pinBody, 200, cpv(315,200));
    oShape->layers = 1;
    cpSpaceAddStaticShape(space, oShape);

    [self addWatchString];
```

Then you set the space updating:

```
[self schedule:@selector(tick:)interval:1.0f/CHIPMUNK_FPS];
}
```

And now you define the first shape to which the other shapes (mainly the tiny gold spheres that make up the chain of the watch) will trail down from. The first link in the White Rabbit's pocket watch is a static shape to which the other chain links are jointed. It is set up as follows:

```
-(void)addWatchString{
    CCSprite *segmentSprite = [CCSprite spriteWithFile:@"tinyGoldBall.png"];
    [segmentSprite setPosition:CGPointMake(pinPoint.x, pinPoint.
        y-(segHeight/2))];
    [self addChild:segmentSprite z:-1];

    segmentBodyA = cpBodyNew(0.1, INFINITY);
    segmentBodyA->p = cpv(pinPoint.x, pinPoint.y-(segHeight/2));
    cpSpaceAddBody(space, segmentBodyA);
    cpSpaceAddConstraint(space, cpPivotJointNew(pinBody, segmentBodyA,
        pinPoint));
```

You then add more links to the chain:

```
for(int i=1; i<numLinks; i++){
```

And attach the sprite—in this case the tinyGoldBall.png image—to the chain links:

```
segmentSprite = [CCSprite spriteWithFile:@"tinyGoldBall.png"];
    [segmentSprite setPosition:CGPointMake
                (pinPoint.x, pinPoint.y-(i*segHeight)-(segHeight/2))];
    [self addChild:segmentSprite z:-1];
```

Next, you'll need to add the rigid body to the sprite, in this case the watch-chain links:

```
cpBody *segmentBodyB = cpBodyNew(0.1, INFINITY);
    segmentBodyB->p = cpv(pinPoint.x, pinPoint.y-(i*segHeight)-
    (segHeight/2));
    cpSpaceAddBody(space, segmentBodyB);
```

And then add a collision shape to the rigid body, in this case the watch-chain links:

```
cpShape *segmentShape = cpCircleShapeNew(segmentBodyB, bodySize/2, cpvzero);
    segmentShape->e = 0.0; // Elasticity
    segmentShape->u = 0.8; // Friction
    segmentShape->layers = 2;
    segmentShape->data = segmentSprite;

    segmentShape->collision_type = 1; // Collisions are grouped by types
    cpSpaceAddShape(space, segmentShape);

    //connect this newly added body to the previous one
    cpSpaceAddConstraint(space, cpSlideJointNew(segmentBodyA,
                segmentBodyB, cpvzero, cpvzero, bodySize, segHeight));

    //also connect the body to the static pinBody
    cpSpaceAddConstraint(space, cpSlideJointNew(pinBody, segmentBodyB,
                cpvzero, cpvzero, bodySize,(i*segHeight)+(segHeight/2)));

    segmentBodyA = segmentBodyB;
    }
}

-(void)addWatch{
```

Now the chain is built; it's time to add the watch itself to the scene:

```
CCSprite *watchSprite = [CCSprite spriteWithFile:@"pocketwatch.png"];
    [watchSprite setPosition:CGPointMake(pinPoint.x, pinPoint.
        y-(segHeight*numLinks)-(watchSprite.contentSize.height/2))];
    [self addChild:watchSprite z:-1];
```

Give the watch physical properties in the scene:

```
cpFloat mass = 0.5;
    watchBody = cpBodyNew(mass, 3000);
    watchBody->p = cpv(pinPoint.x, pinPoint.y-(segHeight*numLinks)
                            -(watchSprite.contentSize.height/2)+10);
    cpSpaceAddBody(space, watchBody);

    cpShape *watchFace = cpCircleShapeNew(watchBody, 112, cpv(0,-30));
    watchFace->data = watchSprite;
    watchFace->e = 0.0;
    watchFace->collision_type = 1;
    cpSpaceAddShape(space, watchFace);

    cpShape *watchNeck = cpCircleShapeNew(watchBody, 50, cpv(0,90));
    watchNeck->collision_type = 1;
    watchNeck->e = 0.0;
    cpSpaceAddShape(space, watchNeck);
```

Joint the watch to the pin at the top of the screen:

```
cpSpaceAddConstraint(space, cpSlideJointNew(watchBody,
            pinBody, cpv(0,(watchSprite.contentSize.height/2)-10),
            cpvzero, 20, (numLinks*segHeight)));
```

And joint the lowermost segment of the chain to the watch itself:

```
cpSpaceAddConstraint(space, cpPinJointNew(watchBody,
            segmentBodyA, cpv(0,(watchSprite.contentSize.height/2)-10),
            cpv(0,-segHeight/2)));
}
```

Creating the "Drink Me" Bottle Scene

Again, you begin by setting up the BottleLabel.h file that imports the relevant libraries.
This file is effectively the same for all pages from now on.

```
#import <Foundation/Foundation.h>
#import "cocos2d.h"
#import "chipmunk.h"
#import "Constants.h"
#import "PhysicsContent.h"

@interface BottleLabel : PhysicsContent {

}

@end
```

At that moment, Alice noticed a table with a little bottle on it ("which certainly was not here before," said Alice), and tied 'round the neck of the bottle was a paper label, with the words "DRINK ME" beautifully printed on it in large letters.

This bottle was not marked "poison," so Alice ventured to taste it, and, finding it very nice (it had a sort of mixed flavor of cherry-tart, custard, pineapple, roast turkey, toffy and hot buttered toast), she very soon finished it off.

Reproduced with permission of Atomic Antelope LTD. © 2010 Atomic Antelope LTD.

Now you begin the BottleLabel.m file, first importing the .h libraries:

```
#import "BottleLabel.h"

@implementation BottleLabel

-(id)init{
    if((self = [super init])) {          CGSize size = [[CCDirector
        sharedDirector] winSize];

        cpBody *zeroBody = cpBodyNew(INFINITY, INFINITY);
        zeroBody->p = cpvzero;
```

Now you add walls around the whole scene:

```
cpShape *wallShape = cpSegmentShapeNew(zeroBody, cpv(0,0), cpv(0,size.
    height), 5);
        wallShape->e = 0.5;
        wallShape->u = 1.0;
        wallShape->layers=1;
        cpSpaceAddStaticShape(space, wallShape);
        wallShape = cpSegmentShapeNew(zeroBody,
                     cpv(0,size.height), cpv(size.width,size.height), 5);
        wallShape->e = 0.5;
        wallShape->u = 1.0;
        wallShape->layers=1;
        cpSpaceAddStaticShape(space, wallShape);
        wallShape = cpSegmentShapeNew(zeroBody,
                     cpv(size.width,size.height), cpv(size.width,0), 5);
        wallShape->e = 0.5;
        wallShape->u = 1.0;
        wallShape->layers=1;
        cpSpaceAddStaticShape(space, wallShape);
        wallShape = cpSegmentShapeNew(zeroBody, cpv(size.width,0),
        cpv(0,0), 5);
        wallShape->e = 0.5;
        wallShape->u = 1.0;
        wallShape->layers=1;
        cpSpaceAddStaticShape(space, wallShape);
```

Now you introduce the sprite that represents the Drink Me bottle:

```
CCSprite *bottle= [CCSprite spriteWithFile:@"potionBottle.png"];
        [bottle setPosition:CGPointMake(550, 700)];
        [self addChild:bottle z:-1];
```

And define the vertexes that make up the shape of this bottle:

```
int numVerts = 12;
        cpVect bottleVerts[] = {
            cpv(-12.4f, -242.9f),
            cpv(-46.3f, -230.9f),
            cpv(-50.6f, -62.6f),
            cpv(-49.9f, 43.5f),
            cpv(-40.0f, 237.2f),
            cpv(-20.9f, 242.2f),
            cpv(18.0f, 243.6f),
            cpv(37.1f, 237.2f),
            cpv(47.0f, 42.8f),
            cpv(49.1f, -81.7f),
            cpv(49.9f, -226.6f),
            cpv(35.7f, -239.4f)};
```

And define its physical properties:

```
cpFloat mass = 0.75;
        cpBody *bottleBody = cpBodyNew(mass,
                     cpMomentForPoly(mass, numVerts, bottleVerts, cpvzero));
```

```
        bottleBody->p = cpv(160, 700);
        cpSpaceAddBody(space, bottleBody);

        cpShape *shape = cpPolyShapeNew(bottleBody, numVerts,
        bottleVerts, cpvzero);
        shape->e = 0.3; shape->u = 1.0; shape->layers = 1;
   shape->data=bottle;
        shape->collision_type = 1;
        cpSpaceAddShape(space, shape);
```

Now you introduce the sprite for the label that dangles off the bottle:

```
CCSprite *label= [CCSprite spriteWithFile:@"drinkMeLabel.png"];
        label.position = cpv(110,802);
        [self addChild:label z:-1];
```

Then define the vertexes that make up its shape:

```
numVerts = 4;
        cpVect verts[] = {
            cpv(-label.contentSize.width/2,-label.contentSize.height/2),
            cpv(-label.contentSize.width/2, label.contentSize.height/2),
            cpv( label.contentSize.width/2, label.contentSize.height/2),
            cpv( label.contentSize.width/2,-label.contentSize.height/2),
        };
```

Give the label a rigid body:

```
mass = 0.01;
        cpBody *labelBody = cpBodyNew(mass,
                        cpMomentForPoly(mass, numVerts, verts, cpvzero));
        labelBody->p = cpv(label.position.x,label.position.y);
        cpSpaceAddBody(space, labelBody);

        shape = cpPolyShapeNew(labelBody, numVerts, verts, cpvzero);
        shape->e = 1.0; shape->u = 0.5; shape->layers = 2;
        shape->collision_type = 2;
        shape->data=label;
        cpSpaceAddShape(space, shape);
```

And finally add constraints so that the label is pinned to the neck of the bottle:

```
cpSpaceAddConstraint(space,cpSlideJointNew(bottleBody,
            labelBody, cpv(0,200),
            cpv(label.contentSize.width/2,
            label.contentSize.height/2), 0, 5));
    }
    return self;
}

-(void)dealloc{
    [super dealloc];
}

@end
```

Alice opened the door and found that it led into a
small passage, not much larger than a rat-hole; she
knelt down and looked along the passage into the
loveliest garden you ever saw, but she could not
even get her head through the doorway.

"Oh," said Alice, "how I wish I could shut up like a
telescope! Then I could fit through".

Creating the Magic Garden Scene

Reproduced with permission of Atomic Antelope LTD. © 2010 Atomic Antelope LTD.

The scene begins by importing the LovelyGarden.h file—effectively the same .h file used by the majority of scenes and defined earlier in the chapter. Then you set up the LovelyGarden.m file, which begins by defining the scene's gravity:

```
#import "LovelyGarden.h"

@implementation LovelyGarden

-(id)init{
    if((self = [super init])) { CGSize size =
                        [[CCDirector sharedDirector] winSize];
        space->gravity = cpvzero;

        GRAVITY_MULTIPLER = 800;

        cpBody *zeroBody = cpBodyNew(INFINITY, INFINITY);
        zeroBody->p = cpvzero;

        NSInteger leftIndent = -20;
        NSInteger topIndent = 290;
        NSInteger bottomIndent = 425;
        NSInteger rightIndent = -230;
```

Now you set up walls that will constrict the movement of the shape attached to the sprite that shows the garden Alice is peeking through the doorway at. First you set the left wall:

```
cpShape *wallShape = cpSegmentShapeNew(zeroBody,
        cpv(leftIndent,bottomIndent),
        cpv(leftIndent,size.height-topIndent), 5);
    wallShape->e = 0.0;
    wallShape->u = 1.0;
    wallShape->layers=1;
    cpSpaceAddStaticShape(space, wallShape);
```

Then the top wall:

```
wallShape = cpSegmentShapeNew(zeroBody, cpv(leftIndent,
        size.height-topIndent), cpv(size.width-rightIndent,
        size.height-topIndent), 5);
    wallShape->e = 0.0;
    wallShape->u = 1.0;
    wallShape->layers=1;
    cpSpaceAddStaticShape(space, wallShape);
```

Then the right wall:

```
wallShape = cpSegmentShapeNew(zeroBody, cpv
        (size.width-rightIndent,size.height-topIndent),
        cpv(size.width-rightIndent,bottomIndent), 5);
    wallShape->e = 0.0;
    wallShape->u = 1.0;
    wallShape->layers=1;
    cpSpaceAddStaticShape(space, wallShape);
```

And finally the lower wall:

```
wallShape = cpSegmentShapeNew(zeroBody,
        cpv(size.width-rightIndent,bottomIndent),
        cpv(leftIndent,bottomIndent), 5);
    wallShape->e = 0.0;
    wallShape->u = 1.0;
    wallShape->layers=1;
    cpSpaceAddStaticShape(space, wallShape);
```

Now you introduce the main sprite to the scene:

```
#pragma mark garden
        int pinX = 550;
        int pinY = 600;
        CCSprite *garden= [CCSprite spriteWithFile:@"tunnelGarden.png"];
        garden.position=cpv(pinX,pinY);
        [self addChild:garden z:-1];
```

And define the vertexes that describe the sprite's shape as you want Chipmunk Physics to see it:

```
int numVerts = 4;
        cpVect gardenVerts[] = {
            cpv(-garden.contentSize.width/2,-garden.contentSize.height/2),
            cpv(-garden.contentSize.width/2, garden.contentSize.height/2),
            cpv( garden.contentSize.width/2, garden.contentSize.height/2),
            cpv( garden.contentSize.width/2,-garden.contentSize.height/2),
        };
```

Next, you add the rigid body to the shape:

```
float mass = 3;
        cpBody *gardenBody = cpBodyNew(mass,
                    cpMomentForPoly(mass, numVerts, gardenVerts, cpvzero));
        gardenBody->p = cpv(pinX, pinY);
        cpSpaceAddBody(space, gardenBody);

        cpShape *shape = cpPolyShapeNew(gardenBody, numVerts,
                        gardenVerts, cpvzero);
        shape->e = 0.0; shape->u = 0.0;
        shape->data=garden;
        cpSpaceAddShape(space, shape);
```

You need to overlay a copy of the background plate that effectively masks the scene so that the sprite can be seen only within the confines of the tiny doorway that Alice is peeking through. You also close the file:

```
#pragma mark overlay
        CCSprite *overlay = [CCSprite spriteWithFile:@"tunnel-overlay.png"];
        overlay.position = cpv(size.width/2,size.height/2);
        [self addChild:overlay z:-1];

    }
    return self;
}
@end
```

"What a curious feeling!"
said Alice. "I must be
shutting up like a
telescope."

And so it was indeed: she
was now only ten inches
high, and her face
brightened up at the
thought that she
was now the right size
for going through the
little door into that lovely
garden.

Creating Shrinking Alice

"What a curious feeling!" said Alice. "I must be shutting up like a telescope!"

And so it was indeed! She was now only ten inches high, and her face brightened up at the thought that she was now the right size for going through the little door into that lovely garden.

Reproduced with permission of Atomic Antelope LTD. © 2010 Atomic Antelope LTD.

This is an interesting scene because it effectively creates telescoping components and then attaches the Alice character's sprites to these components. It's a good example of how you can dream up extremely interesting configurations of physics-objects to produce complex animations. First set up an AliceShrinks.m file as in the previous examples. Now create AliceShrinks.h and define the scene properties:

```
@implementation AliceShrinks

-(id)init{
```

```
if((self = [super init]))
                {CGSize size = [[CCDirector sharedDirector] winSize];
    cpShape *shape;
    float mass;
    int pinX,pinY;
    int numVerts;
    int channelWidth = 300;
    int rightBorder= 20;
    int channelGap = 8;

    space->gravity = cpvzero;

    GRAVITY_MULTIPLER = 800;

    cpBody *zeroBody = cpBodyNew(INFINITY, INFINITY);
    zeroBody->p = cpvzero;
```

Next, add walls around the edge of the shapes that will make up Alice's body:

```
cpShape *wallShape = cpSegmentShapeNew(zeroBody,
        cpv(size.width-channelWidth-rightBorder-channelGap,0),
        cpv(size.width-channelWidth-rightBorder-channelGap,size.
                height), 5);
    wallShape->e = 0.0;
    wallShape->u = 0.0;
    wallShape->layers = 1;
    cpSpaceAddStaticShape(space, wallShape);
    wallShape = cpSegmentShapeNew(zeroBody,
            cpv(0,size.height-50), cpv(size.width,size.height-50), 5);
    wallShape->e = 0.0;
    wallShape->u = 0.0;
    wallShape->layers = 1;
    cpSpaceAddStaticShape(space, wallShape);
    wallShape = cpSegmentShapeNew(zeroBody,
                    cpv(size.width-rightBorder,size.height),
                    cpv(size.width-rightBorder,0), 5);
    wallShape->e = 0.0;
    wallShape->u = 0.0;
    wallShape->layers = 1;
    cpSpaceAddStaticShape(space, wallShape);
    wallShape = cpSegmentShapeNew(zeroBody, cpv(size.width,5),
        cpv(0,5), 5);
    wallShape->e = 0.0;
    wallShape->u = 0.0;
    wallShape->layers = 1;
    cpSpaceAddStaticShape(space, wallShape);
```

Now create Alice's head and add the sprite for Alice's head to the object:

```
    pinX = 600;
    pinY = 860;
    CCSprite *head= [CCSprite spriteWithFile:@"telescope-head.png"];
    head.position = cpv(pinX,pinY);
    [self addChild:head z:-1];

    numVerts = 4;
    cpVect headVerts[] = {
        cpv(-channelWidth/2,-70),
```

```
            cpv(-channelWidth/2, 70),
            cpv( channelWidth/2, 70),
            cpv( channelWidth/2,-70),
    };

    mass = 3;
    cpBody *headBody = cpBodyNew(mass,
            cpMomentForPoly(mass, numVerts, headVerts, cpvzero));
    headBody->p = cpv(pinX, pinY);
    cpSpaceAddBody(space, headBody);

    shape = cpPolyShapeNew(headBody, numVerts, headVerts, cpv(0,42));
    shape->e = 0.0; shape->u = 0.0; shape->layers = 1;
    shape->data=head;
    cpSpaceAddShape(space, shape);
```

Next, create Alice's legs:

```
pinY = 140;
    CCSprite *legs= [CCSprite spriteWithFile:@"telescope-legs.png"];
    legs.position = cpv(pinX,pinY);
    [self addChild:legs z:-1];

    numVerts = 4;
    cpVect legVerts[] = {
        cpv(-channelWidth/2,-20),
        cpv(-channelWidth/2, 20),
        cpv( channelWidth/2, 20),
        cpv( channelWidth/2,-20),
    };

    mass = 3;
    cpBody *legBody = cpBodyNew(mass,
            cpMomentForPoly(mass, numVerts, legVerts, cpvzero));
    legBody->p = cpv(pinX, pinY);
    cpSpaceAddBody(space, legBody);

    shape = cpPolyShapeNew(legBody, numVerts, legVerts, cpv(0,-125));
    shape->e = 0.0; shape->u = 0.0; shape->layers = 1;
    shape->data=legs;
    cpSpaceAddShape(space, shape);
```

Create her right arm:

```
pinX = 470;
    pinY = 650;
    CCSprite *rightArm= [CCSprite spriteWithFile:@"telescope-
    rightArm.png"];
    rightArm.position = cpv(pinX,pinY);
    [self addChild:rightArm z:-1];

    numVerts = 4;
    cpVect rightArmVerts[] = {
        cpv(-rightArm.contentSize.width/2,-rightArm.contentSize.height/2),
        cpv(-rightArm.contentSize.width/2, rightArm.contentSize.height/2),
        cpv( rightArm.contentSize.width/2, rightArm.contentSize.height/2),
        cpv( rightArm.contentSize.width/2,-rightArm.contentSize.height/2),
    };
```

```
        mass = 3;
        cpBody *rightArmBody = cpBodyNew(mass,
                    cpMomentForPoly(mass, numVerts, rightArmVerts,
                    cpvzero));
        rightArmBody->p = cpv(pinX, pinY);
        cpSpaceAddBody(space, rightArmBody);

        shape = cpPolyShapeNew(rightArmBody, numVerts, rightArmVerts,
                cpvzero);
        shape->e = 0.0; shape->u = 0.0; shape->layers = 0;
        shape->data=rightArm;
        cpSpaceAddShape(space, shape);
```

Create her body:

```
 pinX = 600;
        pinY = 480;
        CCSprite *alice= [CCSprite spriteWithFile:@"telescope-body.png"];
        alice.position = cpv(pinX,pinY);
        [self addChild:alice z:-1];

        numVerts = 4;
        cpVect aliceVerts[] = {
            cpv(-channelWidth/2,-290),
            cpv(-channelWidth/2, 290),
            cpv( channelWidth/2, 290),
            cpv( channelWidth/2,-290),
        };

        mass = 10;
        cpBody *aliceBody = cpBodyNew(mass, cpMomentForPoly
                    (mass, numVerts, aliceVerts, cpvzero));
        aliceBody->p = cpv(pinX, pinY);
        cpSpaceAddBody(space, aliceBody);

        shape = cpPolyShapeNew(aliceBody, numVerts, aliceVerts, cpv(0,0));
        shape->e = 0.0; shape->u = 0.0; shape->layers = 1;
        shape->data=alice;
        cpSpaceAddShape(space, shape);
```

And her left arm:

```
 pinX = 670;
        pinY = 700;
        CCSprite *leftArm= [CCSprite spriteWithFile:@"telescope-leftArm.png"];
        leftArm.position = cpv(pinX-50, pinY-80);
        [self addChild:leftArm z:-1];

        numVerts = 4;
        cpVect leftArmVerts[] = {
            cpv(-leftArm.contentSize.width/2,-leftArm.contentSize.height/2),
            cpv(-leftArm.contentSize.width/2, leftArm.contentSize.height/2),
            cpv( leftArm.contentSize.width/2, leftArm.contentSize.height/2),
            cpv( leftArm.contentSize.width/2,-leftArm.contentSize.height/2),
        };
```

```
mass = 3;
cpBody *leftArmBody = cpBodyNew(mass,
            cpMomentForPoly(mass, numVerts, leftArmVerts,
                        cpvzero));
leftArmBody->p = cpv(leftArm.position.x,leftArm.position.y);
cpSpaceAddBody(space, leftArmBody);

shape = cpPolyShapeNew(leftArmBody, numVerts, leftArmVerts,
                    cpvzero);
shape->e = 0.0; shape->u = 0.0; shape->layers = 2;
shape->data=leftArm;
cpSpaceAddShape(space, shape);
```

Now you'll define the joints and relationships between the shapes. First attach the head to the body:

```
cpSpaceAddConstraint(space,cpSlideJointNew(headBody,
                aliceBody, cpvzero, cpv(0,50), 0, 330));
```

Then attach the legs to the body:

```
cpSpaceAddConstraint(space,cpSlideJointNew(legBody,
                aliceBody, cpvzero, cpv(0,-50), 0, 280));
```

Fix Alice's legs to the ground:

```
cpSpaceAddConstraint(space,cpSlideJointNew(legBody,
                zeroBody, cpv(0,-legs.contentSize.height/2),
                cpv(size.width-rightBorder-channelWidth/2,5), 0, 5));
```

Pin the left arm to Alice's body:

```
cpSpaceAddConstraint(space, cpPinJointNew(leftArmBody,
                aliceBody, cpv(32,42), cpv(55,179)));
cpSpaceAddConstraint(space, cpDampedSpringNew(leftArmBody,
                aliceBody, cpv(-46,-49), cpv(-50,60), 20, 500, 10));
```

And pin the right arm to Alice's body:

```
cpSpaceAddConstraint(space, cpPinJointNew(rightArmBody,
                aliceBody, cpv(58,-20), cpv(-75,149)));
cpSpaceAddConstraint(space, cpDampedSpringNew(rightArmBody,
                aliceBody, cpv(-54,11), cpv(-40,0), 200, 500, 10));
```

Finally, close the file:

```
    }
    return self;
}

-(void)dealloc{
    [super dealloc];
}

@end
```

Alice had no idea what to do. In despair she put her hand into her pocket, and pulled out a box of comfits, (luckily the salt-water had not got into it), and handed them out as prizes.

Creating the Caucus Race Scene

First, import the .h file, as in previous examples, and set up the scene:

```
#import "CaucusRace.h"

@implementation CaucusRace

-(id)init{
    if((self = [super init])) {CGSize size = [[CCDirector sharedDirector]
    winSize];
        int pinX = 480;
        int pinY = 700;
```

Now add the Dodo sprite:

```
CCSprite *dodo= [CCSprite spriteWithFile:@"theDodo.png"];
        [dodo setPosition:CGPointMake(pinX, pinY)];
        [self addChild:dodo z:-1];

        cpBody *pinBody = cpBodyNew(INFINITY, INFINITY);
        pinBody->p = cpv(pinX, pinY);

        cpBody *zeroBody = cpBodyNew(INFINITY, INFINITY);
        zeroBody->p = cpvzero;
```

Next add walls to the edges of the page to prevent objects from falling off into oblivion:

```
        cpShape *wallShape = cpSegmentShapeNew(zeroBody, cpv(0,0),
        cpv(0,size.height), 5);
            wallShape->e = 0.5;
            wallShape->u = 0.3;
            cpSpaceAddStaticShape(space, wallShape);
            wallShape = cpSegmentShapeNew(zeroBody,
                        cpv(0,size.height), cpv(size.width,size.height), 5);
            wallShape->e = 0.5;
            wallShape->u = 0.3;
            cpSpaceAddStaticShape(space, wallShape);
            wallShape = cpSegmentShapeNew(zeroBody,
                        cpv(size.width,size.height), cpv(size.width,0), 5);
            wallShape->e = 0.5;
            wallShape->u = 0.3;
            cpSpaceAddStaticShape(space, wallShape);
            wallShape = cpSegmentShapeNew(zeroBody, cpv(size.width,0),
                    cpv(0,0), 5);
            wallShape->e = 0.5;
            wallShape->u = 0.3;
            cpSpaceAddStaticShape(space, wallShape);
```

Then define the vertexes that make up the rigid body of the Dodo:

```
int numVerts = 12;
    cpVect dodoBodyVerts[] = {
            cpv(-180.5f, -45.0f),
            cpv(-183.5f, -32.0f),
```

```
                    cpv(-175.5f, -24.0f),
                    cpv(0.5f, 64.0f),
                    cpv(20.5f, 62.0f),
                    cpv(72.5f, 40.0f),
                    cpv(94.5f, 22.0f),
                    cpv(115.5f, -11.0f),
                    cpv(139.5f, -116.0f),
                    cpv(116.5f, -148.0f),
                    cpv(78.5f, -191.0f),
                    cpv(58.5f, -196.0f)};
```

Assign physical properties to the body:

```
cpFloat mass = 10;
        cpBody *dodoBody = cpBodyNew(mass,
                    cpMomentForPoly(mass, numVerts, dodoBodyVerts, cpvzero));
        dodoBody->p = cpv(pinX, pinY);
        cpSpaceAddBody(space, dodoBody);

        cpShape *shape = cpPolyShapeNew(dodoBody, numVerts, dodoBodyVerts,
        cpvzero);
        shape->e = 0.3; shape->u = 0.5; shape->layers = 1;
        shape->data=dodo;
        cpSpaceAddShape(space, shape);
```

Define the vertexes that make up the Dodo's head:

```
numVerts = 9;
        cpVect dodoHeadVerts[] = {
            cpv(-118.5f, -22.0f),
            cpv(-149.5f, 118.0f),
            cpv(-140.5f, 137.0f),
            cpv(-59.5f, 199.0f),
            cpv(-29.5f, 199.0f),
            cpv(-9.5f, 185.0f),
            cpv(-0.5f, 156.0f),
            cpv(-6.5f, 115.0f),
        cpv(-31.5f, 53.0f)};
```

Set the constraints that make the Dodo bob around:

```
shape = cpPolyShapeNew(dodoBody, numVerts, dodoHeadVerts, cpvzero);
        shape->e = 0.3; shape->u = 0.5;
        cpSpaceAddShape(space, shape);


        cpSpaceAddConstraint(space, cpDampedSpringNew
                            (pinBody, dodoBody, cpv(0,200),
                            cpv(0,130), 70, 10000, 0.2));
        cpSpaceAddConstraint(space, cpDampedSpringNew(pinBody,
                    dodoBody, cpv(0,-200), cpv(0,-130), 70, 10000, 0.2));
```

```
        cpSpaceAddConstraint(space, cpDampedSpringNew(pinBody,
                dodoBody, cpv(200,0), cpv(130,0), 70, 10000, 0.2));
        cpSpaceAddConstraint(space, cpDampedSpringNew(pinBody,
                dodoBody, cpv(-200,0), cpv(-130,0), 70, 10000, 0.2));
```

Now you'll need to add the *comfits* (an old name for the sweets Alice gives out after the race) to the scene. You start by defining their vertexes:

```
cpVect comfitVerts[] = {
        cpv(-40,-16),
        cpv(-50,0),
        cpv(-40,16),
        cpv(40,16),
        cpv(50,0),
        cpv(40,-16),
    };

    mass = 0.5;
```

Then generate them randomly around the screen, and finally close the file:

```
for (int i = 0 ; i < 20; i++) {
        CCSprite *comfit= [CCSprite
                spriteWithFile:[NSString stringWithFormat:
                @"comfit%i.png",rand() % 4 + 1]];
        comfit.position = cpv(rand() % ((int)size.width - 200)+100,
                rand() % ((int)size.height - 200)+100);
        [self addChild:comfit z:-1];

        cpBody *comfitBody = cpBodyNew(mass, cpMomentForPoly
                (mass, 6, comfitVerts, cpvzero));
        comfitBody->p = cpv(comfit.position.x,comfit.position.y);
        cpBodySetAngle(comfitBody,CC_DEGREES_TO_RADIANS(rand()%360));
        cpSpaceAddBody(space, comfitBody);

        cpShape *shape = cpPolyShapeNew(comfitBody, 6, comfitVerts,
                cpvzero);
        shape->e = 0.3; shape->u = 0.5; shape->layers = 1;
        shape->data=comfit;
        cpSpaceAddShape(space, shape);
    }

    }
    return self;
}

-(void)dealloc{
    [super dealloc];
}

@end
```

Creating Bill the Lizard

The interesting feature of this scene is the particle generator used to create the smoke effect when Bill the Lizard bursts from the chimney pot. This is not created with Chipmunk Physics, but instead uses the particle generator in cocos2d. Here's how to create this effect:

```
#pragma mark CCParticleChimneySmoke
@implementation CCParticleChimneySmoke
-(id)init{
    return [self initWithTotalParticles:200];
}

-(id)initWithTotalParticles:(int) p{
    if( !(self=[super initWithTotalParticles:p]) )
        return nil;

    NSLog(@"setting up smoke particles");

duration = -1;

    self.gravity = ccp(0,50);


    angle = 90;
    angleVar = 40;
        self.radialAccel = 0;
    self.radialAccelVar = 0;


    self.position = ccp(400,200);
    posVar = ccp(50, 0);


    life = 5;
    lifeVar = 1;


    self.speed = 50;
    self.speedVar = 10;

    // size, in pixels
    startSize = 60.0f;
    startSizeVar = 10.0f;
    endSize = kParticleStartSizeEqualToEndSize;


    emissionRate = totalParticles/life;

    // color of particles
    startColor.r = 0.8f;
    startColor.g = 0.8f;
    startColor.b = 0.8f;
    startColor.a = 1.0f;
    startColorVar.r = 0.02f;
    startColorVar.g = 0.02f;
    startColorVar.b = 0.02f;
```

```
startColorVar.a = 0.0f;
endColor.r = 0.0f;
endColor.g = 0.0f;
endColor.b = 0.0f;
endColor.a = 1.0f;
endColorVar.r = 0.0f;
endColorVar.g = 0.0f;
endColorVar.b = 0.0f;
endColorVar.a = 0.0f;

self.texture = [[CCTextureCache sharedTextureCache] addImage:
@"particle.png"];


self.blendAdditive = NO;

return self;
}
```

Creating the Caterpillar Scene

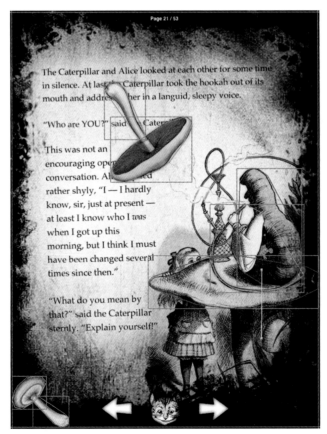

You already know how to create shapes that tumble freely around the page—see the section on the marmalade jar—but you might be wondering how we made the Caterpillar's arm smoke the hookah pipe. Here's the Chipmunk setup that defines the arm and its relationship to the scene. Take a look:

```
#pragma mark arm
        int pinX = 623;
        int pinY = 522;

        //add image
        CCSprite *arm= [CCSprite spriteWithFile:@"caterpillarArm.png"];
        arm.position = cpv(pinX+8, pinY-82);
        [self addChild:arm z:-1];

        cpBody *pinBody = cpBodyNew(INFINITY, INFINITY);
        pinBody->p = cpv(pinX, pinY);

        numVerts = 10;
        CGPoint armVerts[] = {cpv(-65.0f, -103.0f),
            cpv(-110.0f, -76.0f),
            cpv(-129.0f, -31.0f),
            cpv(-121.0f, 18.0f),
            cpv(-78.0f, 80.0f),
            cpv(-47.0f, 107.0f),
            cpv(4.0f, 83.0f),
            cpv(106.0f, -58.0f),
            cpv(58.0f, -93.0f),
            cpv(3.0f, -106.0f)};

        //add arm
        mass = 20;
        cpBody *armBody = cpBodyNew(mass,
                    cpMomentForPoly(mass, numVerts, armVerts, cpvzero));
```

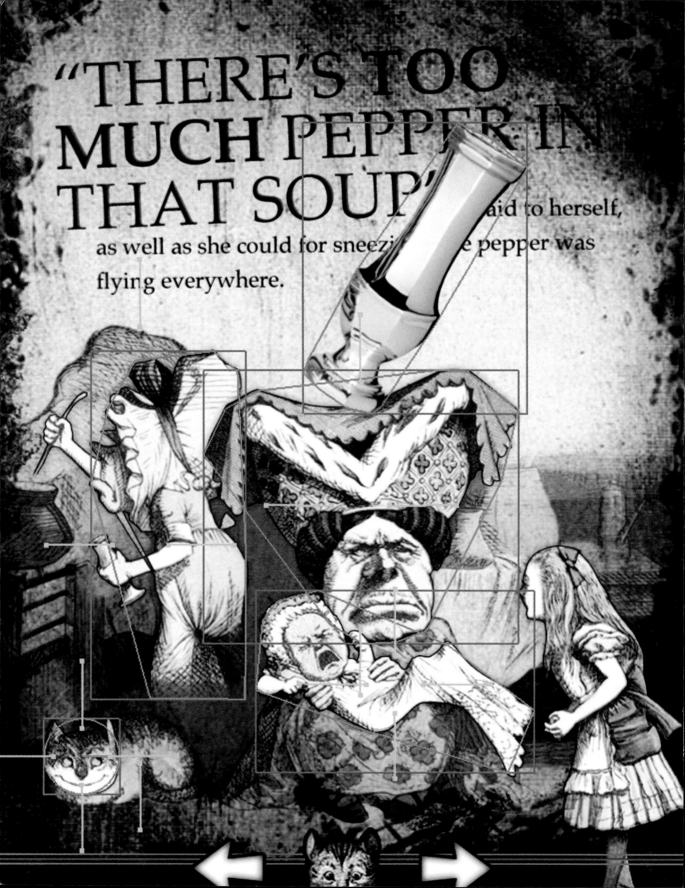

"THERE'S TOO MUCH PEPPER IN THAT SOUP"

said to herself, as well as she could for sneezing, the pepper was flying everywhere.

```
//cpBody *armBody = cpBodyNew(mass, 1000);
armBody->p = cpv(arm.position.x,arm.position.y);
cpSpaceAddBody(space, armBody);

shape = cpPolyShapeNew(armBody, numVerts, armVerts, cpvzero);
shape->e = 1.0; shape->u = 0.5; shape->layers = 2;
shape->data=arm;
cpSpaceAddShape(space, shape);

//joint the arm to the scene
cpSpaceAddConstraint(space, cpPivotJointNew(pinBody,
            armBody, cpv(pinX, pinY)));
cpSpaceAddConstraint(space, cpDampedSpringNew(pinBody,
            armBody, cpv(0,-300), cpv(0,-50), 150, 15000, 10));
```

Creating the Pepper Scene

Reproduced with permission of Atomic Antelope LTD. © 2010 Atomic Antelope LTD.

In this scene a particle emitter is tweaked and attached to the head of the *shape* that out-lines the pepper pot. The pepper pot is set up as follows:

```
#pragma mark pepperPot
        pepperPot = [CCSprite spriteWithFile:@"pepperPot.png"];
        [pepperPot setPosition:CGPointMake(200, 800)];
        [self addChild:pepperPot z:-1];

        cpVect pepperPotVerts[] = {
            cpv(-18.5f, -178.0f),
            cpv(-41.5f, -173.0f),
            cpv(-44.5f, -156.0f),
            cpv(-50.5f, -54.0f),
            cpv(-42.5f, 137.0f),
            cpv(-1.5f, 141.0f),
            cpv(44.5f, 135.0f),
```

```
                    cpv(49.5f, -46.0f),
                    cpv(46.5f, -161.0f),
                    cpv(41.5f, -171.0f),
                    cpv(16.5f, -180.0f)};

        mass = 5;
        cpBody *bottleBody = cpBodyNew(mass,
                    cpMomentForPoly(mass, 11, pepperPotVerts, cpvzero));
        bottleBody->p = cpv(200, 800);
        cpSpaceAddBody(space, bottleBody);

        shape = cpPolyShapeNew(bottleBody, 11, pepperPotVerts, cpvzero);
        shape->e = 0.3; shape->u = 1.0; shape->layers = 1;
        shape->data=pepperPot;
        cpSpaceAddShape(space, shape);
```

And the particle emitter here:

```
#pragma mark CCParticlePepper
@implementation CCParticlePepper
-(id)init{
    return [self initWithTotalParticles:500];
}

-(id)initWithTotalParticles:(int) p{
    if( !(self=[super initWithTotalParticles:p]) )
        return nil;

    NSLog(@"setting up pepper particles");

    // duration
    duration = -1;

    // gravity
    self.gravity = ccp(0,-90);

    // angle
    angle = 90;
    angleVar = 60;

    // radial acceleration
    self.radialAccel = 0;
    self.radialAccelVar = 0;

    // life of particles
    life = 3;
    lifeVar = 0.25f;
```

```
    // speed of particles
    self.speed = 150;
    self.speedVar = 20;

    // size, in pixels
    startSize = 6.0f;
    startSizeVar = 4.0f;
    endSize = kParticleStartSizeEqualToEndSize;

    // emits per frame
    emissionRate = totalParticles/life;

    // color of particles
    startColor.r = 0.1f;
    startColor.g = 0.1f;
    startColor.b = 0.1f;
    startColor.a = 1.0f;
    startColorVar.r = 0.05f;
    startColorVar.g = 0.05f;
    startColorVar.b = 0.05f;
    startColorVar.a = 0.2f;
    endColor.r = 0.1f;
    endColor.g = 0.1f;
    endColor.b = 0.1f;
    endColor.a = 0.2f;
    endColorVar.r = 0.0f;
    endColorVar.g = 0.0f;
    endColorVar.b = 0.0f;
    endColorVar.a = 0.1f;
    w
    self.texture = [[CCTextureCache sharedTextureCache] addImage:
    @"particle.png"];

    // additive
    self.blendAdditive = NO;

    return self;
}
```

Creating the Pig Baby

Alice caught the baby with some difficulty, as it was a queer-shaped little creature and held out its arms and legs in all directions.

Reproduced with permission of Atomic Antelope LTD. © 2010 Atomic Antelope LTD.

Reproduced with permission of Atomic Antelope LTD. © 2010 Atomic Antelope LTD.

This is a nice scene to learn from, so I've included the full code you need to build it. A simple physics setup means that when you rock the iPad, Alice rocks the Pig Baby.

```
#import "PigBaby.h"

@implementation PigBaby

-(id)init{

        space->damping = 0.8;

        int pinX = 325;
        int pinY = 692;

        //add label image
        CCSprite *label= [CCSprite spriteWithFile:@"pigBaby.png"];
        label.position=cpv(pinX+50, pinY-20);
        [self addChild:label z:-1];

        cpBody *pinBody = cpBodyNew(INFINITY, INFINITY);
        pinBody->p = cpv(pinX, pinY);

        int numVerts = 9;
        CGPoint verts[] = {cpv(-114.0f, -99.5f),
            cpv(-105.0f, -68.5f),
            cpv(22.0f, 107.5f),
            cpv(69.0f, 134.5f),
            cpv(110.0f, 100.5f),
            cpv(113.0f, 62.5f),
            cpv(107.0f, 38.5f),
            cpv(52.0f, -52.5f),
            cpv(-15.0f, -114.5f)};

        //add label body
        cpFloat mass = 20;
        cpBody *labelBody = cpBodyNew(mass,
                    cpMomentForPoly(mass, numVerts, verts, cpvzero));
        labelBody->p = cpv(label.position.x,label.position.y);
        cpSpaceAddBody(space, labelBody);

       cpShape *shape = cpPolyShapeNew(labelBody, numVerts, verts, cpvzero);
       shape->e = 1.0; shape->u = 0.5;
       shape->data=label;
       cpSpaceAddShape(space, shape);

        //joint the label to the scene
        cpSpaceAddConstraint(space, cpPivotJointNew(pinBody,
                    labelBody, cpv(pinX, pinY)));
        cpSpaceAddConstraint(space, cpDampedSpringNew(pinBody,
                    labelBody, cpv(100,10), cpvzero, 75, 12000, 10));

        cpShape *sShape = cpCircleShapeNew(pinBody, 20, cpv(0,80));
        cpSpaceAddStaticShape(space, sShape);

    }
    return self;
}

-(void)dealloc{
    [super dealloc];
}

@end
```

Alice was a little startled by seeing the Cheshire-Cat sitting on a bough of a tree a few yards off. The Cat only grinned when it saw her.

"Cheshire-Puss", began Alice, rather timidly, "would you please tell me which way I ought to go from here?"

Creating the Cheshire Cat

This scene is accomplished with a simple graduated fade-in and fade-out on the cat sprite:

```
#import "CheshireCat.h"

@implementation CheshireCat

-(id)init{
    if((self = [super init])) {
        CCSprite *cat= [CCSprite spriteWithFile:@"cheshireCat.png"];
        [cat setPosition:CGPointMake(486, 796)];
        [self addChild:cat z:-1];
        cat.opacity=0;

        CCSprite *smile= [CCSprite spriteWithFile:@"cheshireCatSmile.png"];
        [smile setPosition:CGPointMake(410, 784)];
        [self addChild:smile z:-1];

        id action = [CCSequence actions:
                    [CCDelayTime actionWithDuration:1],
                    [CCCallFuncN actionWithTarget:self
                            selector:@selector(repeatForever:)],
                                nil];

                    [cat runAction:action];
                            }
    return self;
}
```

```
-(void) repeatForever:(id)sender
{

    id action = [CCSequence actions:
                    [CCFadeIn actionWithDuration: 3.0f],
                    [CCDelayTime actionWithDuration:2.0f],
                    [CCFadeOut actionWithDuration: 3.0f],
                    nil];

    CCRepeatForever *repeat = [CCRepeatForever actionWithAction: action];

    [sender runAction:repeat];
}

-(void)dealloc{
    [super dealloc];
}

@end
```

Creating the Mad Hatter's Tea Party

Here you set up two bobble-head systems: one for the Mad Hatter and the other for the March Hare. Here are the Chipmunk instructions used to create the March Hare's bobble-head. You would repeat the process for the Hatter's head, or any additional heads you add to the scene:

```
#import "TeaParty.h"

@implementation TeaParty

-(id)init{
    if((self = [super init])) {int hareX = 380;
        int hareY = 486;
        int hatterX = 652;
        int hatterY = 504;

        #pragma mark hares head
        CCSprite *hare = [CCSprite spriteWithFile:@"haresHead.png"];
        [hare setPosition:CGPointMake(hareX, hareY)];
        [self addChild:hare z:-1];

        cpBody *harePinBody = cpBodyNew(INFINITY, INFINITY);
        harePinBody->p = cpv(hareX,hareY);

        int numVerts = 8;
        CGPoint hareVerts[] = {cpv(10.0f, -94.0f),
            cpv(-12.0f, -82.0f),
            cpv(-70.0f, 67.0f),
            cpv(-68.0f, 79.0f),
```

WHY IS A RAVEN LIKE A WRITING-DESK?" asked the Hatter. He then poured a little hot tea upon the Dormouse's nose.

```
        cpv(29.0f, 95.0f),
        cpv(64.0f, -17.0f),
        cpv(65.0f, -69.0f),
        cpv(53.0f, -89.0f)};

cpFloat mass = 5;
cpBody *hareBody = cpBodyNew(mass,cpMomentForPoly
        (mass, numVerts, hareVerts, cpvzero));
hareBody->p = cpv(hareX, hareY);
cpSpaceAddBody(space, hareBody);

cpShape *shape = cpPolyShapeNew(hareBody, numVerts, hareVerts,
    cpvzero);
shape->e = 0.3; shape->u = 0.5;
shape->data=hare;
cpSpaceAddShape(space, shape);


cpSpaceAddConstraint(space, cpDampedSpringNew
        (harePinBody, hareBody, cpv(120,0), cpv(50,0), 70,
            1500, 0.2));
cpSpaceAddConstraint(space, cpDampedSpringNew
        (harePinBody, hareBody, cpv(-120,0), cpv(-50,0), 70,
            1500, 0.2));

cpSpaceAddConstraint(space, cpPivotJointNew
        (hareBody, harePinBody, cpv(404,420)));
```

Reproduced with permission of Atomic Antelope LTD. © 2010 Atomic Antelope LTD.

Creating the Rose Garden Scene

This is a fairly simple scene, which I've included in its entirety here for you to experiment with. It's similar in setup to the scene where comfits fall on Alice and the Dodo, except in this instance the physics environment is altered to give the rose petals a slower, more ethereal descent:

```
#import "PaintingRoses.h"

@implementation PaintingRoses

-(id)init{
    if((self = [super init])) {CGSize size = [[CCDirector
    sharedDirector] winSize];

        //heavier damping
        space->damping = 0.2;

        GRAVITY_MULTIPLER = 1000;

        cpBody *zeroBody = cpBodyNew(INFINITY, INFINITY);
        zeroBody->p = cpvzero;

        //add walls
        cpShape *wallShape = cpSegmentShapeNew(zeroBody,
                    cpv(0,0), cpv(0,size.height), 5);
        wallShape->e = 0.5;
        wallShape->u = 0.3;
        cpSpaceAddStaticShape(space, wallShape);
        wallShape = cpSegmentShapeNew(zeroBody, cpv
                    (0,size.height), cpv(size.width,size.height), 5);
        wallShape->e = 0.5;
        wallShape->u = 0.3;
        cpSpaceAddStaticShape(space, wallShape);
        wallShape = cpSegmentShapeNew(zeroBody,
                    cpv(size.width,size.height), cpv(size.width,0), 5);
        wallShape->e = 0.5;
        wallShape->u = 0.3;
        cpSpaceAddStaticShape(space, wallShape);
        wallShape = cpSegmentShapeNew(zeroBody, cpv(size.width,0),
            cpv(0,0), 5);
        wallShape->e = 0.5;
        wallShape->u = 0.3;
        cpSpaceAddStaticShape(space, wallShape);

        int numVerts = 8;
        CGPoint verts[] = {cpv(-23.5f, -37.0f),
            cpv(-41.5f, -19.0f),
            cpv(-38.5f, 4.0f),
```

"Would you tell me," said Alice, a little timidly, "why you are painting those roses?"

Five and Seven said nothing, but looked at Two. Two began in a low voice, "Why the fact is, you see Miss, this here ought to have been a RED rose-tree, and we put a white one in by mistake; and if the Queen was to find it out, we should all have our heads cut off, you know."

```
                   cpv(-17.5f, 29.0f),
                   cpv(22.5f, 25.0f),
                   cpv(47.5f, 9.0f),
                   cpv(24.5f, -14.0f),
                   cpv(-4.5f, -34.0f)};

        float mass;
        //create a bunch of randomly placed petals
        for (int i = 0 ; i < 20; i++) {
            CCSprite *petal= [CCSprite spriteWithFile:
                     [NSString stringWithFormat:@"petal%i.png",rand() %
                          4 + 1]];
            petal.position = cpv(rand() % ((int)size.width - 200)+100,
                     rand() % ((int)size.height - 200)+100);
            [self addChild:petal z:-1];

            mass = (rand()%3)+0.5;
            cpBody *petalBody = cpBodyNew(mass, cpMomentForPoly
                     (mass, numVerts, verts, cpvzero));
            petalBody->p = cpv(petal.position.x,petal.position.y);
            cpBodySetAngle(petalBody,CC_DEGREES_TO_RADIANS(rand()%360));
            cpSpaceAddBody(space, petalBody);

            cpShape *shape = cpPolyShapeNew(petalBody, numVerts, verts,
                 cpvzero);
            shape->e = 0.5; shape->u = rand()%1;
            shape->data=petal;
            cpSpaceAddShape(space, shape);
        }


    }
    return self;
}

-(void)dealloc{
    [super dealloc];
}

@end
```

When the procession came opposite to Alice, they all stopped and looked at her, and the Queen said severely, "Who is this?"

Creating the Queen's Crown

Here you can define the outlines of the sprites on the screen, using shapes in the physics world described by their vertexes. In doing so, you create a ledge for the crown to sit on, which it then topples off when the users tilt their iPads:

```objc
#import "TheCrown.h"

@implementation TheCrown

-(id)init{
    if((self = [super init])) {CGSize size = [[CCDirector sharedDirector]
    winSize];

        cpBody *zeroBody = cpBodyNew(INFINITY, INFINITY);
        zeroBody->p = cpvzero;

        //add walls
        cpShape *wallShape = cpSegmentShapeNew(zeroBody,
                    cpv(0,0), cpv(0,size.height), 5);
        wallShape->e = 0.5;
        wallShape->u = 1.0;
        cpSpaceAddStaticShape(space, wallShape);
        wallShape = cpSegmentShapeNew(zeroBody, cpv(0,size.height),
                        cpv(size.width,size.height), 5);
        wallShape->e = 0.5;
        wallShape->u = 1.0;
        cpSpaceAddStaticShape(space, wallShape);
        wallShape = cpSegmentShapeNew(zeroBody, cpv(size.width,
                        size.height), cpv(size.width,0), 5);
```

```
wallShape->e = 0.5;
wallShape->u = 1.0;
cpSpaceAddStaticShape(space, wallShape);
wallShape = cpSegmentShapeNew(zeroBody, cpv(size.width,175),
cpv(0,175), 5);
wallShape->e = 0.5;
wallShape->u = 1.0;
cpSpaceAddStaticShape(space, wallShape);


#pragma mark sprites

CCSprite *crown= [CCSprite spriteWithFile:@"royalCrown.png"];
[crown setPosition:CGPointMake(550, 700)];
[self addChild:crown z:-1];

CCSprite *alice= [CCSprite spriteWithFile:@"aliceStanding.png"];
[alice setPosition:CGPointMake(494, 302)];
[self addChild:alice z:-1];

CCSprite *queen= [CCSprite spriteWithFile:@"queenStanding.png"];
[queen setPosition:CGPointMake(205, 386)];
[self addChild:queen z:-1];


wallShape = cpSegmentShapeNew(zeroBody, cpv(481,550),
cpv(643,550), 5);
wallShape->e = 0.5;
wallShape->u = 1.0;
cpSpaceAddStaticShape(space, wallShape);

cpVect crownVerts[] = {
    cpv(-65,-82),
    cpv(-96,0),
    cpv(-72,41),
    cpv(-12,82),
    cpv(12,82),
    cpv(66,39),
    cpv(96,-10),
    cpv(62,-79)
};

cpFloat mass = 5;
cpBody *crownBody = cpBodyNew(mass, cpMomentForPoly
            (mass, 8, crownVerts, cpvzero));
crownBody->p = cpv(570, 700);
cpSpaceAddBody(space, crownBody);

cpShape *shape = cpPolyShapeNew(crownBody, 8, crownVerts,
    cpvzero);
shape->e = 0.3; shape->u = 1.0;
```

```
        shape->data=crown;
        cpSpaceAddShape(space, shape);


    }
    return self;
}

-(void)dealloc{
    [super dealloc];
}

@end
```

Creating the Duchess

Here the Flamingo pivots in Alice's arms and the Duchess's head bobbles in a similar way to the characters in the Mad Hatter's Tea Party scene. Again, the full code for this scene is shown here so you can dive right into creating a similar setup:

```
#import "AliceAndTheDuchess.h"

@implementation AliceAndTheDuchess

-(id)init{
    if((self = [super init])) {
        space->damping = 0.8;

        int pinX = 210;
        int pinY = 670;


        #pragma mark flamingo
        CCSprite *flamingo= [CCSprite spriteWithFile:@"flamingo.png"];
        flamingo.position = cpv(pinX,pinY);
        [self addChild:flamingo z:-1];

        int numVerts = 8;
        CGPoint verts[] = {cpv(-15.5f, -137.5f),
            cpv(-40.5f, -118.5f),
            cpv(-28.5f, 127.5f),
            cpv(18.5f, 138.5f),
            cpv(32.5f, 133.5f),
            cpv(40.5f, 111.5f),
            cpv(40.5f, -103.5f),
            cpv(15.5f, -136.5f)};

        //add label body
        cpFloat mass = 30;
        cpBody *body = cpBodyNew(mass, cpMomentForPoly
                (mass, numVerts, verts, cpvzero));
```

"You're thinking about something, my dear, and that makes you forget to talk," said the Duchess to Alice.

```
body->p = flamingo.position;
cpSpaceAddBody(space, body);

cpShape *shape = cpPolyShapeNew(body, numVerts, verts, cpvzero);
shape->e = 1.0; shape->u = 0.5; shape->layers = 1;
shape->data=flamingo;
cpSpaceAddShape(space, shape);

cpBody *flamingoPinBody = cpBodyNew(INFINITY, INFINITY);
flamingoPinBody->p = cpv(pinX, pinY);

//joint the arm/flamingo to alice
cpSpaceAddConstraint(space, cpPivotJointNew
        (flamingoPinBody, body, cpv(pinX+10, pinY-30)));
cpSpaceAddConstraint(space, cpDampedSpringNew
        (flamingoPinBody, body, cpv(0,200), cpv(0,100), 50,
            500, 10));

#pragma mark duchess head
pinX = 472;
pinY = 787;
CCSprite *head = [CCSprite spriteWithFile:@"duchess-head.png"];
[head setPosition:CGPointMake(pinX, pinY)];
[self addChild:head z:-1];

cpBody *headPinBody = cpBodyNew(INFINITY, INFINITY);
headPinBody->p = cpv(pinX,pinY);

numVerts = 10;
CGPoint headVerts[] = {
    cpv(-127.7f, -139.1f),
    cpv(-131.3f, -44.8f),
    cpv(-125.3f, 31.6f),
    cpv(-90.7f, 141.5f),
    cpv(15.5f, 165.3f),
    cpv(46.6f, 162.9f),
    cpv(131.3f, 102.1f),
    cpv(127.7f, -3.0f),
    cpv(27.5f, -104.5f),
    cpv(-86.0f, -162.9f)};

mass = 10;
body = cpBodyNew(mass,cpMomentForPoly(mass, numVerts, headVerts,
    cpvzero));
body->p = head.position;
cpSpaceAddBody(space, body);

numVerts = 6;
CGPoint chinVerts[] = {cpv(-114.0f, -145.8f),
    cpv(-129.4f, -53.4f),
    cpv(-95.5f, -35.9f),
    cpv(-13.3f, -93.4f),
```

```
            cpv(-43.1f, -141.7f),
            cpv(-89.3f, -162.2f)};

        shape = cpPolyShapeNew(body, numVerts, chinVerts, cpvzero);
        shape->e = 0.6; shape->u = 0.5; shape->layers = 1;
        shape->data=head;
        cpSpaceAddShape(space, shape);

        numVerts = 8;
        CGPoint headDressVerts[] = {cpv(-97.5f, -35.9f),
            cpv(-111.9f, 38.0f),
            cpv(-88.3f, 136.6f),
            cpv(41.1f, 161.2f),
            cpv(131.4f, 101.7f),
            cpv(128.3f, -9.2f),
            cpv(25.7f, -108.8f),
            cpv(-13.3f, -95.5f)};

        shape = cpPolyShapeNew(body, numVerts, headDressVerts, cpvzero);
        shape->e = 0.6; shape->u = 0.5; shape->layers = 1;
        shape->data=head;
        cpSpaceAddShape(space, shape);

        cpSpaceAddConstraint(space, cpDampedSpringNew
                (headPinBody, body, cpv(0,200), cpv(0,130), 70, 3000,
                    0.2));
        cpSpaceAddConstraint(space, cpDampedSpringNew
                (headPinBody, body, cpv(0,-200), cpv(0,-130), 70,
                    3000, 0.2));

        cpSpaceAddConstraint(space, cpDampedSpringNew
                (headPinBody, body, cpv(200,0), cpv(130,0), 70, 5000,
                    0.2));
        cpSpaceAddConstraint(space, cpDampedSpringNew
                (headPinBody, body, cpv(-200,0), cpv(-130,0), 70, 5000,
                    0.2));

    }
    return self;
}

-(void)dealloc{
    [super dealloc];
}

@end
```

Creating the Tart Fight Scene

You can work out the physics behind this scene by combining the techniques already described earlier in this chapter. But I thought it would be interesting to show you in more detail how this particular scene is layered, and the design process behind its construction.

Creating Mile High Alice

This scene uses a very simple scaling operation to make Alice grow. I have included the full code for the scene here:

```
#import "MileHigh.h"

@implementation MileHigh

-(id)init{
    if((self = [super init])) {
        CCSprite *alice= [CCSprite spriteWithFile:@"aliceGetsBigger.png"];
        [alice setPosition:CGPointMake(290, 370)];
        [self addChild:alice z:-1];
        alice.scale=0.4;

        [alice runAction:[CCScaleTo actionWithDuration:8.0f scale:1.0f]];
        [alice runAction:[CCMoveTo actionWithDuration:8.0f
            position:ccp(285,615)]];
    }
    return self;
}

-(void)dealloc{
    [super dealloc];
}

@end
```

Just at this moment Alice felt a very curious sensation — she was beginning to grow larger again.

Creating the Card Attack

Reproduced with permission of Atomic Antelope LTD. © 2010 Atomic Antelope LTD.

This is the grand finalé to the whole book and uses many of the techniques you've already looked at in combination with each other:

```
#import "CardAttack.h"

// Iterate over all of the bodies and reset the ones that have fallen
//offscreen.
static void
eachBody(cpBody *body, void *unused)
{
    if(body->p.y < -200 || body->p.y > 1500){
        body->p = cpv(-100, -100);
        body->v = cpv(rand() % 1000 + 200,rand() % 5000 + 1000);
    }
}

@implementation CardAttack

-(id)init{
    if((self = [super init])) {cpFloat mass;
        int pinX,pinY;
        cpShape *shape;

        cpBody *zeroBody = cpBodyNew(INFINITY, INFINITY);
        zeroBody->p = cpvzero;


        cpShape *wallShape = cpSegmentShapeNew
                    (zeroBody, cpv(290,800), cpv(400,1100), 5);
        wallShape->e = 0.5;
        wallShape->u = 1.0;
```

```
wallShape->layers = 2;
cpSpaceAddStaticShape(space, wallShape);
wallShape = cpSegmentShapeNew(zeroBody, cpv(400,1100),
    cpv(600,900), 5);
wallShape->e = 0.5;
wallShape->u = 1.0;
wallShape->layers = 2;
cpSpaceAddStaticShape(space, wallShape);


#pragma mark alice right arm

int numVerts = 6;
CGPoint rightArmLowerVerts[] = {cpv(33.5f, -106.0f),
    cpv(-43.5f, -62.0f),
    cpv(-63.5f, -37.0f),
    cpv(-53.5f, -7.0f),
    cpv(54.5f, -74.0f),
    cpv(47.5f, -97.0f)};

pinX = 370;
pinY = 795;

CCSprite *rightArm= [CCSprite spriteWithFile:@"right-arm.png"];
[rightArm setPosition:CGPointMake(pinX, pinY)];
[self addChild:rightArm z:-1];

mass = 3;
cpBody *rightArmBody = cpBodyNew(mass, cpMomentForPoly
            (mass, numVerts, rightArmLowerVerts, cpvzero));
rightArmBody->p = cpv(pinX, pinY);
cpSpaceAddBody(space, rightArmBody);

shape = cpPolyShapeNew(rightArmBody, numVerts, rightArmLowerVerts,
        cpvzero);
shape->e = 0.5; shape->u = 0.5; shape->layers = 1;
shape->data=rightArm;
cpSpaceAddShape(space, shape);

numVerts = 6;
CGPoint rightArmUpperVerts[] = {cpv(-54.5f, -4.0f),
    cpv(7.5f, 73.0f),
    cpv(47.5f, 104.0f),
    cpv(58.5f, 91.0f),
    cpv(63.5f, 67.0f),
    cpv(-15.5f, -29.0f)};

shape = cpPolyShapeNew(rightArmBody, numVerts, rightArmUpperVerts,
        cpvzero);
shape->e = 0.5; shape->u = 0.5; shape->layers = 1;
shape->data=rightArm;
cpSpaceAddShape(space, shape);

#pragma mark alice
numVerts = 17;
```

```
CGPoint aliceVerts[] = {cpv(-177.5f, -262.0f),
    cpv(-161.5f, -94.0f),
    cpv(-104.5f, 137.0f),
    cpv(-67.5f, 210.0f),
    cpv(-11.5f, 287.0f),
    cpv(11.5f, 297.0f),
    cpv(67.5f, 291.0f),
    cpv(92.5f, 271.0f),
    cpv(115.5f, 220.0f),
    cpv(136.5f, 131.0f),
    cpv(146.5f, 28.0f),
    cpv(104.5f, -254.0f),
    cpv(76.5f, -273.0f),
    cpv(49.5f, -282.0f),
    cpv(-0.5f, -292.0f),
    cpv(-68.5f, -298.0f),
    cpv(-129.5f, -293.0f)};

pinX = 495;
pinY = 535;

CCSprite *alice= [CCSprite spriteWithFile:@"aliceBody.png"];
[alice setPosition:CGPointMake(pinX, pinY)];
[self addChild:alice z:-1];

mass = 5;
cpBody *aliceBody = cpBodyNew(mass, cpMomentForPoly
        (mass, numVerts, aliceVerts, cpvzero));
aliceBody->p = cpv(pinX, pinY);
cpSpaceAddBody(space, aliceBody);

shape = cpPolyShapeNew(aliceBody, numVerts, aliceVerts, cpvzero);
shape->e = 0.5; shape->u = 0.5; shape->layers = 2;
shape->data=alice;
cpSpaceAddShape(space, shape);

cpBody *alicePinBody = cpBodyNew(INFINITY, INFINITY);
alicePinBody->p = cpv(pinX, pinY);

//alice pivots about her waist
cpSpaceAddConstraint(space, cpPivotJointNew
        (alicePinBody, aliceBody, cpv(pinX,pinY)));
//spring means she's held upright
cpSpaceAddConstraint(space, cpDampedSpringNew
        (alicePinBody, aliceBody, cpv(0,350), cpv(0,200), 100,
        3000, 30));
//pin her right arm to body
cpSpaceAddConstraint(space, cpPinJointNew(rightArmBody,
        aliceBody, cpv(50,-98), cpv(-74,163)));
cpSpaceAddConstraint(space, cpDampedSpringNew(rightArmBody,
        aliceBody, cpv(40,-98),cpv(-70,163), 10, 20000, 10));
//this spring holds her right arm 'up'
cpSpaceAddConstraint(space, cpDampedSpringNew(alicePinBody,
        rightArmBody, cpv(-250,200), cpv(-45,-35), 50, 1000, 5));
```

```
#pragma mark alice left arm
numVerts = 10;
CGPoint leftArmVerts[] = {cpv(31.5f, -83.0f),
    cpv(-5.5f, -62.0f),
    cpv(-39.5f, 35.0f),
    cpv(-46.5f, 65.0f),
    cpv(-28.5f, 86.0f),
    cpv(-17.5f, 84.0f),
    cpv(-3.5f, 69.0f),
    cpv(47.5f, -38.0f),
    cpv(46.5f, -63.0f),
    cpv(42.5f, -75.0f)};

pinX = 595;
pinY = 625;

CCSprite *leftArm= [CCSprite spriteWithFile:@"left-arm.png"];
[leftArm setPosition:CGPointMake(pinX, pinY)];
[self addChild:leftArm z:-1];

mass = 3;
cpBody *leftArmBody = cpBodyNew(mass, cpMomentForPoly
        (mass, numVerts, leftArmVerts, cpvzero));
leftArmBody->p = cpv(pinX, pinY);
cpSpaceAddBody(space, leftArmBody);

shape = cpPolyShapeNew(leftArmBody, numVerts, leftArmVerts, cpvzero);
shape->e = 0.5; shape->u = 0.5; shape->layers = 1;
shape->data=leftArm;
cpSpaceAddShape(space, shape);

//pin her left arm to body
cpSpaceAddConstraint(space, cpPinJointNew(leftArmBody,
            aliceBody, cpv(30,-70), cpv(130,20)));
cpSpaceAddConstraint(space, cpDampedSpringNew(leftArmBody,
            aliceBody, cpv(30,-70),cpv(130,20), 0, 50000, 10));
//this spring holds her left arm 'up'
cpSpaceAddConstraint(space, cpDampedSpringNew(alicePinBody,
            leftArmBody, cpv(70,400), cpv(-30,70), 220, 1000, 5));

#pragma mark cards
//create a bunch of randomly placed petals
for (int i = 0 ; i < 30; i++) {
    CCSprite *card= [CCSprite spriteWithFile:
                [NSString stringWithFormat:@"card%i.png",rand()
                    % 9 + 1]];
    [self addChild:card z:-1];

    mass = 0.4;
    cpBody *cardBody = cpBodyNew(mass, 1);
    cardBody->p = cpv(-100,-100);
    cpBodySetAngle(cardBody,CC_DEGREES_TO_RADIANS(rand()%360));
    cardBody->v = cpv(rand() % 1000 + 200,rand() % 5000 + 1000);
    cpSpaceAddBody(space, cardBody);
```

```
            //cpShape *shape = cpPolyShapeNew(petalBody, 6, comfitVerts,
            cpvzero);
            cpShape *shape = cpCircleShapeNew(cardBody, 25, cpvzero);
            shape->e = 0.1; shape->u = 0.8;
            shape->data=card;
            cpSpaceAddShape(space, shape);
        }


        #pragma mark lizard
        CCSprite *lizard= [CCSprite spriteWithFile:@"cards-lizard.png"];
        [lizard setPosition:CGPointMake(550, 170)];
        [self addChild:lizard z:-1];

        #pragma mark goose
        CCSprite *goose= [CCSprite spriteWithFile:@"cards-goose.png"];
        [goose setPosition:CGPointMake(200, 200)];
        [self addChild:goose z:-1];

        //checks if bodies have fallen off screen
        [self schedule: @selector(iterateBodies:) interval: 1.0f/4];
    }
    return self;
}

//calls method to iterate over bodies and reset positions if they've
//fallen offscreen
-(void)iterateBodies:(ccTime)dt{
    cpSpaceEachBody(space, &eachBody, nil);
}

-(void)dealloc{
    [super dealloc];
}

@end
```

Emerging from the Rabbit Hole

Now you've had a good look behind the scenes of Alice for the iPad, you should have
a decent grasp of the basic gravity simulations that you can set up using the iPad and
Chipmunk physics. The really wonderful thing about Chipmunk (code.google.com/p/
chipmunk-physics/) is that it works a lot like a kid's construction set. The basic components—rigid bodies, restraints, and pivots—can be used in conjunction with each other
to build extremely sophisticated and powerful mechanisms that can power all kinds of
weird and wonderful book designs. There are no real limits to what you can create with
Chipmunk other than the breadth of your imagination.

Before moving onto the next chapter, where you'll take a look at adding sound to your creations, it's worth mentioning that there is also an alternative physics simulation system that is compatible with the iPad. It's called Box2D (www.box2d.org). Although we didn't use Box2D in *Alice for the iPad*, it is a very capable physics engine, perfect for anyone who wants to create a digital pop-up book, or a physics-aware game.

Whichever system you choose to create your app, the real magic is in imagining how the characters will interact with each other in the story, and how you can use this advanced technology to support and enhance the narrative of the app. Don't just throw together some physics objects and expect to create a masterpiece—the real art to using these techniques is found through intuition, hard work, and genuine love for the source story.

Chapter 11
Starting Out with Sound on the iPad

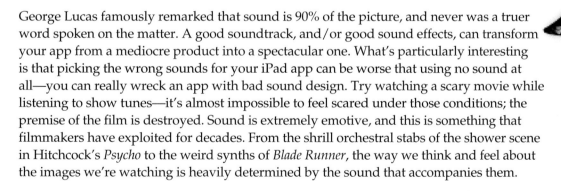

George Lucas famously remarked that sound is 90% of the picture, and never was a truer word spoken on the matter. A good soundtrack, and/or good sound effects, can transform your app from a mediocre product into a spectacular one. What's particularly interesting is that picking the wrong sounds for your iPad app can be worse that using no sound at all—you can really wreck an app with bad sound design. Try watching a scary movie while listening to show tunes—it's almost impossible to feel scared under those conditions; the premise of the film is destroyed. Sound is extremely emotive, and this is something that filmmakers have exploited for decades. From the shrill orchestral stabs of the shower scene in Hitchcock's *Psycho* to the weird synths of *Blade Runner*, the way we think and feel about the images we're watching is heavily determined by the sound that accompanies them.

You may be thinking that sound is not important in your app. Perhaps you're not making an immersive videogame, or an interactive storybook. Perhaps you're making a spreadsheet app or a graphing calculator. Well, don't be deceived: Sound is still essential in your app design. It's essential because the choice not to include sound should be as careful a decision as the decision to include sound.

An iPad app can appeal to only three senses: touch, sight, and hearing. Since hearing is one of just three means by which your app can convey information to your users, it's important to spend some time thinking about how you will use it, and also how you will not use it. As one example of misuse, consider how irritating the system sound effects can become in some operating systems. Personally I know I would rather rip my own ears off than listen to the jolly ping of an incoming email in Microsoft Outlook, and, if you've ever sat next to a coworker who has enabled sounds for almost every action possible on their computer, you'll know that there's something uniquely maddening about a misplaced or overused sound effect. "Woooosh," there he's sent another email. "Keraaghshhh," he's deleted a file. And so on. I'm sure it drives you mad too.

In this chapter I'm going to show you how to use sound to improve your app, and when not to use sound, so you can avoid wrecking your app. Of course, there is the likelihood that the users will not have the sound turned on when they're using your app, so I'll also demonstrate how to use sound to supplement your app design without relying on it.

TIP

Sound can provide a shortcut straight to the emotional core of the audience for your iPad app. You can watch the raw impact of sound in action if you take a look at some of the movie-trailer-redubs that users have uploaded to YouTube. For example, one user has overdubbed a trailer for classic horror movie, The Shining, giving it a new soundtrack and voiceover. The film's plot is transformed: what was originally a murderous rampage by Jack Nicholson's character turns into a film about a caring father figure on a feel-good romp with his family. The images in the trailer are all from the original film, but the sound accompanying them has completely redefined the meaning of these images. Your iPad app can make use of the same phenomena. By picking the right sounds, or soundtrack, and using them tastefully, in the right place, you can create an emotional connection between your users and your software.

Often less is more. Your app could potentially incorporate just one or two sounds, occurring on rare occasions, and still outshine an app packed with sounds. Don't make the mistake of turning your apps into soundboards—very few actions need audio accompaniment. Using sound well in your apps is a skill you'll acquire over time—some people make a career of this field alone—but the advice in this chapter should give you a good idea of where to begin.

How Not To Annoy People with Sound

There is almost nothing more capable of annoying people than sound. Governments use sound to torture people. If you see something you don't like, you can turn away, or as a last resort, close your eyes. If you touch something you don't like, you can let go of it. But if you hear something you don't like, you're pretty much stuck with it unless you find some way to stop it, or run far enough away that the volume decreases. Barking dogs, pneumatic drills, or the neighbor's music blaring through the walls. Sound is uniquely unencumbered by physical boundaries, and perfectly placed to annoy us. Obviously the iPad has a handy volume control to turn the sound of completely, but I want you to start thinking about the way bad sound design will impact on your users: They will reach for the volume control, and turn the app's sound off to escape it. Consider this simple action a vote of no confidence in your app—consciously or subconsciously the users are enjoying your app less. You can forget word-of-mouth recommendations for your app if users are muting the sound; they're not going to sing your praises on forums and all over the web, the life-blood of any indie app developer.

There are three types of sound on the iPad that are guaranteed to annoy users:

- **Repetitive sound:** Any sound that occurs more than once a minute, with the exception of sound in some games.

- **Shrill sound:** Any sound that is unpleasant to listen to. Generally, this means not using shrill or repetitive sound effects.

- **Constant sound:** Any sound or soundtrack that loops without end, not changing pace or style.

When designing *Alice for the iPad*, we quickly discovered that sound could not be done by a half-measure. Either we scored the entire app with the same attention to detail as a movie soundtrack, or we minimized sound to the point where it didn't interfere with the story—almost removing it completely. Anything between these two options and the app seemed clumsy and unfinished. Worst of all, a looping soundtrack with little change in dynamics clashed with the story and actively sabotaged all our hard work on the app. Sometimes it takes a lone, brave voice to point out these kinds of flaws in the sound design of an app. Often you'll find that projects gain an odd kind of momentum and the very fact that someone, or a group, has been assigned to create sounds for the app means that sound will be included, come hell or high water. It takes guts to stop and ask if sound is required at all. Be careful of falling into this kind of trap throughout the design process and don't be afraid to stop and ask: Why are we doing this?

Having cautioned against including sound if you're not prepared to put a significant effort into it, let's take a look at effective use of sound in iPad app design.

Preparing Sound for the iPad

If you've designed sound for the iPhone, you'll have a good idea of what to expect here. As with many parts of iPad app production, you may get better results from this process if you seek the help and advice of a sound professional. However, you may already have the skills to edit sound. For the purpose of this chapter, I'm going to assume from here on in that you do have a basic knowledge of sound editing and mastering techniques. If you don't, you'll still learn something from the advice here, but be aware that audio production is a fairly complex task. You'll need to consider whether the time spent learning to edit and master your own audio might be better invested elsewhere while someone who has already learned these audio editing skills gives you a hand. The advice I'm about to give you applies to preparing sound for any computer software, but there are a few special considerations to be made in the case of the iPad. First, let's run through the three most basic technical requirements of any sound you create for the iPad, covered in the following sections.

© 2010 Apple Inc.

Sound Must Be Audible

Audible sound on the iPad may rely on use of normalization, gain, and compression on the source audio. Apple *GarageBand*, bundled free with all Macs, is a great piece of software for tweaking your audio tracks before exporting them for use on the iPad and allows you to check the audio waveforms and preview the sound output. *GarageBand* also has a fairly decent range of compression options. Compression is a process that reduces the dynamic range between the loudest and quietest sound levels in your recording. These levels are partly a matter of personal taste, and partly a necessity given that the iPad is often used in home and work environments with a fair level of background noise. In these situations, some compression is essential to keep the quieter audio within an audible range. You'll also want to keep an eye on the peak levels of the audio when you play it back; often some gain will need to be added to the audio track to improve the signal-to-noise ratio.

Sound Must Be Clear and Undistorted

Keep checking the peaking point in your audio editor. As a general rule, you want your audio levels to peak around the highest point they possibly can, without clipping. *Clipping* is where the dynamic range of the audio exceeds the maximum amplitude of the sound outputs, and distortion can be heard. You can tell when this is happening either by listening to the sound—although sometimes it may be a very subtle distortion that's hard to hear and may not become obvious until later on—or by observing the audio meters. When the audio meters hit the red range, the audio is either clipping, or dangerously close to clipping. You do not want this to happen, because clipped sound is ugly and crackly. In *GarageBand* there are two little red dots at the end of the level meters; if either of these light up during playback, your audio is clipping. Bad news—turn down either the level of one of your audio tracks, or the level of several tracks, until you get the meters peaking near the top of their ranges, but not in the red.

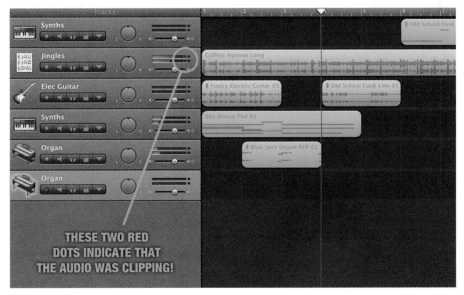

© 2010 Apple Inc.

Sound Must Not Overload the Processor

Unfortunately, only trial and error will determine for sure whether your audio is causing problems for the iPad. Personally, I've not seen any problems with throwing a fair few tracks of audio onto the iPad, but I have previously had problems with games my company made for the iPhone. You're only likely to run into trouble if your app is already pushing the iPad to its processing limits—at that point, adding a few layers of audio may be the straw that breaks the camel's back. The likely consequence of demanding too much audio processing from the iPad is that you experience a slight slowdown in the device's ability to complete other tasks. In some apps this may not be obvious to the naked eye, but in others— such as games that rely on a high frame rate—you may want to experiment with disabling sound temporarily when troubleshooting any glitches in performance, to rule this out as a cause.

Choosing an Audio Format

The iPad accepts a variety of sound formats and you may be deceived into thinking that, as with audio on your computer, you're free to make a choice based on personal preference. However, the iPad handles audio formats in different ways and the processing power required to parse each format varies. Some sound formats are better suited for multi-tracking, whereas others offer higher quality output. In general, compressed sound puts more demand on the processor, but takes up less space in your app.

For uncompressed audio, Apple recommends 16-bit, little-endian, linear PCM audio packaged in a CAF file. Although this might sound horrifyingly complex at first glance, for all practical purposes you can largely ignore what this cryptic format means as long as you know how to create one of these so-called CAF files. The operation is unusually complex for something dreamt up by Apple, but still doesn't present much of a challenge. Follow these steps:

1. First save your source audio file in a lossless format, like an AIFF file. This should be an option in most audio software. In GarageBand, it involves clicking the Share menu and selecting Export Song to Disk.

2. Once the song is saved, you'll need to open a terminal window. Go to the top-right corner of your Mac's screen and click the Spotlight magnifying glass and type terminal. Press Enter.

3. Once you've opened a terminal window, use the following command to convert your audio file: **afconvert -f caff -d LEI16** *[INPUT] [OUTPUT]*.

For example, if you were converting a file called soundtrack.aiff to CAF format, you'd navigate in your terminal window to the relevant directory where the soundtrack.aiff file was located and then type the following: **afconvert -f caff -d LEI16 soundtrack.aiff soundtrack.caf**.

This will create a CAF file equivalent of your AIFF. The iPad also supports IMA/ADPCM audio (IMA4) format, as well as ALAC (Apple Lossless), AAC, and MP3 audio formats. The Apple developer guide provides good instructions on the use of these formats.

Creating Soundtracks and Sound Effects

As I explained at the top of this chapter, sound is the most emotive tool you have at your disposal when immersing users in your app. However, this emotive tool might best be left unused in spreadsheets, word processors, and other utility apps. The decision not to use sound is often the most sensible option and coming to any decision about sound, even the decision to leave it out, should be taken very seriously. The temptation is to wait until your app is almost done and then tack on sound, while the better approach is to consider sound from the very start of the production phase.

The iPad also presents an interesting challenge for sound design: The iPad is commonly used on-the-move, where the device's sound will either be switched off, turned down, or almost impossible to hear on account of all the general hullabaloo of the modern metropolis. This presents tricky unknowns for apps where sound is used heavily—games in particular. In general, I've found the best approach is to avoid relying on sound alone for vital game cues, but be aware that some users love immersive environments coupled with great sound design and may often use the iPad with headphones to avoid distractions. These users will prize your attention to sound and are usually exactly the same users who are enthusiastic enough to post their feelings about your iPad on forums and message boards across the Internet. These same users will also tend to leave reviews on iTunes. So, aside from the fact that good sound makes an entertainment app shine, it is also likely to impress the vocal minority who will go out and shout about how great your app is.

My company has made some apps where I scored entire soundtracks for the software using a mix of Propellerhead's *Reason* and Apple's *GarageBand*. I can personally recommend *Reason* if you're looking for a sequencer that goes beyond what *GarageBand* can provide. It's a pretty neat piece of software and, coupled with a keyboard, I can't imagine exhausting its potential for creating iPad app music. I used *Reason* to compose the title music and in-game music for *Twitch Origins*. Despite the dramatic failure of that particular title (see Chapter 8 for details), I'm still very pleased with the audio on the game.

TIP

*Consider getting hold of **Reason** if you're doing a lot of sound design for the iPad. **Reason** is particularly well suited to retro-style gaming music, which has seen a resurgence lately, driven by indie rock bands who have adopted the "chip" sound of the Commodore 64 and other 8-bit games consoles. There are plenty of free **Reason** "refills" around the web that you can use to equip the software with a full range of 80s-style coin-op arcade sounds to give your game titles that dragged-down-from-the-attic feel. **Reason** is also great for sequencing fairly realistic strings sections and acoustic-style drums. I haven't found much I can't do with the software—it probably sounds like I own shares in **Reason,** but I don't, it's just a very impressive piece of kit for iPad sound design that I find myself turning to whenever I need to soundtrack an app. It won't export CAF files directly, but you can easily convert the lossless files **Reason** exports into CAF by using the terminal command covered earlier in this chapter.*

Part IV
Marketing Your App

I'm going to let you in on a bizarre secret. If you have no money to market your iPad app, you have a huge advantage over your rich competitors. Although this sounds like madness, in this part I'll explain why a wealthy software company tends to fail completely when it comes to marketing their products and why you, as a small indie developer, with barely enough money to buy mittens to keep yourself warm through winter, can outgun the big boys.

Before you explore some zero-budget solutions, I'd like to give you a little inspiration. *Alice for the iPad* is on hundreds of thousands of iPads and appeared in every major newspaper in the world. Sounds great, right? Now, can you guess how much this press coverage cost us to achieve? Fifty thousand dollars? A hundred thousand dollars? Surprisingly, no, it cost absolutely nothing. Not even a dollar. The reason why it cost nothing is that we considered the marketing potential of our app idea before we built it. We marketed it to the right people and we put every ounce of heart we had available into building an app that we knew we could sell through YouTube and word of mouth. In this part, I'm going to show you exactly what you need to do if you want to sell your way to a million dollars on the App Store.

Chapter 12
Zero Budget Solutions

Here's the extraordinary truth of the matter. I've worked some of the biggest online publishers in the world, some of the most wealthy media corporations and the biggest TV companies, and one thing they had in common was this: Nobody knew what they were doing. There was too much money and too many marketing meetings, and little by little we went insane. It was a godless world where people shouted each other down and reduced good promotional ideas to bland mush. For some reason I've never managed to get to the bottom of, marketing managers are among the least inventive, most uninspiring people I've ever met. Of course a small number are brilliant minds fighting against the tide, but most are complete idiots. I attended party after party where some marketing lunatic would drone on and on about a new flat screen TV or a new motorbike, but no one was listening. These people would spend anything up to $200,000 on a party that lasted two or three hours, and think nothing of it. Marketing by big business is horribly wasteful, clumsy, and ineffective. Often it's no more than an opportunity for the CEO's ego to jog around the room, showing off.

I can't count the number of times I was flown to places like Paris, Italy, New York, and Amsterdam to watch a marketing lizard pull a velvet cloth off a new MP3 player, or laptop. Can I remember any of these products; did I care? Did it excite me? No. Because there was so little artistic sensitivity, and so little creativity in these marketing methods. If you show even a glimmer of aptitude at promoting your products in the way I describe in this chapter, you'll become more clued up than 99% of "marketing" companies out there.

The efforts of big business to market products in print or online are often even worse than the parties. I've seen advertisers stick adverts called "interstitials" on the front page of major websites I've worked for. An interstitial advert is one that displays before you get a chance to look at the site—it effectively hijacks the front page for a moment, supposedly giving the advertiser the user's full attention. However, what it actually does is massively irritate the user, and the user then associates that brand with being irritating. Who thinks this stuff up?

If you want to know how a big marketing department promotes a new piece of software, I'll give you the unvarnished truth of this industry. The marketing department is given a budget, let's say $50,000, to promote a new app. Now, I don't know how many new-media marketing people you've met, but their first instinct on seeing any sum of money is to start visualizing means of using that money to throw a party. At least 80% of this money will now be spent on the party. Now, I'm not knocking public relations parties, but in my experience they tend to be populated by journalists, half-blind on drink and canapés, with about the same ability to retain any memories or interest in the product as that guy in the movie *Memento*. I've personally watched technology journalists, from magazines you probably read, falling drunk into ice sculptures, throwing up into promotional bags, and in one particularly memorable case, drop-kicking a demo product off the VIP balcony of the *World DJ Championships* and into the crowd. You can see where I'm going with this: The big marketing departments have gone mad. Completely mad. The only people madder than the marketing departments are the journalists that are umbilically attached to the pulsing of this reckless creature. Corporations regularly hemorrhage money on wild schemes with little thought behind them, and the bigger the company, the worse the excess.

So, while this is hilarious and bewildering, and generally disappointing for the human race, it's very good news for indie developers. Because the big corporations are so awful at marketing, you can use your guile and cunning to outwit them. In this chapter I'm going to show you exactly how you can eclipse anything they can do. All you'll need is a video camera and your imagination. Before I get onto the practical side, let's take a look inside the belly of the media beast.

Understanding How the Press Works

The press is a valuable promotional tool when it comes to selling your iPad app. Luckily for you, newspapers and magazines are now so chronically underfunded that an ethical void has developed. Where it was once reasonably difficult to convince a journalist that your product was newsworthy, now most news desks are happy to rehash press releases and print marketing material as if it were news. There just isn't enough money or manpower to vet the stories. As a former journalist for two of the UK's top newspapers, I've seen this effect in action.

TIP

*In a nutshell, to promote your app in the press, the trick is to tie your marketing message to a human-interest story, so it looks like news. Forget what your iPad app **is**, focus on what it **does**. Now dream up an interesting story about someone using your app to do something quirky. For example, if your app diagnoses car problems, maybe it would make a good story if someone used it to save themselves from freezing to death after their car broke down on a deserted road in Vermont?*

As funding in journalism decreases even further, you can often pick out lots of articles in your newspaper that are thinly disguised marketing messages from corporations. Many journalists don't have time to go out and research stories, so the majority of news comes off something called the "news wire." This is a feed of news from a number of journalists across the world, which is then shared between all the newspapers. In effect, the source of your news might have a different masthead on the front page, but the news inside is usually the same as any other paper. In rare cases, you might be able to get your iPad app on the wire; there are plenty of examples of this happening, but it is hard to pull off.

Personally, I'm opposed to manipulating the media into accepting a press release disguised as news, and I only mention it because it's what your competition may be up to—keep an eye on them. Manipulating the press is unnecessary if your iPad app is a genuine killer-app. If you've followed the steps throughout this book, you should have ended up with an app that requires only one thing to send it skyrocketing: a critical mass of public awareness.

I define critical mass as the number of people you need to communicate with before word-of-mouth marketing takes over and almost every iPad owner knows about your app. If your app is a killer, this critical mass is around 50,000 people. Once this many people know about your app, awareness will snowball to near 100%. At this point, as I found with *Alice,* the press will automatically kick into action without much prompting. So, how do you reach these people, your first-wave of customers? Simple: use YouTube.

Harnessing the Power of YouTube

Just in case YouTube has become normalized to you, I'm going to recap on what YouTube is. Ten years ago, if you wanted to promote your software to millions of people, you would have to buy airtime on a national television channel. Your advert would cost a minimum of $100,000 to make, and millions of dollars to air. Today, because of YouTube, you can reach the same audience for less than a dollar. If YouTube doesn't seem like the most extraordinary marketing tool ever invented, I'm not sure how to impress you. YouTube is invaluable in promoting your iPad app: It's free, but it's also invaluable. Odd, hey? Welcome to the 21st century.

If your app goes atomic, there's another great advantage to promoting it through YouTube—it has the resources to deal with all the web traffic you can throw at it. Believe me, if your app gets even a fraction of the success of *Alice for the iPad*, your website servers will not stand up to the demand, and your site will crash and burn. This is the last thing you want because it means information about your app will be inaccessible at the same time that interest in it is at an absolute peak. Having your videos on YouTube will avoid this happening. There are few other hosting services that will survive trending on Twitter, and simultaneously featuring on *Gizmodo*, *Oprah*, the *BBC*, and *Slashdot*, but YouTube does.

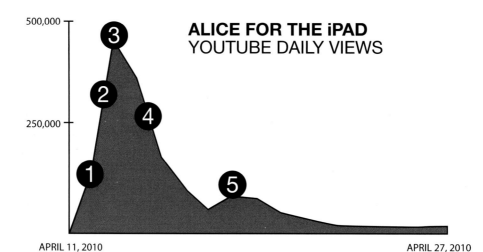

When **Alice for the iPad** became a global hit, YouTube was serving millions of users the **Alice** trailer in the space of just one week, and it didn't cost us a penny for all this advertising. YouTube is run by Google, and the site is used to handling massive traffic spikes, so there's no need to worry about everything falling apart at just the wrong moment. If you want to promote your app from a bullet-proof platform, there's not much to compare to this.

Making a Video

If a picture is worth a thousand words, then a video is worth millions of the suckers. Nothing—and I really mean nothing—is going to sell your app better than a good video. Video production is an art in itself—whole books could be written on the subject of making an iPad app promo video—but I'm going to distill all this information into a bright gleaming flame for you. First I'm going to explain the technical aspects of creating a video of your iPad app—how to light and film the device itself, and then I'll describe tried-and-tested methods of structuring the contents of your video, the narrative that will sell your app.

Know Your Camera

First: Know your video camera, or find someone who does. You're either going to have to rely on your camera's automatic settings—which is pretty risky when shooting the iPad—it tends to create challenges even for the experienced photographer —or, more likely, you'll have to manually set focus and aperture (the size of the hole through which light is captured by the camera—determining the exposure). If you don't know what exposure is, or how to set it on your camera, then it's going to take you at least an hour of experimentation to figure that out to a basic degree of competency. Again, you might find it easier to find someone who knows about this stuff already.

Get the Proper Exposure

Assuming you've got to grips with the basics of how exposure works on your video camera, you'll now have to balance the brightness of the iPad with the brightness of the environment you're shooting in—to give a picture that you're happy with (see the images here as examples). A video camera can't capture images as well as our eyesight, so you have to be careful not to include too many extremely dark areas in the frame with extremely bright areas. This spread of contrast is known in the trade as the *dynamic range*. With a set exposure, above a certain brightness level, video cameras see parts of the image as pure white. They're unable to capture the detail in these areas and so simply show them as white holes in the picture (your eyes do this too, if you look at something really bright).

Generally, with default settings, your video camera is likely to overexpose the iPad (the screen will appear washed out, or completely white), and under-expose the bezel and the user's hands (everything except the iPad's screen will seem too dark). Or, your camera might do the exact opposite. There are two options here, either you decrease the brightness of the iPad's screen, or increase the brightness of the surrounding environment. If you're really careful, you might be able to use your camera in an automatic setting, and attempt to balance the light in the environment to match the light from the iPad's screen—either by adding ambient lights to the environment, or by dimming the iPad's screen. This will take a bit of trial and error, but eventually you're likely to discover the biggest problem with filming the iPad: reflections.

Avoid Reflections

The iPad is a big slab of glass, and it loves reflecting everything, especially you, and the video camera you're filming it with. The best low-budget solution to this problem I've found is to make the artistic decision to underexpose the actor's hands and the room, and then correctly expose the iPad screen. This requires you to have direct control of the lighting in the room. The brightness of the iPad's screen will always be a starting point for the exposure you set on the camera, so expect to spend some time shifting this up and down using the brightness control in the Settings app until you get the effect you're looking for. The darker the room, relative to the iPad's screen, the less it will be reflected in the display. Any light sources around the iPad may also reflect in the screen so, often, it's best to film the iPad with a camera directly overhead, pointing down, its line of sight perpendicular to the floor and ceiling—since it's more likely that you will not get reflections from the ceiling. If you're new to video, avoid windows, shooting outdoors, and shooting in a space where you cannot control the lighting and environment.

BASIC LIGHTING SETUP USED FOR THE *ALICE FOR THE iPAD* **VIDEO**

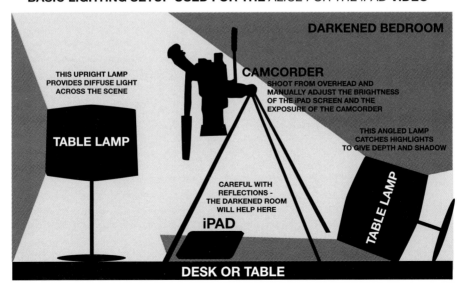

The biggest challenge, even for an experienced camera operator, is the reflectivity of the iPad screen. However, you can purchase anti-glare coatings for the iPad, which may be useful if you're shooting outdoors or in an environment where the iPad will be moved about. Generally, I'd advise beginners to stick to relatively static shots, with a tripod-mounted video camera. It's also a good idea to focus purely on the iPad and the hands of the user, rather than add all the complication and distraction of full or half-body shots. Keep the emphasis on the app, unless you have a very good reason not to.

Get Creative

Experienced videographers will discover that there are many other ways to shoot an iPad video, and endless creative alternatives to the setups described. It's early days for iPad promotional videos and I'm looking forward to seeing more material shot out on the streets, with the iPad in real-world situations. However, video shot with the iPad outside is not for the faint hearted—if in doubt, get help from someone with more experience.

Before you attempt any video whatsoever, be aware that filmmaking is one of those arts that is deceptively accessible. You might think, "Oh, I can just point this video camera at the action and it'll all work itself out," but the reality is that it's a hell of a lot easier to buy or rent the video equipment than it is to use it. It's very easy to make video look cheap and dull. Although I'm tempted to suggest hiring a "professional" to shoot your iPad promo, in my experience most of these people are a glorified rental outlet and have very little understanding of what makes a compelling showcase for an iPad app. If you really want good results, take the time to learn how your video camera works, and concentrate on the story you're telling. The money you'd otherwise spend on a "professional" is better spent on food while you learn your way around the equipment—nobody will care as much about your app promo video as you do, so who better to shoot and direct it than you?

Tell a Good Story

Now you have an idea of the technical requirements for shooting an iPad promo, I'm going to explain exactly how to structure the visual story, or narrative in your video. The story in your video is more important than anything else. If you tell a good story, you could potentially shoot your video with the webcam in your laptop computer and still get a million hits on YouTube. Production values, sound, flashy editing, and music are all secondary to the story. So, what is a story?

For the purpose of creating an iPad promo video, I'm going to define story as follows: A short crescendo of moving images that establishes a need for your app, and compels the viewer to buy it. The story might take a traditional form, with a beginning, middle, and end, or, like the promo for *Alice for the iPad*, it might use highlights from the app, set to music, which work their way into a frenzy. Or, more likely, it will be something entirely different. When you tell the story of your app in video, make sure that you answer the golden question, "What is it?"—see the next section for more about this.

Do not make your iPad app promo video longer than 60 seconds, and preferably make it 30 seconds. The attention span of viewers will be stretched after two or three seconds and very few users will watch the whole promo. Stick the good stuff up front—you have about five seconds to convince the viewer your video is worth watching. Restricting yourself to a 30-second time limit will also force you to refine and clarify the idea behind your app. This helps you and helps the consumers of your software because they'll have a clearer idea of what you're offering. As discussed in Chapter 1, if you can't sell your app in a 30-second YouTube clip, then—unless you have a lot of money to throw at traditional advertising—don't even attempt to make that app; it will almost certainly crash and burn.

If you really want to blaze your way to the top of app charts, your iPad promo video must have at least one of the story qualities covered in the next sections, and preferably a number of them.

Funny

People forward each other funny adverts all the time, and it's a great way to get attention virally. Because the story is funny, the product gets lots of coverage as a side-effect. Don't, however, make the mistake of creating a funny video in which your iPad app is not a vital plot device. It might be hilarious to watch a man falling over with an iPad in his hand, and the video may get millions of hits, but what does this have to do with your app? Using *Alice for the iPad* as an example, imagine a video where someone dressed as the Queen of Hearts digs into a freshly-baked tart, spots something odd in it, plunges her hand in, pulls an iPad out from the pastry and filling, wipes it off, and begins playing the *Alice* app. This makes quite a funny video concept and emphasizes the app *and* the situation, not just the situation. The whole video is about the app; it's not just tacked on to the funny circumstances. The imagery in the video is also strongly app related—the Queen of Hearts, the tart, the iPad, the app. Include strong app-related imagery and your advertising message becomes hard to ignore. There are lots of ways to make your app funny, and you don't necessarily need costumes or a set. Think laterally about how you can show off your app in amusing ways.

Quirky

Videos that are quirky can also become quite popular on YouTube. I define quirky videos as those that are more odd than funny, but make you look twice at what's going on. As an example, let's suppose you're making a cookery app. What if the chef using the app was shown in the video selecting a recipe, then reading instructions to cut up an onion, she reaches into her knife drawer, ah! There are no knives. She looks around. No knives anywhere. In desperation, she picks up the iPad and uses the edge to quickly dice the onion. Pretty quirky hey? I'd forward friends a video like that. What would make the video even better is if the capabilities of the app are more tightly integrated into the story. Let's imagine this cookery app includes great video demonstrations by top chefs. We could have our protagonist clumsily trying to carry on watching the video demonstration with her head tilted sideways, bobbing, while chopping the onions. Think story, and think app.

TIP

Don't take your iPad app too seriously. It might do a serious task, but serious doesn't traffic well on YouTube. Funny sells iPad apps, so don't worry that you're devaluing your product or brand; it's almost impossible to genuinely undermine yourself with good comedy. Consumers love companies that can laugh at themselves. They feel like they're part of some jolly consumer-capitalist in-joke, and ignore the reality—that they are being manipulated to buy a product. Remember: Funny makes money.

Unique

If your app does something that's never been tried before, and you can explain what it does quickly and easily, you're in a very special position. You don't need to worry too much about your video being funny or quirky, you just need to make sure that your video is clear, compelling, and convincing. But don't think you're off the hook: It must be exceptionally clear why any user would want your app, especially if you've invented a new category of app. A good example of such an app is *Flipboard*—which you read about in Chapter 9. *Flipboard* repackages content from various websites into a personalized magazine. The makers of *Flipboard* paid a lot of attention to the way they made the promo video for the app, and clearly had a decent budget to do this with. Take a look at the promo on the site, it closely resembles Apple's in-house style and helps attach familiarity and gravitas to what was, at the time, a completely unknown product.

So, this is the first step: Create certainty around your new app category by framing it in the language of a familiar video format. The *Flipboard* video then goes on to explain, using an actor speaking in a plain, down-to-earth tone, what *Flipboard* does. Here I feel it falters a little because it relies on voice narration, a better approach is to show users what the app does— try to refrain from telling them what it does. I have to confess that I did not download *Flipboard* after watching this promo video; it was only after a personal recommendation that I took a look at this genuinely remarkable app. The problem with the *Flipboard* video is that I did not come away from it understanding what *Flipboard* was. This is always a big risk with defining a new app category. I also felt that the *Flipboard* video didn't tell a story, it was, in the end, just a man in a room talking about an app. It would have been much more effective if the video could have depicted people actually using the app, in everyday life.

Take a look at the recent iPhone and iPad adverts by Apple for good examples of this approach. None of them talk about the features of the devices, or what they do, they simply show actors using the device in plausible real-life situations. The subtext of this kind of video is: "You could be this person"—this a raw, appealing idea, especially if you admire the character portrayed. The subtext of the *Flipboard* video can only ever be: "You could download this app," which is an infinitely less convincing appeal to our human psychology.

Reproduced with permission from Flipboard. Flipboard and the Flipboard logo are trademarks of Flipboard, Inc. © 2010 Flipboard Inc.

TIP

If you have actor friends, or a bit of money to spend, consider using actors in your video. Videos that depict actors, in character, using your app can be extremely convincing. When you involve humans in the story, viewers are more likely to identify with the purpose of the app, and aspire to own it so that they can be like the people in the video. The idea that you can be a more sophisticated, happier, better person if you own a particular app is much more compelling than any spec sheet. However, there's nothing worse than bad acting, and a lot of actors are pretty awful. Cast very carefully, and be sure of your story, or it might be better to stick to safer ground and focus on the mechanics of the app itself.

WATCH OUT!

Be very careful if you think you've invented a new genre of iPad app. Although your idea might be revolutionary, it's going to need explaining to new users. Keep boiling down the essence of your app and try to end up with a video that anyone—even a non-iPad user—could watch and then explain back to you what the app does, without confusion.

Useful

If you're lucky, and you've thought carefully about marketing at the early stages of designing your app, you may find that your app idea is just so damn useful that this alone can be the focus for the story in your video. This is especially true if you are designing your app for a niche audience. By niche, I don't mean an app aimed at a very small number of people (I can't recommend that kind of development), but I mean an app aimed at some number less than every iPad customer. Personally, I'd stick to apps that could appeal to any iPad user, but if you're making an app for a special industry, let's say the restaurant industry, presumably your audience comes predisposed with some interest in your app idea, and will be happier to sit through a longer presentation.

In cases like this, especially where you're selling to businesses, you may find that a slower, more informative approach to explaining what your product does in video can be effective. However, don't forget that business people are the same people that slump in a sofa at the end of the day and watch 100 adverts a night. Just because you're selling to businesses, it doesn't earn you the right to be boring—although judging from some PowerPoint presentations I've sat through, many managers seem to think it does. The same techniques that appeal to a broader consumer—humor, quirkiness, and so on—work just as well in a business situation, and sometimes better. Businesses don't expect a compelling presentation, so are all the more delighted when you provide one.

Good examples of useful apps include *CloudReader* and *SketchBook Pro,* as shown in the images. *CloudReader is* a brilliant document viewer that accepts most text formats you can imagine—I couldn't live without this app, it's simple, well-executed, and unflashy. *SketchBook Pro* is another useful app—there's no easier way to sketch out quick ideas on the iPad. There are lots of useful apps for the platform, and very often they sell very well, most likely because they offer a very straightforward answer to The Golden Question— see the next section for more on this.

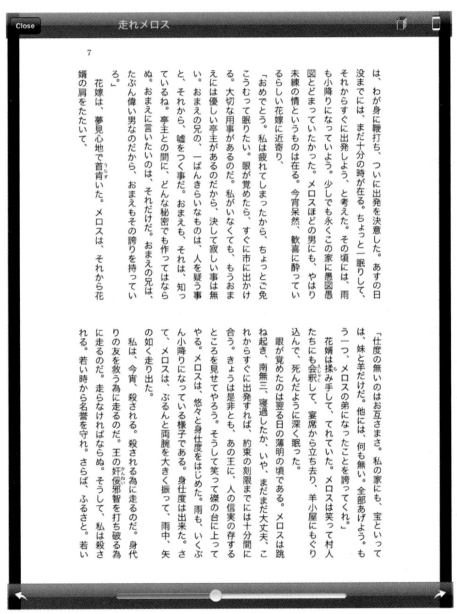

Reproduced with permission of Satoshi Nakajima. satoshi.blogs.com/uie © 2010 Satoshi Nakajima.

Reproduced with permission of SketchBook Pro. © 2010 Autodesk Inc.

Amazing

Some apps are just so wildly beyond what's gone before that just a few frames of video is enough to provoke users to download them. One good example of this is *Uzu*, the crazy visualization masterpiece, and another is *Apple Pages*, which, on launch, just looked so far ahead of anything else in the software world that it was one of the first apps most users downloaded when getting their iPads. Another great example of an amazing app is *Epic Citadel*, shown in the images, which was the first iPad game that really made me understand just how well the iPad will compete with traditional gaming platforms. *Alice for the iPad* was also fortunate enough to fall into this category—it surprised and shook up both the publishing industry and millions of users across the world who had never imagined what a digital pop-up book might look like.

Reproduced with permission of Citadel, Epic Games Inc. © 2010 Epic Games Inc.

Reproduced with permission of Citadel, Epic Games Inc. © 2010 Epic Games Inc.

Reproduced with permission of Citadel, Epic Games Inc. © 2010 Epic Games Inc.

Reproduced with permission of Citadel, Epic Games Inc. © 2010 Epic Games Inc.

Reproduced with permission of Citadel, Epic Games Inc. © 2010 Epic Games Inc.

Reproduced with permission of Citadel, Epic Games Inc. © 2010 Epic Games Inc.

There is plenty of scope to build iPad apps that wow great swathes of iPad users, but you shouldn't enter into a project with the dense expectations of potential fame and fortune hanging over you. Don't feel that you have to do something revolutionary; simply create to the best of your abilities and trust in the process—in fact, embarking on a project with intentions of fame distracts you from the task at hand. Great apps, like many great creative works, aren't built out of dreams of fame, but out of hard work and perseverance. We didn't build *Alice for the iPad* with visions of fortune and glory, we built it because it we loved the concept and respected our audience.

The Golden Question: What Is It?

There is one simple question that you must be able to answer in a short sentence if your iPad app is to have any chance of success. The question is: "What is it?"

Let's ask this question of a few best-selling apps. Here I've listed some best-selling apps and their implicit answers to that golden question:

- *Apple Pages:* It's a word-processor you can touch.
- *SketchBook Pro:* It's a sketchbook you can draw on with your fingers.
- *Need for Speed:* It's a racing game that you steer by tilting the iPad.
- *Alice for the iPad:* It's a digital pop-up book based on the book, *Alice in Wonderland*.

Okay, so from these descriptions you get a strong sense of what the app in question is. Let's apply the same question to my company's massive flop of an app, *Twitch Origins*. So, what is it?

Twitch Origins is a four player game where each player puts one finger on the device and silhouettes of object appear on the screen, and if the shape matches the changing descriptions on the screen, you lift your finger as fast as you can, and score a point if you are the fastest to lift.

Can you see why *Twitch Origins* failed to sell many units? It's almost impossible to easily explain what it is, and even in the briefest description I can provide, it's still not really clear to the consumer what the hell the app does. Nobody bought *Twitch Origins* because nobody knew what it was. It was an unsellable concept, a dead-weight of complexity, and confused the customer in the app store. Although *Twitch Origins* may be a cleverly designed app—and boy did we think we were smart little pumpkins putting it together—in fact it's much too damn clever. We over-thought the concept from our perspective, as geeks, and forgot that at some point we would have to actually sell the thing to a normal human being. I learned the hard way that unless you can answer the question: *What is it?* with a single, quick sentence, your idea is worthless in the App Store. There are just too many other apps competing for attention, and these apps can answer that question.

Now, let's make no mistake about this, you don't want to be in a situation where you're trying to invent a clear purpose for your iPad app after it's been built. You must have an answer to the question, "What is it?" before you begin. It's horrible to watch a software designer try to shoehorn a clear marketing message into an app that is already completed but horribly doomed on account of its complexity—as was *Twitch Origins*. As I explained in Chapter 1, your marketing plan should be hatched well before any design or pre-visualization work is attempted. Ideas that are not easy, concise sells should be discarded before any time is wasted on them, no matter how seemingly great they are—because they will almost certainly languish in obscurity. Obviously, if you're convinced you have a revolutionary new idea on your hands that will slowly creep its way into the public consciousness despite being almost impossible to explain, go ahead and roll the dice, but you better not bank on it paying the bills.

If you cannot explain your iPad app in a short, compelling sentence, using language a person-in-the-street would understand, you won't sell many copies. The world is stuffed with exciting alternatives to your app—television shows, magazines, movies, and games—that all have a clear and digestible purpose. If a consumer can't grasp your iPad app concept in a couple of seconds, you'll be lost in the roar of modern life. Keep it simple, powerful, and direct.

Naming Your iPad App

"What's in a name? A rose by any other name would smell as sweet," so wrote William Shakespeare, who in many regards was a genius, but on this issue was, I think you'll agree, a total idiot. The name of your iPad app is critically important and an iPad app by any other name may very well not smell as sweet. In fact, the name of your app is potentially so important that it's often worth coming up with app names and then thinking about app ideas that might fit them—after all, many consumers will only ever read the name of your app—they may not see a picture of it in action, or even see the icon—so it's in your best interest to grab their attention with a good name. Conversely, there is a trend, since the advent of the Internet, to invent names that are almost total nonsense—Google stands out as one example, Skype another, and apps like O-GAWA and Shazam have pretty odd sounding names. However, I think these are the exception to the rule, and the most effective app names are both thought-provoking and relevant to the app. Let's take a look at some of the most popular apps and determine what influence the app name has had on consumers.

Angry Birds HD

If I didn't know this app already, I wouldn't be able to figure out what it did from the title, however *Angry Birds* sounds peculiar enough to make me want to find out, it's also a fairly apt description of the content of the game.

Pages

A simple and straightforward name that directly relates to the main function of the app—word processing. The name is nice and short, and makes users think of the task it enables: writing on pages.

Note Taker HD

This is a great example of not going overboard with your app name. The app name *Note Taker HD* is nothing but raw description. Nobody sat around a boardroom table throwing around ridiculous quirky names for this app, and as a result it's sold very well. If I wanted to take notes on my iPad, would any other app stand out in the App Store as clearly as this one? Probably not.

The Calculator for iPad

Again, what could be more obvious? This has also sold extremely well on the App Store and makes good use of simple naming techniques. I don't need to see a photo of this app in action, or see the icon, or even read a description of it. I can tell from the app name that, if I'm looking for a calculator for my iPad, this is app going to do the trick.

So, you can see from these examples that the name of your app is vitally important in the trench warfare of the App Store. A good name won't save a bad app, but a good app will sell even better if its name is descriptive or intriguing enough to compel users to click on it to find out more.

TIP

*I would advise leaning towards brutally descriptive app names, rather than inventive ones. You might not win any prizes for artistic creativity by naming your travel app **World Travel Guide** rather than **GlobeZipper,** or something similar, but you're likely to sell a lot more of the former, more simply-named app. The more descriptive and obvious your app name, the more likely a consumer is to understand what your app is and consider a purchase. Most people will ignore apps that do not have an immediately obvious purpose—don't get lost in the crowd, keep it descriptive.*

The Problem with Journalists

Journalists are fickle creatures. I know because I was once one of them. You will almost literally have to smack one around the head before they pay any attention to you. With a few wonderful exceptions, journalists have no real clue what is good and what is bad in the world of technology. They mostly rely on formal press releases from the big brands before they stir themselves into action. This is an awful situation for indie developers. I'm going to give you an insider's perspective on how the major newspapers and websites operate.

First, I'd like you to imagine the person you're pitching coverage of your app to. I want you to imagine the haggard, hung-over, overworked, broken-dreamed moral vacuum of a human we call the journalist. I'd like you to picture this journalist sitting at his desk, picture him clearly, picture this miserable blot on humanity, this word lizard. Do you see him (her)? Okay, now this word lizard is receiving an email from you. Ping! It's just hit the inbox. The first thing the word lizard will do is flick its eyes over the title of your email. It better be a pretty spectacular subject line or the lizard will flit onto the next 200 emails waiting to be read. The word lizard does not have time to investigate your email any further if the subject line bores him. What's worse is that even if your subject line is good, and you're pointing the journalist towards an exceptional app, he still probably won't care. Journalists like this mainly care about one thing: not getting sacked. Taking the time to investigate an app that is not made by a massive corporation they already recognize is too much for most technology journalists. Your other alternatives are to phone the journalist, or mail him something bizarre enough to stir him into action. Both of these tactics are also likely to result in nothing.

TIP

My personal suggestion is not to bother contacting the press directly, it's a complete waste of energy 99% of the time. If your app is fantastic, promoting it through YouTube will be enough, and the press will flock to you. Alternatively, you can use some of the story-building techniques I discussed in "Understanding How the Press Works," earlier in this chapter, and you might also get their attention. Much as they hate it, eventually the word lizards need to fill the pages with type, and they do watch YouTube and follow Twitter. Don't expect the media to promote you, the more likely scenario is that they'll cover you only after you're already popular as a result of your own promotional efforts.

Chapter 13

Tracking Sales and Adjusting Prices

Ever since the first goat-herder took his goats to market, humankind has pondered the essential question: How much can I charge? It's always the first question I get asked by iPad developers about to launch an app. They expect me to have a definitive answer—sometimes I'm tempted to lean close to their ear and whisper in a very serious and slow way, "Three dollars ninety-nine cents. Now don't tell another *soul*."

Unfortunately there is no magic number and the short answer is simply: Charge as much as the market will sustain. The more desirable and novel your app idea, the more cash you can demand from the purchasing masses. There is also the iPad's innate pricing advantage to consider: Because the iPad is bigger and more computer-like than the iPhone, many consumers are prepared to pay more for iPad software—so much more in fact that *Gizmodo* felt compelled to write an editorial titled "iPad app prices are out of control and will kill us all," in which they complained about the high cost of iPad apps and made the quite reasonable suggestion that "We're not arguing against the power of paid, we just want it to continue in the best way possible: cheap."

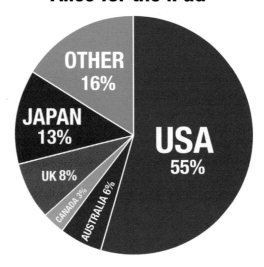

Geographical sales of Alice for the iPad

The iPad pricing dilemma has generated more than its share of angry consumers. Many were particularly affronted by the way established publishers priced their iPad magazine content. The writers at *Strange Attractor* were upset with apps like the *Wall Street Journal*, who charged $17.99 a month for its iPad app, but just $1.99 a week for a subscription to its website. *Attractor* characterized this as a "last act of insanity by delusional content companies… If any company thinks that the iPad will allow them to rebuild the monopoly rent pricing structure of the 20th Century… you've blown yet another chance to build a credible digital business."

Some "experts" will offer you detailed strategies for pricing your iPad app, but at the most basic level you will have to make a very personal pricing decision using what you know about the market your app is competing in, based largely on intuition. Don't believe anyone who tells you they have a perfect model for predicting how your app will sell at various price points—the psychology of pricing goods, especially software, is extremely complex, and often counter-intuitive. It can't be worked out on a spreadsheet because there are too many human elements to the mechanism. In some cases an app will sell more at a higher price point that it would at a lower price point, because when the perceived value of the product increases, so can the perceived quality.

With *Alice for the iPad*, we were able to charge $8.99 and sustain extremely high sales because the app had excellent media exposure and absolutely no competition at the time. I also chose this pricing strategy because I did not want Alice to lead a race to the bottom—as I watched happen with the iPhone—where all apps quickly gravitated to 99 cents. I also did an emotional comparison between the *Alice* product and its closest equivalent—a pop-up book—and then priced the app around the cost of a pop-up book. A fair deal given that it was emulating all the functions of this existing product, and more besides.

This may be one effective way to go about pricing your app: Try to view what you are selling as a pure experience, and price it accordingly. How much do equivalent experiences cost elsewhere in life, not just in the world of software? I was tempted to show you a lot of graphs and charts that illustrate how app sales are affected by price changes, but the data I collected was all so wildly contradictory and varied so massively from app to app, that I've been forced to conclude that there really is no simple mathematical calculation that will help you decide how to price your iPad app. If you twisted my arm and made me spit out a rule it's this: What is the most you could reasonably charge? What is the least? Pick a point somewhere between and carefully observe sales data when your app hits the store.

 Be aware that changing the price of your iPad app once it's in the store does not happen in a vacuum. If you've been charging $14.99 for three weeks and then discover that you've only sold 100 apps, reducing the price to $3.99 may sell 500 apps in the next three weeks, but you've now potentially enraged the 100 loyal users who bought your app when it was $14.99—be prepared to see a lot of angry reviews in the App Store. The better policy is to think hard about your app pricing strategy before you enter the store. If you treat app pricing like an auction and reduce the price every week, hoping you hit a sweet spot, you're actually more likely to alienate your most vocal audience. It's a tricky business; move carefully.

Marketing Lite Apps

Lite apps are an extremely valuable tool for selling users up to the full version of your app (although Apple doesn't want you to frame it that way). A lite app gives a taste of the full app, but is free to download and makes great advertising for your product. However, Apple explicitly states that it will not accept lite apps that are demos. The app must be fully functioning and useful as a self-contained experience. This presents another interesting dilemma: How do you give away enough to make the lite app desirable and useful and functional without making it so good that there's no point in buying the full app?

With *Alice for the iPad*, we took a common approach: We limited the scale of the experience. In the case of *Alice* this meant stopping the lite app 30 pages into the book. In the case of a game, it might mean stopping the lite app at level 5 of 40. This type of withholding assumes that by page 30, or level 5, the user is deeply involved in the experience and wants more of the same. The alternative method of withholding is to limit features. This is trickier because Apple states that a lite app cannot appear to be missing features—although in practice there is some leeway given here.

As an example of limiting features, let's say you create an app that simulates a piano. The lite app might include three different piano sounds, but the full app includes 20 piano sounds and the option to record what you're playing. In this case, the user is persuaded to purchase the full app because, although the experience is not limited in scale, it is limited in opportunity. The user wants to do more than the lite app allows, and is tempted to purchase the full version.

Although it's rewarding to have shifted 100,000 free apps, is it better than shifting 10,000 apps at 99 cents? Sometimes your decision to go free can make the difference between not being able to pay the rent, and being able to pay the rent. Of course, shifting 100,000 of any product is a remarkable achievement, so there is clearly an emotional satisfaction to that. Sadly you can't deposit emotional satisfaction in the bank, although I'm sure Goldman Sachs' vampire squid is working on it. If you are going to go free with your app, make sure it's part of a bigger plan—either to upsell to a paid app, or to establish a name for yourself.

Don't make the mistake of thinking that "free" counteracts negative reviews or unrealistic expectations in your customers. People expect free stuff to work just as well as paid stuff. Users make almost zero concession for the fact they paid nothing for your app. Take a look through the App Store at the reviews on lite apps. Nobody holds back on venting their anger when free stuff doesn't work properly.

The two main ways to convince users to switch from the lite version of your app to the full version is to limit either the scale or opportunity in the software—make it clear that there is either much more content, or much more that can be done with the existing content. However, you don't want to make your lite app appear half-hearted or restrictive because this will not impress your customers. The best way to sell-up to the full version is to really blow users away with the lite edition. Make the lite app amazing and the full app spectacular.

Marketing Limited-Time Offers

I've noticed recently that several iPad app developers have chosen to initially release their app for free and then charge for it. The first few weeks are used to gain traction for the app, to get it onto a huge number of iPads, and then the following weeks the app is priced up—no longer free—and word spreads via the users who got it for free. I think this is an extremely effective approach for some apps, particularly apps that are hard to explain but easy to demonstrate. Word-of-mouth advertising is exceptionally compelling, and you can't get a better salesperson than a friend showing you how cool the app they just downloaded is.

© Colordodge Labs Inc.

A great example of an app that used a limited-time offer to its advantage is the app *Uzu*, which you read about in Chapter 8. *Uzu* is impossible to explain to people. I could talk on the phone with someone for 20 minutes and still not effectively describe to them what *Uzu* is and what *Uzu* does. Nobody in their right mind is likely to buy *Uzu* based on a description of what it does. It makes no sense. You have to see it (this makes it an interesting exception to some of the marketing strategies discussed in relation to The Golden Question in Chapter 12). Obviously the makers of *Uzu* figured this out pretty quickly, and offered the app for free initially. Now everybody I show my free copy of *Uzu* to wants a copy of it on their iPad and downloads the paid edition. I'd wager that if *Uzu* had cost money to begin with the developer wouldn't have sold a tiny fraction of the apps they've sold today.

Not all apps are suitable for limited-time offers. What if the bulk of your target audience downloads your app in the first few days—how will you recoup development costs? I recommend that you only use the limited-time offer approach if your app has considerable mainstream appeal and begs to be shown off. This way you should be able to recoup the initial "losses," because for every person who downloaded your app when it was free, two or more may be persuaded to buy it when this non-paying user shows it off to friends in the future.

Analyzing Your App Sales Data to Improve Profit

Is your iPad app selling well in Japan? Maybe it would sell even better if you translated it into Japanese? Why did you sell twice as many copies in Italy this weekend than you did last weekend? Why are sales so high in Russia on Wednesdays? These are all questions I've asked myself when reviewing data from the App Store. Sometimes there is no apparent answer to these questions and the data just shows the inevitable quirks and randomness of the universe, yet other times it's possible to use this data to improve sales. Often you'll find that spikes in sales correlate quite directly with press coverage in some magazine or newspaper somewhere on the planet, or on a popular website like *Slashdot*. Sometime the things you think will cause a spike in sales, such as an appearance on *Oprah*, won't actually cause much of an increase at all, whereas others, like a mention in a distant Russian newspaper, will send purchases skyrocketing. In the photo here, you can see me holding a copy of *The Daily Telegraph* newspaper, which ran a huge double-page feature on *Alice.*

*Keep an eye on international sales. Japan is a particularly good market for **Alice for the iPad** and we've had incredible sales in this region. This is something I could never have anticipated, but was quick to react to. We got in touch with some Japanese magazines and television stations and provided them with everything they needed to demonstrate **Alice** to their viewers. Regional translations are always worth looking into. Very few app developers take the time to translate their apps into foreign languages, but the most unexpected markets can develop if you give customers in different countries a chance to buy your app in a local language. Often you'll have friends who can speak another language who can give you a hand with the translations—but it's probably worth getting their translation double-checked by another native speaker before setting a localized app live on the App Store.*

Dealing with Investors

This is an interesting time to be a developer because investors have gone crazy for the iPad. If you have any degree of success, you're likely to be approached by venture capitalists looking to make money from your genius. Venture capitalists are crawling all over the iPad and iPhone scene. Atomic Antelope had lots of approaches and there's a huge amount of money available if you want to sell your soul. The pros are that you get a lot of cash from the venture capitalists, the cons are that they eventually want a lot of money back in return. It'll likely end up with your door getting kicked in and a man in a ski mask smashing your legs to pieces, but sometimes these offers are hard to resist.

If you're offered a contract, check it carefully and discuss it with the best lawyer you can afford. The industry is cutthroat and often takes advantage of designers and illustrators who foolishly assume that the business world shares their intrinsic love of art. Do not expect to grasp the details of a contract, however innocent seeming, unless a professional lawyer has combed it half to death. Corporations are designed, from the ground up, to take advantage of any opportunity to make money—don't expect them to have ethics, or any sense of what is fair. If you find yourself in a position in which investors want to finance your projects, or another company offers help, look very closely at the small print. Remember what excited you about designing for the iPad in the first place, and ask yourself why these people want you. Usually they will step in and quickly kill the dream because they just don't get it.

There are sharks circling the iPad scene. A lot of money has flooded into the industry and, as usual, the MBA grads have woken up from their slumber and stumbled over to the developer community. If you have a successful app in the App Store, expect to be courted by investors with dollar bill signs spinning in their greedy little eyes. Some investors are fine upstanding members of society, but many will take your dream and mismanage it into oblivion. If you really love developing apps, the quickest route to hating your job is to partner up with the wrong venture capitalist.

Index

Apple
    communicating with, 96–97, 100
    documentation for programmers, 219
    Flash subjugated by, 89
    GarageBand sound editor, 292, 293, 295
    history of, 97–99
    humanistic approach of, 99
    image versus reality, 99
    Objective C implementation of, 94
    patents filed for gestures, 117, 118, 119
    realism recommended by, 161
    sales as core interest of, 99–100
    silence of, 96, 100
    submitting apps to, 7
    support for independent developers, 91, 97
    UI guidelines enforced by, 7
Applied Cognitive Psychology, 82
apps
    analyzing sales data for, 326–327
    Apple's core interest in, 99–100
    in complete solutions, 24–25
    describing concisely, 316–317
    ergonomics and possibilities for, 20–21
    evolving from iPad features, 60, 109–111
    Flash, avoiding adaptation of, 88
    inspiration for, 34–35, 41
    iPhone, adapting for iPad, 7, 17–21, 49
    lite apps, 323–324
    market size for, 23, 24–25, 63
    naming, 317–319
    pitching ideas to clients, 87–88
    planning, 102, 103
    pricing, 321–323
    profitability of, 23–24, 49, 76–77, 95
    registering names of, 101–102
    storyboarding, 102, 103
    submitting to Apple, 7
    UI guidelines enforced for, 8
    visual-emotional response to, 47
audio. *See* sound

B

Bauble Christmas app, 31, 32, 36–37
BBC News video app, 44
beauty, balancing with usability, 144

books on the iPad. *See also Alice for the iPad*
    capturing the tone, 198
    concerns about, 207
    copyright-free art for, 200–207
    iBooks store, 163–165, 178, 194–197
    illustrations for, 198, 200, 207
    matching the original material, 181
    newspapers versus, 81–82
    pitfalls to avoid, 179–181
    public domain sources for, 37
    publishers' skepticism about, 177–178
    scaling text in, 125
    strong source text for, 198
    suitability of, 81–82
    taste and restraint for, 180–181
    textbooks, 66
    traditional books versus, 177–178, 181
    turning pages in, 152, 154, 155, 208–213
    typography considerations, 124–127
Box2D physics simulation system, 288
brainstorming groups, avoiding, 82
business contract for team, 102–103

C

CAF files, creating, 294–295, 296
The Calculator for the iPad app, 318
Calendar app, 161, 162
Carroll, Lewis (*Alice* author), 198
children as app testers, 175
Chipmunk Physics engine, 217–223, 287
choices (user options)
    making instead of offering, 141–144
    maximum menu options, 143
    prototype menu designs for, 154–161
    stock UI components for, 161
    UI flow for, 155
    users confused by, 142–143
chord, 119. *See also* gestures
Christmas, marketing around, 31, 32, 36–37
clients, working with, 85–90
CloudReader document viewer, 310–311
Cocoa Touch APIs, 219
Cocos2d programming framework, 94
collision shapes, 221–222
colors, legibility affected by, 127